MAN UNPLUGGED
JOHN BROADBENT
SECRET MEN'S BUSINESS
For Men & Those Who Love Them

Man Unplugged – Secret Men's Business For Men
& Those Who Love Them

First published in Australia in 2014 by: Man Unplugged Pty Ltd
Second Edition published in Australia in 2025 by:
Realise Potential Pty Ltd

PO Box 346
Terrey Hills NSW 2084
ACN 118 320 362
www.manunplugged.com.au

All rights reserved. No part of this publication may be reproduced, stored in a retrieval system, or transmitted in any form or by any means, electronic, photocopying, recording or otherwise, without the prior written permission of the copyright holder.

© John Broadbent – 2025

Author:	Broadbent, John, 1957-
Title:	Man Unplugged – Secret Men's Business For Men & Those Who Love Them / John Broadbent
ISBN:	9780992417826
Subjects:	Men—Psychology Self-perception in men Self-actualization (Psychology)

Dewey Number: 155.332
Edited by John Broadbent
Cover design by Verve Designs
Cover photo by Absolute Photography
Layout by Sweetlip Graphic Design

For Benjamin and Nathanael:
Two extraordinary sons
who have taught me what it means
to love, unconditionally.

For Sara:
Your unbounded Joy lights up my life.
Thank you for 'adopting' me
all those years ago ...

For Amanda:
Your vivacity mirrors my passion for life.
Thank you for saying, "YES!"

For Men:
To the good men, everywhere,
who show up, every single day
in so many ways.
You know who you are ...

WHAT OTHERS HAVE TO SAY

You have in your hands a blueprint for the Male Spiritual Journey. As more and more men realise that their identity or sense of self can no longer be determined by the one-dimensional aspect of what they do, questions then need to be asked and answers found. John Broadbent has elegantly shared his soul and laid bare his journey in answering the big questions in his life. Man Unplugged sheds a much-needed light on a vital pathway for any man who seeks more from his life than what appears on the surface. Scratch that surface, open this book... and thus begins a close encounter of the first kind!

Andy Roy – *Author of Raising Teenage Boys, mentor and rites of passage group facilitator*

Man Unplugged cuts through layers of complex issues facing men, often woven into our most trusted relationships and masked by social norms. John combines personal insights, real-life experiences and practical tools from experts, inviting readers to engage with this second edition through their unique journey and worldview. Those who do will find themselves deeply challenged and emerge richer for the experience.

Blake Woodward - *Founder of Suit Tie Stroller*

From a man who has been on a journey for over 30 years to understand my masculinity more deeply, I have found this 2nd edition of Man Unplugged to be both a liberation and a deep invitation to reflect on my current journey as a man in my Autumn years. John expresses insight and elements of his personal journey as a man, to unpack what 'men's work' is all about. The more authentic and personally aware we are as men, the more we can unlock the stereotypes and the stuckness that holds us back from playing our part to be partners in liberating the world.

Brendan Sullivan *– Cofounder of TASMEN Org and Executive Coach*
Working to rehabilitate and improve the outcomes of incarcerated men

The most male-friendly book I've ever read!

Dave Golding *– Men's Retreat Facilitator*

POWERFUL! I found Man Unplugged comprehensive and nourishing, and a must-read for men and women. John skillfully weaves his own rites of passage into the Great Journey all men must take, and much, much more. The reader is obliged to question, "Who am I in this matter?" John potently engages with both his head and his heart, and his chapter on Eldership directly mirrors my 82 years of lived experience!

David Dyke *– Public speaker, film creator, mentor, rites of passage leader, wildlife activist*

In the 2nd edition of Man Unplugged, John has skilfully crafted and updated an already great book – he has a keen eye for the dynamics of the insincere and insecure nature of our prevailing consumer culture, where the burden of masculinity serves neither men nor women. Well worth a read!

David Mallard *– President, Melbourne Men's Group Inc & Facilitator*

'Man Unplugged' is like an atlas of the man's heart. It traverses the wide terrain of mountains and valleys, vulnerabilities and strengths, light and dark, of the experience of men. Importantly, John speaks to the everyman hero in a way that is calm, balanced and down to earth. I hope that many men will read it, and draw inspiration to continue walking their path toward being caring, healthy, whole versions of themselves. The world certainly needs them right now.

David Pointon – *Co-Founder and CEO, The Men's Table*

I have just finished a marathon. I started reading Man Unplugged and could not put it down until I finished it. What a wonderful book it is - so many topics covered with lots of anecdotes and statistics and truths! I agreed with every single chapter and am thrilled that John has written it. My hope is that every woman purchases it for the men in their lives and that men buy it for themselves and their mates. Let's make a difference in this world and come together to create peace, in our own lives, in our family, our community and the world. With thanks and gratitude.

Diane McCann – *Director of Beyond The Ordinary: Seminars for the Soul*

What a journey of discovery with John Broadbent's book, Man Unplugged. In my professional experience, the forgotten art and value of the rites of passage for boys into manhood has revealed men feeling adrift and seeking a deeper connection with their partner, children and friends. John shines a light on this very meaningful journey of masculine unfoldment, a significant quest waiting for every man. I trust this treasure by John will pave the way for many more men to connect with their own True Man and be the best partner, father and friend he can be.

Reading Man Unplugged by John Broadbent was both stimulating and thought-provoking—a book I wish I had come across much earlier in life. Now, at 71, with 13 grandchildren, I found myself nodding in agreement, sometimes wincing at memories, and often reflecting on my own journey from boy to man, to father, and now grandfather.

One of the moments that made me squirm was recalling the very awkward sex discussions I had with my own father as a boy—conversations that were just as uncomfortable years later when I had them with my son. If only we had better guidance back then!

John's insights into how we arrived at our current situation as men made complete sense, and I was encouraged to see that we are, albeit slowly, improving things.

John does more than just analyse the issues—he shares his own lived experiences with remarkable vulnerability, something I deeply admire. His call for an Office for Men's Health is spot on. Simply lumping men's and women's health together in generic services doesn't serve men well. We must invest more in men if we truly want to see change.

The powerful metaphor of Kintsugi—broken pieces being reassembled with gold to become even more valuable—resonated deeply with me. Just as Kintsugi restores broken pottery, Man Unplugged offers a path to repair and renewal for boys and men. This is a must-read for anyone who wants to better understand, support, and empower men on their journey through life.

Ian Westmoreland OAM – *Founder of Mentoring Men*
Founder & CEO of Kintsugi Heroes

Man Unplugged provides incredibly valuable insights into the importance of a present and engaged father/father figure. In an ever-changing, confusing and expanding world, in which the role of the contemporary man and father has become convoluted and even demonised at times, Man Unplugged elicits clarity and steadies the ship for those who want to know how to best show up for their children.

Fathers, father figures and single mothers alike will close the final pages of this book, understanding the vital importance a masculine role model plays in a child's life, and will feel empowered to raise happy, healthy, kind, compassionate, loving and strong children that dare greatly, while feeling loved and supported to do so.

The research overwhelmingly shows that the role of a father is not only distinct from that of a mother, but also vital to a child's overall development. A child's mental health, emotional stability, physical well-being, decision-making skills, problem-solving abilities, attitudes toward school, work, relationships, and life in general are all significantly enhanced when they feel the love and support of both an actively engaged mother and father.

While each parent contributes differently, it is the presence and involvement of both that create the most stable and nurturing environment for a child to thrive. John Broadbent, in Man Unplugged, has done a fantastic job in packaging this research into concise and actionable messages that can help us as parents bring out the best in ourselves and our children.

Josh Wiggins - *Community Dads Group Manager (NSW/QLD/ACT/NT) at The Fathering Project*

Man Unplugged is a synthesis and evolution of all the disparate strands of 'men's business' written in an intimate, layered and authentic voice.

Katerina Cosgrove – *Author*
(www.www.authorcosgrove.com/books)

It is time we all recognised how much good men bring to the lives of their partners, children and society in general. Man Unplugged helps show the way, by encouraging men to have a newer, bigger vision for themselves.

Maggie Hamilton – *Author of What Men Don't Talk About and What's Happening To Our Boys*

Reading John's "Man Unplugged" feels like pulling up a chair with a wise mate, laughing at the mess, then quietly facing the big stuff together.

The book opens with the reminder, "When a child is born, a father is born", a line that slams home the truth our culture keeps missing: dads are made, not pre-installed, and they need support every bit as much as mums.

John strolls through stereotypes, mid-life meltdowns and the Kintsugi image of shards rebuilt with gold, proving men can break and come back better.

John's Fatherhood chapter is pure gold: practical tips, raw confessions and a cracking image of a newborn as "paper" and dad as "pen" writing the first chapter. In a moment when headlines yell "boy crisis" and schools struggle with disengaged lads, John offers a road map that swaps blame for responsibility and invites dads to show up, not show off.

What I absolutely love the most is the tone: equal parts deep, authentic, caring conversation and evidence-based brief, with figures linking present fathers to lower youth crime and better mental health. No BS virtuous preaching, just straight talk and a nudge to try a men's group, switch the phone off and be fully present for thirty minutes that matter more than three distracted hours.

If you care about the future of boys, grab this book, read it, pass it on, then take your son, nephew or mate for a walk and ask, "What story are we writing today?"

Well done, John, I'm sure this gem will be the start of bigger conversations!

Michael Ray – *Author | Speaker | Advocate | LinkedIn Top Voice for Gender Equality, and most importantly, Charlie's dad.*

Got myself a copy. Man Unplugged is one of those essential road maps for the masculine soul.

Terry McArthur – *Author/poet/songwriter*

Man Unplugged is a comprehensive overview of the intriguing and thoroughly necessary world of "men's business", made real and accessible by the author's selfless and generous sharing of his own journey. It is like chatting with a mate, whilst having some real nuggets of gold put on the table. We men, still with work to do, will find this book acts as a gentle, non-prescriptive guide to where we might best exert our energies and focus our attention.

Will Douglas – *Secondary teacher, father, farmer, conservationist, activist, malcontent, optimist*

CONTENTS

FOREWORD	i
WITH THANKS	xiii
1. INTRODUCTION	1
2. STEREOTYPES	9
3. HISTORY	17
4. MOTHERING	25
5. FATHERING	35
6. INTELLIGENCE	45
7. MATURING	61
8. STATISTICS	75
9. HEALTH	85
10. RELATIONSHIPS	93
11. SEXUALITY	105
12. SHAME	123
13. DIVORCE	133

14. DEPRESSION & SUICIDE	145
15. THE MAN CAVE	159
16. AN ACKNOWLEDGEMENT	169
17. WOUNDEDNESS	175
18. RITES OF PASSAGE	191
19. MASCULINE & FEMININE	203
20. BOUNDARIES	215
21. THE SHADOW	227
22. SECRET MEN'S BUSINESS	239
23. FATHERHOOD	251
24. SEASONS	261
25. ELDERSHIP	277
26. AUTHENTICITY	287
27. NEXT STEPS	297
EPILOGUE	301

FOREWORD TO THE FIRST EDITION

John Broadbent's book Man Unplugged is all of compelling, insightful and a timely read for both men and women at a time when the rapidly emerging Men's Movement is still struggling to earn a credible, mainstream, public voice.

It is significant also that Australia is at the forefront of this evolving world-wide Spiritual movement, and that John Broadbent writes from first-hand experience of his own journey to becoming a self-aware man, partner and father - and of his encounters and observations with both "mainstream" men not yet on the journey and those well-experienced in the "Heart-centred" Australian Men's Movement.

This quiet but steady revolution is showing up in many ways. A survey commissioned by a leading women's magazine recently revealed that more men than women now rate having an intimate long-term partnership and children as a key measure of life success.

If we are to create balance in our culture and evolve as a society for the sake of our children and future generations, it is vital that the journey of men and boys is understood and supported equally with that of women and girls.

John Broadbent writes with clarity, compassionate balance and gender inclusiveness, in a way that gets beyond rampant stereotyping and gives a real measure of where modern men are at. Each chapter concludes with a thoughtful summary and there is a valuable resource of references and complementary published works.

Women who have the awareness and curiosity to read Man Unplugged - especially the chapters on Secret Men's Business, Fatherhood and Authenticity - may gain much in understanding, enhanced relationships – and maybe a few surprises!

Whereas men have consistently been called on to support Feminism, women's causes and gender equality, men themselves are often blocked in their own journey by misunderstanding, stereotyping and ironically outright opposition from some of the very social forces that demand their support. While many women see the importance of and support the Men's Movement, bureaucracies and media everywhere have a tendency to be far less than supportive.

Misogyny has become a popular catchphrase to describe anything men might do to disadvantage women. Yet it is still politically incorrect to mention the word "misandry", the equally-pervasive stigmas, attitudes and disrespect men and boys face in the cultural dumbing-down and derision of males in the media and on-line blogs. And in the systemic feminisation of our education systems that are failing boys at a catastrophic rate, along with the institutionalised denial of health and social services funding for men.

Apart from their own personal struggle to become more authentic men, better fathers and more emotionally-aware partners, modern men also face a battle to redefine masculinity in a culture which even some seasoned Feminist writers say has in many ways become antagonistic towards men and boys.

Society has spent several decades criticising men for their shortcomings, both real and perceived, creating what some sociologists call a cultural attitude that: "Women HAVE problems, Men ARE a problem". Yet there has also been an endemic denial of the social challenges and obstacles facing men and boys. Left unaddressed, these are already creating a generational gender imbalance that will eventually impact women equally.

And while wellbeing, parenting and life balance challenges faced by women have been a staple diet of mainstream media coverage for several decades, the equally pressing issues faced by men are only recently starting to register – and often in a blaming or scolding tone! To tell the men's story with any real accuracy and authenticity, men are borrowing a famous slogan from Feminism: "Sisters are doing it for themselves."

Authors like John Broadbent now are producing a steady stream of work from the best source possible. From inside the Men's Movement and their own experience, men are "doing it for themselves" in telling the modern story of masculinity that mainstream media largely still has shrouded in distorted stereotypes and misinformed perceptions.

John Broadbent includes a crucial gem of wisdom in his chapter on Masculine and Feminine - that the way men relate to their inner feminine aspect and the way women relate to their inner masculine has a great influence on how we each relate to the opposite sex.

Men and women both have work to do in learning to understand themselves and each other. It requires each to have the emotional intelligence to let go of judgements and hold a supportive space for each to do their inner growth work. The healthy relationships of our children and future generations depend on this.

Paul Mischefski

(Paul is an Elder of the Men's Movement in Queensland and a facilitator of lifestyle programs with Mens Wellbeing Inc, one of the leading men's organisations in Australia. Based on the Gold Coast, he is a journalist and writer on social and gender issues and a long-time advocate and lobbyist for men's and boys' health issues. He has 35 years of experience internationally in running Spiritual development seminars and groups for both women and men. - *paulmis@powerup.com.au*)

FOREWORD TO THE SECOND EDITION

I get the feeling that the exceptional information and insights presented to us within this splendid book have been conspiring, waiting almost for the right person with the commitment and skills needed to frame them in a way that makes this complex topic accessible to the reader. It typifies John Broadbent's generous clarity of knowing and intention to create for us the opportunity to understand the shifting world of contemporary masculinity and have it relevant to us men and a wider readership. There certainly will be many signposts, challenges and reflective insights ahead for the reader.

On reading it for this foreword, I felt a sense of homecoming. A deep dive into the masculine. A nourishing and enriching ponder … and … a call to action.

So Welcome!

Paul Mischefski's excellent foreword to the first edition and John's own Introduction to this second edition will already give you a taste of what's to come.

The present post-Covid 2025 circumstance of the 'masculine' in a social context has amplified since 2014 when the first edition was published. Men are in the spotlight and usually, for wrong or misunderstood reasons. John's new title has broadened the invitation and territory of his enquiry. It engages with a wider potential readership along with the potency of his updated comprehensive insights. Much has happened to him and us since 2014. There is an increased urgency around men's issues. This book will be a primary source document from which, hopefully, a new future for men evolves.

It also establishes John Broadbent as Australia's most important voice in this new era of emerging contemporary men's issues. He prepares us for the journey with solid facts and information about men. He uses examples and statistics as a background of relationship for what's to come. He coaches us with some useful processes on what parts of our individual intelligence come into play, particularly in challenging situations. He emphasises the benefits of engaging with other good men as an essential factor in every man's development. Men were not designed to go it alone and tough it out. It's the quality of the men we are with that makes all the difference.

It's like packing the bags with the prerequisite materials and documentation for the journey. John is invitational about this, and as a reader, I felt safe, curious, informed, prepared and understood. Strange, for me as this unfolded. I could re-examine where I stand in the whole matter of who I am and how I was or have been, all at once!

I forgot to let you know that I am 82 and somewhat obliged to be 'old'.

If you are a bloke, you will find yourself somewhere along this continuum. The male journey is like that, but you can trust the internal scenery and climate to let you know where you are in the matter of being a man.

This is John Broadbent the craftsman at work. His sense of service directed towards his readership is impeccable. He layers information into acceptable chunks and mindfully traverses complex and varied situations with skill, leavening his flow with examples from his own life where he has stuffed up. Not just anecdotes but often the deepest of heartfelt anguish. The highs and lows of how it is, or was for him, on his journey, wrapped in the hope it will help others.

The middle part of the book is the rollercoaster/slow train wreck concerning Midlife. John tells it like it is. For many men and those who love them, this will be the most challenging, essential, and potentially rewarding aspect of engaging with these chapters. For some, your life may depend on how you respond to what you read. Midlife is the fulcrum of the sea-saw, and it is for the midlife man to decide where he stands in the matter of ups and downs and more importantly, what to do about it.

This conundrum is in the domain of 'letting go' and holds fundamental realisations, sometimes phrased as 'new beginnings'. In my early facilitation days, the phrase was 'I need to re-invent myself.' If this brings up 'stuff' for you, make sure there is someone with whom you can share your considerations.

In another time this is where Elders would provide a safety net to guide the midlife man. He would already know that this transition was coming his way, and he was about to enter the valued and generous part of his life, as a contribution to both his gender and his community.

Not now, and it is in this contemporary setting that the widest range of seemingly uninvited interventions, ambiguities and anguish gain a foothold in the bewildered man. John gently takes and talks us through this most tender time in manhood. For some, as you read this section, hidden forces may emerge, ambiguities, issues of trust, or self-worth perhaps.† This section is a perfect read for a men's group to discuss.

As well, he opens the aspect of 'secret men's business' and breaks into the myth of concealment. In my first paragraph, I describe John's 'clarity of knowing' and chose that phrase carefully as there is that part of a man's longing to be understood, acknowledged and blessed by men who are important to him. John opens this topic and eloquently journeys into the domain of the male's caution of disclosure, and particularly that elusive 'knowing' that sometimes becomes palpable within a group of men. Somehow, for me, admiration for my gender shows up here also. We can be exceptional! Just a week ago, prior to this writing, the Australian Open gave us the young Alcaraz (20) battling it out with the victorious Djokovic (37). For me, watching this took me deeply into the elusive force field of the masculine, much more than just a game of great tennis. I am not sure I would know how to describe this feeling or even wish to. Primal energies were at play, especially as, two days later, Djokovic had to graciously say to the world, 'I'm done'. Summer to Autumn.

As an aside, my colleague Wes Carter and I used to run a three-hour program called 'Secret Men's Business for Women Only'. Best fun ever, and wow… amazing curiosity and questions.

Further, John takes us into the world of the Shadow. All cultures have their way of engaging with this powerful and elusive force of the human condition. It is something we all need to 'know' about. John explains this well. Strange, this 'knowing', as for men this an essential step on the pathway towards Eldership and a primal echo across the valley of life's journey. An opportunity for us men to truly celebrate our later life's purpose. It is not the intention of this book to universalise and ponder the Dark Side, but the magnitude of the collective shadow and its malignant stealth has global implications.

And so, to the latter part of John's book.

John and I met because of Eldership. In fact, we have spent a total 24 days together sitting in and around an Elders Circle ... three Elder's Way programs in Bali. The first, in 2018, John was a participant and I a facilitator, and then after the COVID intervention, John re-emerged as the program organiser and Elder of this remarkable program, which we jointly facilitated twice in 2024. If you are in late midlife and curious, this section of the book has much to inform you about Eldership. It is, after all, A Castle Without Walls, a collective of good men graciously holding space for other men to make their glorious accomplishments and mistakes!

I have deliberately left one aspect of the book until last. It includes Fathering and the many painful life distractions that preclude the father's attention towards his son's dependence on him as a primary guide. And then, in Chapter 18 on Rites of Passage, there is one of two sentences sitting almost alone as the last Key Point:

- ***Our education system is not designed to help boys become men.***

I gasped when I read it, emphasising the potency of this bewildering and awful truth.

This is a double whammy!!! Distracted fathers are all but precluded from being proper Dads and our education system is not designed to help boys become men!

This is Australia, we can do better than that. This is a national disgrace. When you also look at John's overwhelming stats on percentages, outcomes of rehabilitated unhealthy male behaviour, and consider the hyper-massive costs to us all, of crime, incarcerations, recidivism, rehabilitation, policing, family law, mental health and violence, tragic family outcomes, and the massive infrastructure that supports this, a mighty wake-up call is needed. Blind Freddy can see we are not looking at the causes, and we are running out of band-aids.

John has armed us with the best possible information to address this. This is Australia's most expensive neglect. Not even a Ministry for Men's and Boy's Affairs. We need male teachers in Schools, especially in the primary area and Dads who demand time out to be purposefully with their sons and other good men.

And we need women to help us do this.

This is finger extraction time. Australia is good at change, and we are in a perfect position to model this for the rest of the world. Phew ... don't get me started!

This book and its purpose.

This is a book about men getting their money's worth from being a bloke. Finding their voice and being the man they want to be.

It is a source document, exceptionally well informed and impactful at many levels of readership ... as John says, 'for Men and those who love them.'

It offers exceptional insights into the primary aspects of the masculine journey.

It is invitational and helpful, and it provides for a much-needed breadth of readership.

It has a personality: author John Broadbent shows up, warts and all.

It has lots of ingredients, you get to choose.

It holds potential, a signpost to a better future for men.

Thank you, John.

Peter Efford

(John's invitation to write about myself is a fair call, but I have long ago packed away my trumpet and in truth, it is the Australian men's movement that has me happen. Reading Steve Biddulph's book Manhood in 1995 on a plane up to Jakarta. Attending countless men's Gatherings (29 in Western Australia alone). Being a member of the same Compass Men's Group since 1996. Sitting with Indigenous Elders, Co-founding The Menswork Project with Wes Carter OAM (formally since 2001). Apart from many public workshops and presentations, we created two remarkable Men in Bali programs: A Man's Journey and The Elder's Way, the 40th iteration of which will happen with John in 2025 and be part of my goodbye to 'Menswork' as my shelf-life reaches its use by date. My meeting and working with John has been an essential part of my development.

I'm keeping up with men's breakfasts at my place 8 times a year since 2004. If I have the puff there will be a third edition of 'The Momentum Concept' first published 2017, to place it into a more contemporary setting. It looks in part at the unhealthy appropriation of the masculine 'force field', by power and patriarchy.

I regularly get to 'sit' with younger men. A precious privilege.

Actually, I am an Artist, an Academic career in the School of Design at Curtin University for 30 years, and I now, for the past 20 years, have been running a regular life drawing group and go bush to paint landscapes.

Mostly my life's journey has been safe and satisfying. Fifty years of loving marriage with my fellow artist and accomplished partner Georgia Efford OAM, and all the blessings of family. As the lens distances, there is much to hold with tenderness ...)

† *Dear reader, if you are or know of any midlife man who, for whatever reason, is struggling with his situation please seek support. There is information both in and at the back of this book that can help.*

WITH THANKS

Writing a book depends on many factors to come together, in sequence, each of which ultimately involves remarkable people. I would like to thank the major contributors as follows:

Back in June 2012, I attended an event aimed at educating entrepreneurs how to become a 'Key Person of Influence' (KPI and renamed Dent Global) in their chosen field. Its founder, Daniel Priestley, the Australian KPI team led by Glen Carlson and the mentors they'd assembled, all inspired me that day, so I joined their program. This book is a direct output from their 40-week 'business accelerator' and I feel blessed to have met the Dent Global team and the wonderful peers who journeyed with me. Gratitude to all of you for your unending support, 'tough love' and friendship to get the first edition to print.

On that program, one individual stands out as a mentor and I have been doubly fortunate to have been personally supported by the inimitable Andrew Griffiths, Australia's leading small business author, entrepreneur, speaker and publishing wizard. I affectionately call him Saint Andrew since his generosity of spirit knows no bounds. Gratitude Andrew for all your guidance and freely shared wisdom. You're an amazing midwife to so many budding authors!

When a manuscript is finished it needs to be edited, which is a scary step for an author, since I had no idea whether my months of effort would come back cut to ribbons or be returned relatively unscathed? As synchronicity would have it, thankfully in my circle of friends I stumbled across an author, writer and editor who offered her expert help. Gratitude Katerina for your enthusiasm, encouragement, insights and professionalism.

The realm of design and graphic arts is an interesting world for those of us who sit outside such a specific and creative pursuit. I'm again fortunate enough to know a graphic artist who is so much more – a communicator of thought and purpose, who can listen, ponder and create with depth. Gratitude James of Verve Design for your persistence, insights, attention to detail and your creative light.

James had the idea for the book cover and I'm sure he sensed my resistance to his idea of my face, in close-up, taking up the entire page. Never to be swayed, James put me in touch with the fabulous Vanessa from Absolute Photography. From the very first moment we met, your manner allowed me to feel so much at ease, that the photo-shoot was actually fun! Gratitude Vanessa for your art, professionalism and infectious passion.

Saint Andrew put me in touch with a designer to complete the final layout and once again, exactly what I needed appeared when it was time. Gratitude Susan of Sweetlip Design for agreeing to help at such short notice, and for your collaborative 'no problem' spirit in taking my manuscript and converting it into the book it is today, including this second edition.

I wouldn't be living in Australia if my parents had not had the courage to leave their home and family in the UK in 1968, to find a new life for our family in Australia. Arriving at Sydney harbour on the morning of my birthday was the beginning of a new life for me. Dad joked Australia was too big a present to wrap. Gratitude Mum and Dad for all that you did for me and my family, your enduring love, support and generosity. I miss you both every single day.

As you may have noticed, this book is dedicated to my two sons, Benjamin and Nathanael, who have taught me so much. They of course wouldn't be here without the commitment shown by their mother, who birthed them both at home, in water, providing them with an extraordinary start to life. Gratitude Claire for the wonderful mother you are to our two sons, who are both becoming fine men-in-the-making.

You'll read about the beginning of my journey and an eventful experiential workshop in June 1991. The facilitator of that workshop became my closest friend, and it was with him that I travelled during the 1990s and met Shaman in Alaska, Elders at Uluru, healers in Bali and sages in India. When he died in January 2000 just after the euphoria of the dawning millennium, I felt shattered with grief and utterly lost. However, I committed to continue my journey, to keep walking on my path of self-realisation, to honour all that I had experienced and learned. Gratitude Stuart for your unconditional acceptance, without which I most certainly would never have found myself.

Sincerest gratitude to Andy, Elizabeth and Maggie for your testimonials, Paul Mischefski for taking the time to read my book, provide feedback and write the original foreword.

Thank you, Peter Efford, for your friendship, guidance,

mentoring and foreword to this second edition. Your support of me and my 'men's work' in recent times has been critical to my ongoing evolution.

You may have noticed the reviews at the beginning of this edition, each of which willingly made the time to read the daunting 160-page A4 PDF draft version, provided their feedback and contributed their gem of wisdom, into how they perceived this edition. Thank you to all of you for your generosity and encouraging words.

To those who have supported the men's movement, such as Robert Bly, Steve Biddulph, Robert A Johnson, Dr Warren Farrell, David Deida and all the writers, male and female, who have worn their Hearts on their sleeve in their selfless pursuit to improve men's lives. I am humbled by your deep commitment and wisdom and have learned much from all of you.

And finally, to my last partner in this lifetime, and wife, the Adorable Amanda, whose gregarious infectious spirit and bubbly personality, coupled with an uncanny ability to 'make friends' with just about anyone, has taught me so much about how to move past my own introverted limitations. Your evident love for me, the love we share, and the life-changing work we do together via our relationship education business, is a true partnership. Thank you for all that you do for me, and the difference you make in the lives of those who choose to get to know you.

1. INTRODUCTION

As an author, I can never know who will be reading my words, so firstly, I'd like to thank you for being interested enough to take the first step by opening this book, and secondly, to learn more about men as this book is unapologetically men-centric.

The first edition's title was, *Man Unplugged – Exploring The Inner Man*, and as you can see on this book's cover it's changed to, *Man Unplugged – Secret Men's Business For Men And Those Who Love Them*. The thinking behind this change is that in the ensuing years since the original manuscript, penned in late 2012 and into 2013, much has changed in the world of contemporary masculinity.

In my endeavours, coaching and mentoring men privately, running men's retreats and events, and working as a couple's relationship educator alongside my wife, I've realised that much of what is found within the pages of this edition, remains a mystery to men themselves. This is not due to any malicious intent or withholding of information. It stems from the simple reality that the vast majority of men don't share what's troubling them. Consequently, many men who find a way forward through challenging times unwittingly keep their insights to themselves! This, of course, reinforces the idea that everyone else is doing fine, and it must only be me who's struggling.

We've come a long way with men's health awareness, such as *R U OK Day* and *Movember*, and yet the health of men measured across mental, physical, emotional and spiritual dimensions still shows we're making little, if any, progress. So, whether you're reading this book purely for self-interest, or to gain a deeper understanding of the men in your life (husband, partner, brother, father, son, friend, co-worker or boss), I hope that it will help you understand the often-hidden dynamics at play, in the inner world of men. The world needs more awareness of what it means to be a man in this 21st century.

I wrote the Introduction to the first edition sitting on a plane flight from Sydney, Australia, to Queensland's Gold Coast, to attend my first-ever weekend 'men's gathering' in November 2012. Over 100 men descended on the hinterland to share their experience and wisdom, discuss some challenging topics and raise awareness of those attending just that little bit more, as well as to provide a supportive environment for the courageous attendees who were seeking to know more about themselves. It was a pivotal moment for me and one that galvanised my resolve to share my *personal experience of transformation*, in the hope that it would encourage other men to embark on their Hero's Journey.

This second edition has emerged more than a decade later, simply because so much has happened in those intervening years, both for me and the world at large. On a personal note, I've navigated the death of both parents, a divorce, a marriage, starting a new business, navigated an additional decade of being a parent, had much deeper exposure to 'men's work' both as a participant and a facilitator, a coach and a mentor, so you might say life has been anything but boring! I felt that with the benefit of hindsight, coupled with another decade of lived experience and much more activity in the 'men's space', I could substantially enhance the original edition and incorporate the wonderful and supportive feedback I received about the first edition.

The old and somewhat stifling models that informed men of our roles and how to be in the world continue to not serve society nor men. We men used to be defined by our work, which fulfilled our role as both *provider* and *protector*. Ongoing economic shifts have resulted in the loss of predominantly male jobs. More women are entering the workforce, and men are finding connection in caring for their children. We are seeking deeper and more meaningful relationships. We're searching for ways to redefine who we are and at the same time attempting to live more authentic lives. We cannot do this in isolation, and we must seek the company of those courageous and pioneering men who have already paved a path forward and laid down beacons of direction. A more formal role of Eldership for those men who've gathered important wisdom, is one way men can do this, and I address this toward the end of this book.

Women play a key role in men's evolving journey too, simply by acknowledging that the roles and rules have changed, and that we stand on shifting sands with new models of masculinity emerging. Women can support this transformation by being their authentic selves too.

The #metoo movement has seen a further shake-up with men in powerful positions being 'called out' for completely unacceptable behaviour, and society at large is acknowledging the courage it's taken for women to speak up. As with all shakeouts such as these though, collateral damage has been an unwanted outcome. For some men, just as they are stepping up, becoming more 'emotionally available' and learning to be vulnerable and express their innermost feelings, some elements of the #metoo movement have demanded that it's time for men to 'shut up' and finally listen to what women have endured. Both points of view are valid, and within that lies the conundrum, so perhaps in this example, we have understanding that it's not about 'either/or', but '*and*'.

There's no doubt that men need to listen to the stories of pain and suffering these women have endured. However, there's much confusion in many men, wondering how best to respond more actively, other than only listening. For some, it's committing to calling out bad behaviour when they see it, whether male- or female-initiated. After all, bad behaviour is bad behaviour no matter who perpetrates it.

In the long run, no one benefits from a win-lose situation and sadly, extremes of both the misogynistic men's rights activist movement on the one hand, and misandrist feminism on the other (both most likely being driven by personal and unresolved pain), hijack a more inclusive narrative and fuel a gender-based *divide*, which ultimately divides society itself, rather than unites it. These extreme perspectives are never likely to agree with the 'other' or convince them to change their views, yet the battles continue, unabated, often vicious and sometimes violent.

Together is the only way we can create a society that respects our differences, supports our individuality and understands that women and men both require human connection, understanding, safety, equality, respect and love.

My intention is to take you on a journey into the often-hidden and perhaps secret world of men, by exploring current stereotypes, how we have arrived where we are and where we might be headed, as each day we're confronted with news of violence: wars, murders, rape, shootings, abuse, glassings, suicide – the list goes on. One could be forgiven for tarring all men with one brush, however, to do so ignores the extraordinary and varied grass-roots men's movements that are quietly emerging, as we acknowledge that the outdated views of masculinity are tarnished and collectively, it's imperative we do something about it. The comments at the start of this book from various organisations and groups support the much-needed work required, if we're to be empathetic to the needs of our boys and men.

We're seeing the emergence of men's groups, men's 'sheds', workshops for men, attempts to recruit more male teachers, men not accepting the media-driven stereotypes of the bumbling fool, books on manhood, weekend warrior events, father-son experiences and Rites Of Passage programs.

If one looks closely there really is an underground movement, mostly shunned by the mainstream media, for who knows what reason? Maybe in challenging the stereotypes the media loses its fodder. This is something we'll explore at the beginning of this book. The good news is that the underground movement is making progress.

(Throughout this book I've used the term 'Heart' rather than 'heart' when referring to our core of connectedness, the centre of our being where we feel so much emotion. This is to delineate from the organ that beats in our chest.)

I've listened to many men speak from their Heart and share openly about the love they have for their children, their relationships, family, parents and society at large, and I'm always humbled by the depth of emotion sitting just beneath the surface. In safe environments, often facilitated and surrounded by other open-Hearted men, I've seen men of all ages in heaving sobs of pain-release, exposing their raw and vulnerable centre, opening up and expressing unresolved sources of that pain, sometimes carried in silence for years. I too have been, and continue to be, one of these men.

At retreats for men that I have co-facilitated, I've come to realise that *life is the great leveller*. It doesn't matter what job we do, what car we drive, the size of our house, the money in our bank account, or what other trappings of material 'success' we think might make us happy, we all have our pain to bear. Whether it's the death of someone close, a parent, partner, sibling or child perhaps, or dealing with illness, infirmity, physical pain, hospitalisation, radical surgery, or mental health, no matter what role(s) we choose to fulfil, in the end, no one gets out of this life, alive!

Every single word written in this book comes from my fundamental desire to support the healing work currently underway, to educate those who may not know what really goes on in 'men's business', and to encourage women and men alike to put the past behind us, take a breath and a little leap of faith, and build a new paradigm for female/male relations based on *mutual respect*. I have no doubt there will be readers who disagree with some my views, after all, there are more than 8 billion of us on this "pale blue dot" (as Carl Sagan called our planetary home), however, these are perspectives driven by my lived experience, so neither 'right' nor 'wrong', simply my perspective and learnings shared here with the intention to *educate*.

I sincerely believe that if we can suspend our past hurts and judgements, we are more than able to forge a new egalitarian future, one that is so much brighter for our children, society and the planet as a whole. Only then will we be able to create a balanced, safe, functional and sustainable world.

Our children deserve nothing less.

I am hoping that the wisdom I have gained from an additional decade of living, coupled with my various roles and participation in what's known as *men's work*, coaching, mentoring and retreat facilitation, strengthens this edition, expands your wisdom and, in doing so, helps you live a more fulfilling and aware life.

In service,

John Broadbent, Sydney 2025

2. STEREOTYPES

We made a mistake. We thought that 'liberation' meant that we were liberated to go out and be like men and we sacrificed some very feminine aspects of ourselves in the name of Feminism. We came up with a generation of hard women and soft men and it didn't work for anybody.
— **Marianne Williamson**

As we embark on this journey exploring the inner world of men, it's important to understand one's own perceptions, as these will deeply affect the information you read here and the opinions you will subsequently form. We all view life through lenses of our own creation, so it's often *not what we're looking at, it's where we're looking from*! Therefore, it's vitally important we understand our perspectives and the influences from which they've been created.

The Oxford English Dictionary defines a stereotype as, *"a widely held but fixed and oversimplified image or idea of a particular type of person or thing."*

We know that male stereotypes are everywhere: on billboards, in magazines, television shows, advertising, movies, the Internet, social media, computer games – and I'd like you to pause for a moment, whether you're a woman or a man, and really think about your views of men.

Where do you see male imagery or what do you hear about men? Do you give it a second thought, or do you simply ingest whatever view is being pushed? How influenced are you by what you see and hear? What history do you have with men, which has influenced the way you perceive and relate?

If you're a woman, I'd suggest that your views are most coloured by your relationship with your father, and it is often said that a woman's first male love *is* her father. Was he a dedicated, loving, caring, available, emotionally intelligent, present, respectful, responsible father who fulfilled your needs for protection, love and safety, or was he an absent, quiet, stern, withdrawn, surly, perhaps abusive father whom you never really knew, and maybe still don't?

And if you're a man, perhaps the positive qualities you were looking for from your father, were leadership, mateship, strength, fun, presence, vulnerability, integrity, connection and honesty, but instead your father was removed, shutdown, alcoholic, workaholic, distant, dishonest and maybe even abusive.

Of course, these are extremes at opposite ends of the spectrum, so most likely your father was a composite of some of these attributes. What's important as we begin this journey together into contemporary masculinity, is to be really honest about the perceptions we carry, so that we can perhaps minimise subjectivity, understand our perspectives and see our fathers, and our relationship to them, a little more objectively.

Here's a quick exercise for you to do, that might help you deepen your understanding of your perspective and the lens through which you look at men. Grab a couple of sheets of blank paper and a few quiet minutes. Close your eyes and ponder your father, or what you know of him. Whether he is alive, estranged, present, absent or no longer here doesn't matter, as his influence (or lack of) will have some bearing on you. If you never knew your father at all, you may have feelings of loss, longing or abandonment.

On the first sheet, think of your father and simply write whatever words flow onto the page. Don't filter! Simply let them flow anywhere on the page. You may find that you have strong emotions attached to some of the words, however, don't get caught up with these for now: simply let the words flow and see what emerges.

Did you write anything that surprised you? Are you able to see an emerging picture, an amalgam of a whole range of characteristics some of which may ring true for the way you navigate your world, especially relating to men?

Now look at them again. Do certain words conjure up feelings, and if so, which ones? Do you feel sad, angry, perplexed, aggrieved, joyful, happy, unsure, frustrated, relieved, distant, numb, warm, cold, depressed, hurt? Perhaps sit with these for a moment to really imbibe and feel your relationship to the words and therefore your perceptions of your father.

I'd like you to now put that aside and on the other blank sheet draw three columns. Think of the stereotypes you see in all the various forms of media that *portray men as invincible*, superhero types in action movies, advertisements etc. and write a list of words in the *first* column that describe how you see them, which may be as invincible, indestructible, strong, immutable, immortal, sexy.

Again, let the words flow, unfiltered, until you have ten or so.

Now, the second column. We've developed an acronym, 'SNAGS', for 'sensitive new-age guys', perceived as having Heart but no spine, soft but without direction, and often met with sloppy 'wet-fish' handshakes. As Marianne Williamson stated in the opening quote, we've created a generation of hard women and soft men. Sons of these women and men are a casualty of that generation. Chances are that they have never experienced a completely functional masculine presence in their lives, unless they've decided to embark on a journey to reclaim this part of themselves through men's workshops or suitable therapy. Now, think of a 'chick flick', TV series or men in your life who might fit the 'SNAG' label and add to your list of descriptive words the characteristics that you like about these men in the *second* column, words such as warm, loving, connected, considerate, open, empathic, available, etc.

The third stereotype popular today can be seen in TV sitcoms and advertisements showing the bumbling fool of a man, or the inept dad. This character is so one-dimensional I feel appalled that somewhere, a young woman or man believes that this is 'normal' masculinity. Again, think of these types of men and in the *third* column, write another list of words to complete the list.

I'd like you to pause again and deeply review your list. Is there a man you actually know who has a majority of all or some of these attributes, or have we all been duped by Hollywood and the various forms of media, into building a completely unrealistic model that no man can ever attain? Or is the spread of characteristics so disharmonious that they can't possibly be applied to one man, so we view all men as a combination of various and different attributes, and if so, which ones are important to you? If they don't have all of them, are they viewed as deficient?

We must take the time to understand our views of men, the lens through which we look, how it has been created and formed, and how our views continue to be adjusted by often unconscious forces outside of ourselves. The media has much to answer for here, and we're often oblivious to its insidious influence, especially on social media.

As an example of gender bias, I'm reminded of a road safety campaign shown in New South Wales, Australia some years ago, where the catch phrase of, "Speeding ... no one thinks big of you", had a photo of a young woman holding up a curled little finger. The message of course, is that anyone who speeds must have a small penis. While there's no doubt that the statistics demonstrate that the majority of drivers in accidents or fatalities are young males, I know from personal experience that young women also speed. So, imagine the advertisement was reversed with a young man holding his hands and fingers to form a large circle, with the message, "Speeding ... no one thinks small of you", suggesting that someone who speeds must have a large vagina. I think you'd agree that an advertisement such as this would never be conceived, let alone make it to prime time TV or billboards, as it would be considered highly offensive. And rightly so!

How about a Florida-based clothing company whose catch-cry is, "Boys are stupid, throw rocks at them!" available on t-shirts, which was also turned into a smartphone game for girls. Again, what outcry would there be if the word 'boy' was replaced with 'girl'?

Here we have all the classic hallmarks of misandry, exposed as a gender double-standard. And there are many more if we choose to be aware of them.

I also wonder what this approach is doing to our young maturing boys who are turning into men. Do they see supermen, SNAGS, incompetent fools, or a combination thereof? From which attributes do they draw their reality principle? Isn't the combination of these attributes not only confusing but also conflicting? Where does that leave them on the journey and yearning to grow into good men?

In *The Myth Of Male Power* by Dr Warren Farrell, he argues that the 'patriarchy' has not served men either, and its modus operandi is out-dated and ill-fitting. When hundreds of thousands of men were killed in a single battle in WW1 at The Somme, we didn't label that anything other than glorifying the men who died as 'serving their country'. High-risk activities such as war, search-and-rescue, manufacturing, mining, construction and other heavy industries are all predominantly 'manned' by men. In 2023, 95% of industrial deaths in Australia, were male. Are boys starting to believe that being born male is being born into a disposable gender?

There's no question that the weight of history regarding male-female relations is peppered by systems that murdered millions of women in the name of religion and witch hunts. Men who were suspected of dabbling in these realms were also targeted. What saddens me is that this is being used to label men of today as 'the patriarchy', creating a further rift.

To quote Farrell, "I am a men's liberationist (or "masculist") when men's liberation is defined as equal opportunity and equal responsibility for both sexes. I am a feminist when feminism favours equal opportunities and responsibilities for both sexes. I oppose both movements when either says our sex is THE oppressed sex, therefore, "we deserve rights." That's not gender liberation but gender entitlement. Ultimately, I am in favour of neither a women's movement nor a men's movement but a gender transition movement."

As you might now be able to see, our views of contemporary masculinity are greatly influenced by our fathers, male relatives, media, advertising and a less than savoury history. It's important to be clear of one's own views as they will colour our perceptions and expectations of the men in our lives, and how we believe they should behave, respond, communicate and act.

We all view life through lenses and filters of our own creation and as noted at the start of this chapter, *it's not what we're looking at, it's where we're looking from*. You may be more influenced by stereotypes than you think! By becoming aware, you will start to see the world and the men in your life a little differently, and perhaps become a little more 'unplugged' from an ill-informed narrative.

So, now we've raised our awareness about our perceptions of men, let's move on and explore the inner world of men in more detail.

Key Points:

- ◆ *Our relationship with our own father greatly influences our perspective of men*

- ◆ *Media-driven stereotypes and history further colour our perspectives*

- ◆ *We need to make the effort to be vigilant regarding these influences and challenge our thinking, especially about gender-based double standards, and even more so if we're bringing boys into the world*

- ◆ *It's not what we're looking at, it's where we're looking from and our beliefs, values, upbringing, education and exposure to all forms of media, colour what we perceive.*

3. HISTORY

Manhood isn't a an age that you reach, it's more like a flow of knowledge and skill, like a river, which you receive and grow strong in, and then pass on downstream to others. Unless you can connect to the inherited masculinity of generations of older men, your manhood may never flourish or grow.
— **Steve Biddulph**

Steve Biddulph is the seminal Australian author who has done more to further the cause of men, men's issues and boys' education than any other. Through reading his books I came to understand the evolution of masculinity and why we seem to have lost our way. Before Biddulph, author Robert Bly brought attention to the issues we face today as men, so here is a brief summary to put some context regarding a man's journey through life.

Prior to the Industrial Revolution some 250 years ago, boys were raised mostly by men. They were born, weaned and then involved with their father's craft, whether he be a potter, thatcher, cooper, smithy, saddler, farmer or whatever trade or skill enabled the father to make a living to feed, clothe and shelter his family. These three factors were a father's primary focus and for many men, still are today.

In most situations, the trade of the father became the trade of the son and often it was a group activity, so the boys were immersed in a world of men performing their trade. Boys also may have been apprenticed to another tradesman to learn a skill outside of the family tradition.

We can see this alive today in the many indigenous cultures that have not lost their way due to Western intervention, with boys being educated and trained by their father *and* a community of men. In these cultures, boys have an end-state, an image of what they might turn out to be, a template, and although rites of passage ceremonies are often secret, the boys know there is some magical, mysterious process that they will undergo, which will turn them from a boy into a warrior. (We will touch on this later in the book as we consider modern rites of passage in Chapter 18.)

Tens of thousands of years of masculine ancestry and the processes refined by eons of time were delivered with precision and purpose, in ways that ensured survival of the entire tribe. These societies were highly synergistic, with a place found for every member, whether it was the best hunter, tracker, herder, spear-thrower, story-teller or healer. There is no doubt that these processes were modified and refined as they evolved. However, it was most likely driven by the rhythms of nature and the requirement to adapt to changing conditions.

So, what has this to do with the Industrial Revolution?

With the advent of mechanisation, standardisation and the ability to mass-produce, it was the wealthy industrialists who financed factories and mines, and of course, workers were needed. Boys would often become factory or mine fodder at a young age, however, the child-rearing period before that was now the mother's responsibility, as the father was often absent. In almost a single generation, the flow of masculine wisdom went from (as I once heard Biddulph describe it), 'a six-lane superhighway to a strangled drip feed.'

Mothers were ill-equipped for this role as they did not understand the foreign world of boys, and so the boys were either left to their own devices or (s)mothered. Farming families were probably the exception since the sons continued to help around the farm, however we know from history that sons were tempted by the lure of emerging cities and stories of money-earning in The Big Smoke, that farming couldn't possibly provide.

And so the change began.

We only have to look around today to see how boys have not adjusted well to this lack of fathering, as it pervades so much of modern society. Under-fathered boys abound, and it is a topic covered by many authors. I have first-hand experience of boys whose sense of masculinity is lacking and whose image of themselves as a maturing male is almost non-existent, due to their development in a masculine vacuum.

There are several authors who've written about how, as children, due simply to a lack of awareness of our parents, we become 'wounded' in a psychological sense. These wounds, often referred to as the 'mother wound' and 'father wound' can greatly influence our adult behaviour, as it's our relationship with our primary carers that sets the tone for how we will view all future relationships.

For example, a young boy comes from a family where his mother and father have separated, and he lives between two homes. When he's with his mother he hears her denigrating his father with terms like useless, an idiot, loser, no-hoper etc. and so the boy's view of masculinity is negatively influenced. He doesn't like hearing his mother speak about his father like this, yet he needs her love, so at a young age, he decides to not be like his father (whether the criticisms are valid or not) and diminishes his sense of masculinity. He now carries a 'mother wound' into adult life, which may emerge as choosing a dominating female partner who bosses him around, calls him 'useless' (since he has little sense of how to carry himself in a functional, masculine way), and if he becomes a father, the cycle continues.

If the boy receives unwarranted criticism from his father with denigrating, negative, put-down comments, the boy never gains a sense of self-worth or self-esteem. When inflicted by his father (who's supposed to 'love' him!) the boy becomes wounded with a 'father wound'. Feelings of being less-than, unworthy, not being good enough, unloved, unsure, ego-driven with bravado, and even becoming an adult bully, are all manifestations of this. These men often become 'loners', unable to navigate their inner world of emotions with any sense of competence, which doesn't bode well for interpersonal relationships or parenthood.

Sadly, we see the impact of this initially emerging in our schools, then in teenagehood, and in various work cultures.

For these men, there's an inner ache of unresolved pain, a lack of a sense of self and how to 'be' in the world. These men can become 'islands' and struggle in relationships where their partner is looking for a deeper, emotional connection and intimacy (into-me-see), yet the man can be oblivious or simply unable to navigate the complexities of his emotional inner world. In other words, the man was never shown or able to model a functional way to express healthy emotions, so they either become buried or prone to outbursts of anger and rage.

We see this often in our media-driven stereotypes mentioned earlier, who become their role models, and to find the leadership they so desperately need, gangs are a natural progression. Boys seek some structure to which they can belong, even though the 'leaders' may be mere boys themselves. '*Lord Of The Flies*' by William Golding comes to mind and we see manifestations in various forms today in dysfunctional gang cultures.

There is a lot we can learn from cultures that still provide meaningful and functional paths for their boys' transformation into manhood, however, we have to be careful not to 'cherry-pick' what we believe might be adaptable processes, for to pluck some obscure event from another culture and try to transplant it within our own, may demean and dishonour the very culture we are attempting to emulate. We need to be very mindful that these processes have evolved over millennia, and we can't possibly be cognisant of all the underlying purpose and meaning that these processes imbue. The culture in focus may not even know why these processes do what they do; they simply know that over the test of time and refinement, they have achieved the goal of turning boys into men.

The result of generations of dislocated men losing their way in a haze of lack of purpose, is that men are being viewed as 'suspicious beings.' Add the recent Australian announcement of a significant paedophile enquiry into religious organisations aimed squarely at men and there's no doubt that modern masculinity has a severe image problem. When we hear of the multiple acts of violence that keep being perpetrated, one could be forgiven for thinking that it's well deserved.

The poignant truth is that this lack of effective fathering has emerged from only the last 10 generations on the genealogical path. We see this also reflected in many dog-eat-dog corporate cultures of today, as disenfranchised men strut their stuff on the corporate stage in modern power struggles, ego-driven, with scant regard for their fellow humans, sustainability or humanity at large.

How many generations it will take to restore this is anybody's guess, however, the men's movement is gaining momentum and if the men's gatherings and retreats I've been to are any indication, we're on a road to recovery. I've also heard that Australian men are leading the (r)evolution, with more men's groups per capita than anywhere else in the world.

Men have a way to go to restore their rightful place as providers and protectors of the nest, and the process will unfold more rapidly if women more deeply understand the world of men. Men also need to make the effort to reclaim their rightful place, to challenge the distorted perceptions of masculinity and be proactive in creating opportunities for boys to learn from other men and mentors.

Key Points:

- *Prior to the Industrial Revolution boys were brought up by their fathers and often learned their father's trade*

- *The removal of fathers into factories and mines interrupted the natural flow of man-to-boy learning*

- *Men can claim their place and start to repair the maturing process*

- *Women can also support this process.*

4. MOTHERING

I've also written the book to honour men, their skill, their intuition, their pragmatism and their humour and their extraordinary ability to become boys again at a moment's notice, whatever their age. I also want to suggest to women, in particular mothers, that, consciously or unconsciously, they're preventing men from using their talents in raising their boys. The challenge remains for we women to accept who the men in our lives are and to stop wasting our energy trying to make them into something they're not.

– Celia Lashlie author of He'll Be OK

I've read many a book and heard many a story about a mother's first reaction to discovering the sex of their newborn child. Some say that the wonderment of the moment masks any response regarding whether it's a boy or a girl, as simply being in the euphoria of birth is enough. Other mothers say that they feel a distinct 'oh-my-God-it's-a-boy' moment, especially if it's their first child, and wonder how they will ever raise a son.

The whole nurturing of children during their early years is often quite different for boys and girls. Social experiments have shown that people who play with a blue-clothed child assume the child is a boy and play more rough-and-tumble activities than when the same child is dressed in pink. We all hear the *big boys don't cry* mantra that in effect prevents boys from expressing their feelings, often being told that to do so is a sign of weakness. From the moment boys are born we're talked out of our feelings, being encouraged to suppress them and 'toughen up.'

The only emotion that is encouraged for boys, especially on the sports field, is *anger*. I remember coaching my youngest son's under-8 soccer side, standing on the sideline at a match, when the opposing coach, standing just a few meters away, put his arm around the player he was about to send onto the field and loudly proclaimed, "GET OUT THERE AND SMASH 'EM!"

I remember turning to the coach and commenting, 'Dude, under 8s!! Seriously?"

Minmia is a female Aboriginal Elder who wrote a wonderful book, *Under the Quangdong Tree* in which she asks a direct question: where are the mothers of the men who commit heinous crimes in society? While there's no doubt about the possible lack of fathering, Minmia's question points to a lack of good mothering in preparing sons for social responsibility. Minmia appeals to mothers to teach their sons about sustainability, the environment, interpersonal relationships, and taking care of themselves, each other and this planet.

In not doing so, mothers are unwittingly making dependent men who will have no choice but to seek a partner who will *mother them*. Often, men raised this way lack the resilience necessary to navigate life. Unless boys have been given the opportunity as children to experience feelings of grief, sadness, setbacks or even a broken Heart, and understand that these feelings can be moved through, they will not know how to cope with them later in adult life.

When these feelings are experienced in adolescent life for the first time, they can seem insurmountable. The knock-on effects can be seen in men with a lack of empathy or care, emotionally shut down and disconnected, and often leaning toward substance abuse.

If or when a man finds a partner to mother them, on whom they'll continue their dependence, any sons they have are likely to be dependent in later life, and so the cycle repeats.

I often hear women today complain about their male partners being 'emotionally unavailable'. By this, they mean that they rarely know the emotional state of their partners, as men have learned from a young age, how to mask their feelings. To me, this is simply men taking on board their early training of not showing emotion and becoming quite good at it!

Society at large fails to recognise that most boys are raised by their mothers, have female preschool and kindergarten teachers, have mostly female primary school teachers and it's only in high school, that a boy may have access to male teachers and even here, rarely in the majority.

Do we have a combination of ill-equipped mothering, absent fathering and poor male role models?

What can mothers do differently?

It's important for mothers to recognise that there are various stages of their son's development. In the early stages of life, it's vitally important for mothers to become aware of their language and try to ensure that any references to feelings being 'bad', inappropriate, or unnecessary are not used. Comments like, "what's *wrong*?", "Don't cry!", "Brave boy!" (to avoid tears), all reinforce that expressions of feelings are not a good thing. I know from personal experience that as parents this language is so ingrained that we do this unwittingly and more often than we realise.

When a man does express emotion, particularly emotional pain or sadness, it's often such an uncomfortable place for others, that even the media reminds us that when men express emotions such as this, we are *broken*. Try entering "man breaks down in tears" into an Internet search and you'll see many headlines such as "Man breaks down in tears as he can't even afford food this Christmas." Language such as this has become so endemic, that sadly, we don't even give it a second thought. There is nothing broken about a man who has the emotional agility to cry, especially when something means so much to him.

It is also important to develop a boy's emotional vocabulary and by that, I mean explaining emotions and putting names to them. Chapter 6 contains a diagram of feeling words and their nuances that can help with this. I discovered at the beginning of my journey that I too was emotionally shut down, unable to feel, let alone put a name to any feelings I was having. It was only through deciding to embark on a psychotherapeutic process and consciously develop my *emotional intelligence* that I realised feelings themselves had 'tones' and that we have words to express them. It's almost as if I had to learn a new language, a language of feelings and their associated nuances, as well as to recognise them in my body when they were occurring, because that's where they start. If we don't support this process in our boys, then we send them out into the world bereft of a dimension of emotional expression, and unable to communicate with their partners and children, essentially emotionally illiterate and therefore disadvantaged.

As a boy matures, his relationship with his mother continues to change, as he learns more about who he is and his place in the world. This is a transition from what I call 'me' thinking to 'we' thinking, where the boy gradually discovers that he isn't the centre of the universe and that to contribute to the world, he has to start by contributing to the family unit in which he lives. For mothers, transferring tasks such as making his school lunch, or his bed every morning, doing his laundry, and learning to cook a meal on a regular basis, all contribute to increasing his sense of self.

Dads need to be involved in this transition as well by demonstrating they too contribute to home care and parenting, and although this can be a challenge for those men who might not be home when their children get out of bed in the morning, they can still be actively involved when they are home. As our children mature, dads often fill the role of more 'bloke' stuff like changing a tyre, looking after a car's needs (tyres, air, water etc.) as well as basic handyman skills such as safely using tools (more on this later in Chapter 15).

If you imagine what life skills you'd like your son to have when he's 18 then you can start the process at about age 10 or 11 with clear directions. If you wait until he's 17 and 11 months and try to cram it all in the last month, of course, it'll be a disaster, so it's best to lay out a plan *with him* and explain that these are skills he will need to lead a fulfilling and self-reliant life.

Robert Bly, introduced in Chapter 3, is the author and poet who kicked off the *mythopoetic* men's movement in the USA in the 1980s. His famous book, Iron John, published in 1990, is based on the Brothers Grimm fairy-tale of a golden-haired boy whose parents are the King and Queen. The boy finds his inner primal man in the country (Iron John) but the King and Queen decide to imprison Iron John. The golden-haired boy knows the key to Iron John's prison is under his mother's pillow and so he has to decide at some point whether to free his primal, passionate man by stealing the key from under the pillow, thereby betraying the Queen (his mother) and freeing himself.

It's a powerful story, well worth reading and one that men can relate to. Many of us might remember an incident in our boyhood lives, where we took the courageous step to steal the key. Of course, the mother can play a significant part in this growth opportunity by being aware that this is a necessary step by not only looking out for it, but also actively supporting it when it happens. Boys who do not do this miss an opportunity to commence the separation from their mothers, in preparation for manhood.

The opening quote from Celia Lashlie is taken from her excellent book, *He'll Be OK*. The author uses a bridge as a metaphor, the bridge of adolescence, and calls on modern-day mothers to allow their sons to get on the bridge, alone, at the beginning of their adolescent journey (around 12-13), and meet them at the other side when they reach around 18 years of age. Lashlie even comments that today, many mothers not only get on the bridge, but they are also camping in the middle of the road and holding up traffic! Mothers who understand that their sons need to embark on their journey of self-discovery with a sense of autonomy are allowing a natural separation process to take place.

From what I've experienced, as a society, we do little to acknowledge this process, which for mothers can be *a profound grieving process*, of letting go of the boy she birthed, wondering if they will ever be as close again. It's a significant leap of faith for mothers and we can do more as a society to honour this letting-go process and support mothers in their grief. Having a conversation about it is a good place to start.

Of course, dads can play a vital role in this process for mums, so we men need to pay attention and honour and acknowledge a mother's role in all that she has done for her son, and that feelings of grief and sadness are a natural part of this process. It is, however, a necessary step in helping the boy grow into a functional and independent man. Indigenous cultures that still have rites of passage ceremonies, often include mothers, as they understand that the boy needs to separate from his mother to move from boyhood into warrior(man)-hood, and that this is a defined and necessary process for the good of the whole community. There is a lot we can learn from cultures both present and past that do this well and later, in Chapter 18, we'll consider contemporary rites of passage.

Another resource for mothers is author Alison Armstrong, who has produced an excellent resource called 'The Amazing Development of Men', which we explore further in Chapter 7.

In it, she explores the major stages of a man's life: Page to Knight to Prince to King. Personally, I found her work beautifully insightful, balanced, and rich with ideas and relevance. As an audiobook, hearing men openly and vulnerably speak at her events of their personal experience of identifying these stages within their lives, and how they navigated them, gave it a deep level of relevance and authenticity. I remember listening to this alone, on an extended car trip, wishing I'd been aware of these stages in my earlier life, and reflecting on how it might have been different if I'd understood what was happening at the time, and why!

Mothers play a vital role in raising boys to become healthy, emotionally-competent and empathic men, which ultimately supports boys in knowing how to navigate, master and express their emotional state, leading to deeper levels of relationship intimacy.

Key Points:

- *Mothers can teach their sons to be emotionally mobile and understand that feelings are not fatal*

- *Mothers, with support of dads, can put a plan in place for their sons to acquire necessary life skills, gradually increasing over a number of years*

- *Mothers can choose to be aware of their son's Iron John and understand that 'stealing the key' is a necessary step on the road to maturity*

- *Mothers need to let their sons embark on their adolescent journey with minimal interference and support dads in their fathering role.*

◆ *Boys move through several stages of their evolution and knowing these can equip mothers with insight into how best to navigate them.*

5. FATHERING

When I was a boy of fourteen, my father was so ignorant I could hardly stand to have the old man around. But when I got to be twenty-one, I was astonished at how much the old man had learned in seven years. **– Mark Twain**

We now have some context about the issues facing growing boys, the language we use around them regarding feelings and emotions, and the requirement to create an environment that encourages their growth from boyhood to manhood, and the role mothers play.

Continuing author Celia Lashlie's metaphor of the adolescent bridge from Chapter 4, a father's role is also not to get on the 'bridge of adolescence', but to walk alongside, so the son knows he's safe and that his dad *has his back*. If the boy falls off the metaphorical bridge, it's the father who puts him back on, and chances are, that may occur more than once!

Ideally, mother and father both meet the transformed boy at the other end, and hopefully with an idea of what the 'end' looks like. Mothers find this *stepping back* difficult to do, to let go of their baby boy into a world of uncertainty, and a burning question they ask is, "Will the father be there for our son?"

Lashlie's view and experience is that pragmatic dads will hang back while mum is doing the parenting, following the adage, "If it ain't broke, it doesn't need fixing!"

One mother I know who'd read Lashlie's book on recommendation, commented that she knew she had to let her son go on his adolescent journey (bridge), however, to 'hand-over' she needed to know her husband would be there to 'step up'. Lashlie counters this by suggesting that a father will not step into the role while there is no space for him to step into. Her experience is that as mothers step back, fathers notice the vacuum and invariably step in.

Only when mothers take a leap of faith and step back, possibly seeing the wheels fall off for a couple of weeks, will the father then provide some guidance, in the way that only dads know how to do. Often, the son will naturally try to amplify his masculinity to fill the vacuum, now that he has space to do so, and in some ways unconsciously challenge his father's role as 'the man of the house'! Simply put, the son is looking for the masculine boundary and testing whether his father really has his back, as he starts on his next phase of masculine development.

It helps of course if there's some dialogue between the parents that this is about to happen, and although the mother may not believe it until she sees it, in the large majority of cases dad fills the gap, albeit not the same way a mother might do. Yes, it's a leap of faith, and there will be exceptions, but Lashlie's research shows that a considerable percentage of fathers realise it's now their turn to be the hands-on parent. It's also a time when any disrespect from the emerging teenage boy toward his mother, can be firmly addressed by his father, since the boy needs to continue to learn how to respect women, which will serve him well in his future.

I'm sure many mothers know their relationship with their sons will undergo a metamorphosis, however, they also often wonder whether the boy's father will make the necessary changes required to support the process. When dads are ensconced in their career aspirations, working long hours, and believing that *being a good provider* is all it's about, they can miss this critical juncture. We now know boys need their father (or father-figure) to be present in their lives, so they have someone to *model*. Without this, boys take their modelling from other boys, social media, movies and whatever other influences are in their lives.

When it comes to exploring their sexuality, boys are exposed to school playground banter, social media and pornography, which sadly fill this gap too (more on this in Chapter 11), so fathers must build a relationship with their sons that includes conversations about things such as sex, safe-sex, informed consent, and to provide a safe environment for our sons to ask questions.

I remember when my eldest son was in his last year of primary school and 11 years of age. We could tell his interest in sex was evidently piqued by some questions he was asking, so I took the lead role, and sat with him privately in his bedroom before bedtime. I started by explaining that I would answer any questions he had, however, he had to allow me to choose how I would answer them, plus give me the right of veto if I felt he wasn't yet ready for the detail. He agreed. What I didn't know was that it would take an entire week!

I learned much during that week, about 'bases' (1 to 11?), 'dry sex', 'wet sex', and a whole heap more in our multiple marathon sessions. What surprised me the most was the level of detail, correct or otherwise, that my son had gleaned from his friends and schoolyard conversations. By the end of the week, I think both of us were sex-talked out, so much so we never had similar conversations again. I believe his lack of shame or embarrassment around sexual conversations as an adult, evidently feeling comfortable in his skin as a sexual being, all stemmed from that one week's deep-dive. Thankfully, my psychotherapeutic journey, which involved unpacking my shame and embarrassment about sex and any such discussion (influenced by being raised by a prudish father and often inappropriate mother, resulting in my father's evident disapproval and discomfort), all happened before becoming a parent and paid huge dividends at this time. I dread to think what might have happened if he and I hadn't had that week, albeit sometimes uncomfortable and edgy for me.

The alternative is that boys keep being mothered and mothers get frustrated that they're unable to step back and let go, when something in them knows they *must*. The boys then don't get a sense of male leadership, and the family is put under unnecessary stress. It also provides a once-in-a-lifetime opportunity for father and son to get to deeply know each other, an opportunity for the father to get real and show his soft underbelly as well as his backbone, and an ideal modelling environment for the son to experience being *fathered*, which will directly affect his fathering style in his future.

If the father doesn't really know how to be a dad in this context, often due to a disconnected relationship with his own father, all is not lost. I've been in an audience of some 200 men, when Biddulph asked the men assembled to indicate the nature of their relationship with their father. He has repeated this exercise on numerous occasions and empirically, 30% of men have no relationship whatsoever, 30%

have a 'birthday and Christmas' relationship but don't talk about anything meaningful, 30% can talk with their fathers but on a limited range of subjects, and only 10% indicate they have an open and healthy relationship.

During the initial COVID lockdowns of 2020, Blake Woodward, an ex-management consultant, fatherhood advocate and founder of the social enterprise *Suit Tie Stroller*, conducted a survey to understand the impact of the lockdowns on fathers. He asked insightful questions of several hundred dads (me being one of them), mostly in white-collar roles, who'd had the opportunity to work from home during lockdowns.

One question was, "Are there any aspects of this isolation (the enforced COVID lockdowns) that you value and want to incorporate into your ideal 'new normal' when COVID restrictions are lifted?"

Men had experienced not having to commute to work, home-schooling, co-parenting, spending time with their family, shopping, organising dinner and a whole host of other activities. While this pressure-cooker environment had the potential to create increased tension in the home, only 3% of men answered that they wanted 'things to go back exactly the way they were'. In comparison, 67% wanted to 'continue spending more time with their kids once lockdowns were lifted'.

There were other fascinating insights in the report too, which question the generally held narrative about fathering, and you can find the full report at www.suittiestroller.com/dad-survey-report/ as well as other excellent resources on the website

Sadly, under-fathered boys are everywhere: boardrooms, government, factories, small businesses, schools and universities, and any man wishing to be a good father must understand their own modelling and relationship with their father, alive or dead. If they are still alive, then this is an extraordinary opportunity to mend their *father wound*. It does, however, require awareness in the approach since if the relationship is strained, walking in and accusing your father of being an uncaring, distant and cold-hearted bastard is not going to start it off on a good footing!

If you're a woman reading this, then you may be in a more objective position to encourage your partner/husband/father of your children to consider his relationship with his dad. I know from personal experience in talking with women, that buying a good book that addresses this specific issue (such as Biddulph's *The New Manhood*), often provides a door-opening opportunity, especially if the man can be honest with himself about his true father-relationship. Many men have locked their feelings of being under-fathered away in a deep, deep cave, believing that in doing so, it can all be forgotten.

If only it were so.

At the men's event I mentioned in the Introduction, there were several opportunities to discuss our memories of growing up and our relationship with our fathers. For many, we were looking for guidance, a hand on our shoulder, some acknowledgment that we were doing okay and on track, being told we were loved, that our dads were proud of us, and they had our back.

For other men it was the complete lack of a father in their lives, having no one at all to provide a model. For others, it was an abusive, addicted, workaholic or depressed father who might have died an early death or suicided. In all cases, father-hunger manifested itself within our lives in various ways, however, the underlying emotions were sadness, grief, deep yearning and loss.

If we're to be better fathers to our sons (when compared to our fathers), if our *intention* is to not repeat the behaviour of our past, then we must do the inner healing work with our fathers, irrespective of how clever we think we are, as the underlying patterns of behaviour we modelled aren't necessarily conscious, and if they're lurking in our unresolved past, they emerge at often the most inappropriate of times.

Many caring parents under duress have 'lost it' with their child and most, if not all, feel a deep sense of shame, vowing to never repeat such behaviour. However, unless addressed at its source, it continues to lurk like a shark in the ocean, waiting for another stressful opportunity to surface and take another bite. In understanding and acknowledging that the ancestral flow of father/mentoring wisdom has been choked to an occasional drip, at least we create awareness and the possibility of different choices.

Today, more and more men are questioning why they work 60 hours a week in corporate jobs, enslaved to large mortgages, lavish lifestyles and debt, while missing out on the most joyful days of their child's development. I know of cases where men have simply decided that they've had enough and have thrown in the 'keep-up-with-the-Jones's' towel and opted for a simpler, down-sized lifestyle.

If parents can truly understand this and be prepared and supportive of downsizing, every time I've seen this happen, the family unit is much, much happier. The social cost of under-fathering in our society is enormous. Boys without leadership, especially in their teens, are a force to be reckoned with. Strong, determined, supported fathering prepares boys for the responsibilities of manhood.

In Andy Roy's book, *Raising Teenage Boys*, he comments that the impending change afoot is change for the whole family, not just the boy, and that if the family doesn't understand or accept this, the entire change burden lands squarely on the shoulders of the boy who carries it for the whole family. As if the changing boy hasn't enough to contend with.

Of the 1 million single-parent Australian households, approximately 80% do not have a father present in the home, and when a dad is estranged from his children's mother, the poignant stories that emerge in a safe 'circle' will stir emotion in anyone listening. It's not uncommon to sit in a room of men, as a man shares his story of losing access to his children (sometimes as a malicious act designed to hurt), and experience how deeply this affects him and most of the listeners as they empathise.

For single mums, finding suitable men or mentors can be a challenge, especially in the climate of 'stranger-danger' so prevalent today. It takes courage, effort, commitment and trust to find strong, safe, clear mentoring for their sons. Various groups, such as sporting clubs, scouting groups and the like can provide enough opportunity for mentoring, as can other families where the father is an involved parent with his son(s).

One exercise for single mums is to take a sheet of paper and make a list of all the men you know either in your area, school, social network or clubs, in no particular order. Then draw 3 concentric circles and put your son's name in the centre. Each circle represents a level of 'fit' for your son in terms of safety, structure, values and qualities, with the inner circle providing the best fit. As you read down the list of men, intuitively place their names in one of the circles.

I'm hoping that from doing this exercise you reveal there are more capable men in your various networks than you initially thought, and that combinations of them might provide a broad section of beneficial values, skills and attributes for your son.

These men will never replace your son's real father, however, several men can be called upon to fulfil various roles, singularly or together, and provide much of the practical guidance that he needs. As the primary parent you need to be clear about what it is you're seeking and communicate that with the men you choose.

Some women who've read this in the first edition, either single mums or in a lesbian relationship, have contacted me for clarification, with some attempting to justify that they can provide ALL that their sons need. I don't have any evidence either way, but I do know that men bring a different dimension and perspective to boys, and that if feasible, they will be richer for the experience.

For nuclear families, the same applies. Having your son(s) involved in groups where other fathers are around, allows your son to see how things are done elsewhere. It's also good to discuss beforehand with the other dads how you'll go about setting boundaries for each other's kids. It can be as simple as including all the boys into one statement, "Come on lads, you know that's not OK to do", or if it's a singular boy creating havoc, "Hey Joe, I know your dad would be pretty upset if he knew you were doing that!", or if you don't feel able to bring it under control, then, "Hey Joe, I think it's time you headed back to your dad (if he's there and if not, to 'the adults') and took a breather for a few minutes to settle down."

I've discovered that boys not only need firm, loving, consistent boundaries, they often push the envelope just to see where the boundaries are, so they can relax knowing someone competent is in charge. It's almost as if once boys know who's got their back, the rules of engagement, and that they will be fairly applied, then they can get on with being boys and have fun.

Key Points:

- *Fathers need to be prepared to step into the void as mothers step back during early teenage years, otherwise disaster will reign*

- *The change needs to be borne by the whole family and not just the boy*

- *Single mums can get the support they need from various networks and organisations*

- *Dads are often yearning to be more involved with their kids but feel unable to break free of the treadmill*

- *Dads must address their relationship with their own fathers, which will make them better dads themselves.*

6. INTELLIGENCE

Your assumptions are your windows on the world. Scrub them off every once in a while, or the light won't come in.
— Isaac Asimov

In this chapter, I wish to explore the role of various intelligences and how they apply to men and our overall development. Generally, there are five accepted and broad categories of intelligences: physical intelligence (PQ), cognitive intelligence (IQ), emotional intelligence (EQ), relational intelligence (RQ) and spiritual intelligence (SQ).

Physical intelligence (PQ) refers to one's ability to be in-body with a high degree of body-awareness. For example, a great dancer, martial artist or high-performing sportsperson would have a high degree of PQ. High PQ people watch what they eat and consider the importance of nutrition, know how to manage stress, get regular exercise, understand the need for recuperating sleep and listen to their body, especially when it needs to rest.

Aiming for a high PQ gives growing boys a greater sense of self in terms of body image. A healthy, active, sporty, well-fed boy feels good about himself, has a better sense of his place in the world and is generally more confident. We know the value of sport for growing boys, both as an outlet for their exuberant energy and as an opportunity to be with other boys (and hopefully other men as either coaches or fathers), to learn how to be part of a team. A sport that has regular training sessions also provides some discipline and educates boys that to get really good at something, they have to show up and practice.

As for diet, mothers and fathers can guide their sons into eating good food (I know it can be difficult) by having only good food at home, as a hungry boy will eat just about anything rather than go hungry! A good diet, free of refined sugars, artificial colours and preservatives, coupled with organic fresh fruit, vegetables, and exercise will increase his PQ, plus provide the necessary fuel for his energetic lifestyle. If your son is a screen-bound gamer or couch-potato, then do him a favour that will impact him for the rest of his life and feed him good food and organise regular exercise. Doing this for yourself also provides good modelling, as children quickly spot hypocrisy!

Some men may have a combination of PQ values, yet my observations, especially around nutrition and the fast-food culture, are that food is an area that needs the most focus. In Australia (from the 2022 Australian Bureau of Statistics survey), approximately 8% of under-18 boys were living with obesity, and almost 20% were classified as overweight.

For men, approximately 35% were obese and 40% overweight, resulting in a combined 70% of all over-18 men either overweight or obese! (www.aihw.gov.au/reports/overweight-obesity/overweight-and-obesity/contents/summary/)

In the 2022 OECD reporting, Australia was ranked 3rd highest, behind the United States and Finland (www.oecd.org/en/data/indicators/overweight-or-obese-population.html?oecdcontrol-9202e3bf52-var3=2022/).

Evidently, we have a health crisis as do many other western countries.

Stress management is also an area in which many men don't do well. If the man in your life isn't taking care of himself in the PQ area, he needs encouragement and support to do so, and that might be as simple as cooking a healthy meal or heading out to a café or restaurant that serves nutritious food. Stress management, via exercise and massage, are also great ways for men to get into their bodies, for this is where we need to be, to *feel* what's going on inside and around us.

IQ, or Intelligence Quotient, is a well-known measure of one's intellectual or cognitive capability regarding various problems presented in some form of standardised test. Its purpose is to provide a scale on which various skills such as abstract reasoning, mathematics, reading, spatial capabilities, memory recall, vocabulary, and general knowledge are measured and compared. It doesn't, for example, present any notion of how a person might cope with psychological stress. It is a way to try to measure one's *rational mind*.

Since the early 1900s, there has been much research on Emotional Intelligence, or EQ, which in summary (thanks to Wikipedia) *"is the ability to identify, assess, and control the emotions of oneself, of others, and of groups."* Some refer to it as EI, however, I prefer the term EQ (emotional quotient), to parallel it with IQ and PQ.

As with most attempts to standardise individual humans (we are after all, completely individual) there is contention regarding the various views of EQ measurement, what they tell us about a person and how useful this information really is. What is accepted though, is that EQ tests try to quantify our *emotional mind*.

It is also generally accepted that unlike IQ, which tends to have a parental and societal inheritance bias, EQ is considered as being influenced more by our immediate surroundings and upbringing, that is, it is a *learned capability*.

In 1995, Daniel Goleman wrote what is probably the most widely read book on the subject entitled (unsurprisingly!) *Emotional Intelligence*, which became a New York Times bestseller. His model struck me as relevant to the situation we find ourselves in today, regarding boys and men.

Goleman's model has five constructs for EQ, which are:

1. Self-awareness

2. Self-regulation

3. Social skill

4. Empathy

5. Motivation

Goleman defines the first four of these as requiring a high degree of *emotional mobility*. For example, you can't be empathic to another's feelings if you don't have a strong sense of your own. Goleman states that emotional literacy can be *learned*, and my personal experience supports this.

In the early 1990s when I embarked on my journey of self-discovery, it was only with the benefit of hindsight that I realised I was very emotionally *illiterate*. It took me many years to understand *what* I was feeling in my body and then some time to be able to articulate it. I now know I had been talked out of my feelings to the degree that I didn't feel much at all and so couldn't explain what I was feeling.

Imagine living in your head, so you can only *think* your way through life, with the band between your neck and your hips dead to internal emotional feeling, but then the band below that, around your groin, is very much alive. Robin Williams' explained this, "See, the problem is that God gives men a brain and a penis, and only enough blood to run one at a time!"

So, my journey began with learning to become aware of the sensations I was feeling *in that band of my torso*. Fortunately for me, I had an extraordinarily empathic mentor who could sense the feelings I was experiencing in my body. He would ask me questions, which guided me to the sensations, and then we would work together to put words around them. As I became more and more emotionally literate, I was then able to expand my emotional vocabulary to include the *nuances* of feeling.

Women tend to be much more fluent in the language of emotion, simply because of their social environment and conditioning. As I mentioned in Chapter 4, boys are often talked out of their feelings from a young age so the challenge for parents, especially mothers, is to take every opportunity to allow their son's emotional expression and guide them into understanding what it is they're feeling, then attach *feeling words* to the feelings. The following diagrams show primary feelings in the centre, with *nuances* of these central feelings around them.

Read these carefully and you'll hopefully agree that the nuance words are not something you would hear your son use, nor perhaps the men in your life. If you're the father of a boy, these feeling words may seem strange, flowery, too 'feminine' and most likely not a part of your vocabulary either. You may know most of them, but they wouldn't form part of your everyday language, yet to be armed with such an array of options provides us with more opportunity to communicate exactly what it is we're feeling:

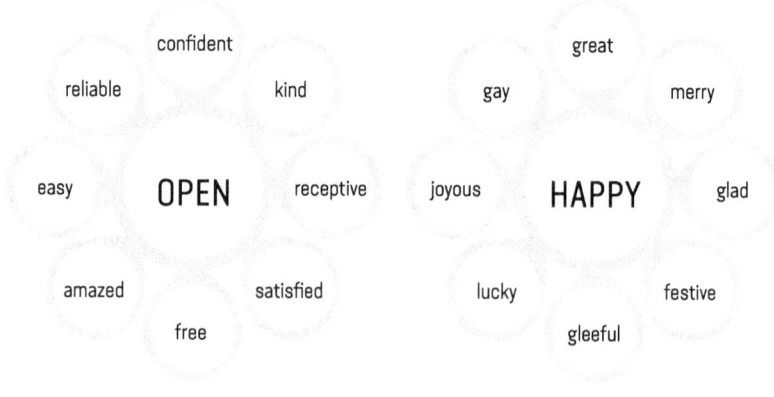

```
                    lifeless                    anxious
     insensitive              cold      terrified              alarmed

     dull    INDIFFERENT   bored    fearful    AFRAID      panic

           neutral           weary            nervous            worried
                    reserved                    scared


                    aching                     lonely
        offended           injured      grieved              unhappy

     crushed    HURT      rejected    tearful    SAD        desolate

           deprived         tortured          pained            anguish
                    pained                      grief
```

(Adapted from http://www.psychpage.com/learning/
library/assess/feelings.html)

As you can see, we're blessed with a language of such variety and choice, but only if we're educated to do so and can accurately access the words we wish to use. Authors, poets and songwriters use many of these nuance words, which are necessary to convey the breadth and depth of feeling, to add colour to phrases and to express what is in the writer's Heart.

When I hear a woman say that her partner is *emotionally unavailable*, she's not only seeking more conversation about what's really going on inside a man's head, but also seeking to understand what's going on inside his Heart. I often have to explain to women in my couples work that their man is emotionally unavailable, most likely due to his upbringing. Men need support and encouragement if they're to delve into the depths of their emotional being, and to unlearn the narrative that imprisoned them in an unfeeling body in the first place.

As the Jungian analyst and author Robert A Johnson explains in his book *The Fisher King & The Handless Maiden*, "Sanskrit has 96 words for love; ancient Persian has 80, Greek three, and English only one. This is indicative of the poverty of awareness or emphasis that we give to that tremendously important realm of feeling."

In English, we use that one word we have for love with qualifying words to describe its application: the love of adoration, romantic love, love of compassion, Platonic love etc. Not knowing Sanskrit I am unable to even imagine 96 versions of love, let alone their application in language!

The above quote by Johnson is from a man who contributed much to us learning about who we are. He comments that when a society doesn't notice that our ability to feel and express our feelings has almost disappeared, we're a society in trouble. In his book *WE - The Psychology of Romantic Love,* Johnson takes us on a journey using the myth of Tristan and Iseult (a precursor story to Romeo & Juliet) where Tristan learns to differentiate his use of the 'sword' and the 'harp'. As a man, I love this metaphor. It speaks to me and calls on me to be conscious of when to use which. Sometimes as men, we need to be decisive and sometimes, we need to be gentle. I believe a good leader knows not only that he has both a sword (head?) and a harp (Heart?) in his arsenal; he also knows when to use which and to what degree.

I asked the author Steve Biddulph in private dialogue, how he would define contemporary masculinity and his reply is along the same line as Johnson's, with an appeal to parents, especially fathers, to play an active and vital role in shaping their sons and therefore, the future of our society:

"Today we are making real progress in raising boys to be fine men. The breakthrough has been realising that two elements are needed in balance. Those elements are backbone and heart. Backbone is being strong, trustworthy, loyal, and being able to stand firm under pressure. These were more the traditional male qualities we valued in the past. Heart is the ability to be warm, empathic, affectionate and close to others, and in touch with one's own grief, anger and fear rather than converting this to displacement activities such as alcohol or violence.

Mothers can raise sons very well, but the role of dads and other men in showing boys how to be male and emotionally healthy, really helps. Many men are looking to their own development, spurred by the need to be more connected to their kids. Fathering programs and men's groups, counselling that is male-friendly, and a cultural change towards being more real, are all helping this along. I am very optimistic that we will have more good fathering, and better-loved boys and girls, in the future."

Heart and backbone.

These words have been echoing around my head ever since I read them and along with their parallels, the harp and the sword, call on me to be self-aware, to choose wisely. They also direct me as a parent as sometimes I do need to choose between them for my own two sons. These can also be seen as *feminine* and *masculine* qualities, but more on that in Chapter 19.

I cannot stress enough how much mothers play an important part in their son's ability to become emotionally articulate, so if you wish to see men in the world with a degree of emotional intelligence, bear this in mind when engaging with your son(s) or other boys in your life. I'm convinced that emotionally intelligent men take care of the planet, do not initiate war, fulfil their role as protectors and make far better partners, lovers and fathers.

In recent years there has been an emergence of a new kind of intelligence, RQ or relational intelligence. RQ is our ability to understand and navigate the complexities of relationships, which after all, unless you live alone on a deserted island, means *every* interaction with people.

RQ is the ability to understand and effectively navigate interpersonal relationships. It involves being able to perceive and interpret the emotions and intentions of others, and to respond to them in an appropriate and effective way. EQ is an evident and related component of RQ too.

People with high levels of RQ are generally able to establish and maintain positive relationships with others, and are skilled at managing conflicts and resolving problems in a constructive manner. Couples with high RQ tend to have the most rewarding relationships because they can effectively communicate and empathise with others, which helps build trust and cooperation.

Some key skills that are associated with RQ include:

Emotional awareness: The ability to recognise and understand one's own emotions and the emotions of others.

Emotional management: The ability to regulate and control one's own emotions, as well as to effectively manage the emotions of others.

Empathy: The ability to understand and share the feelings of others.

Social skills: The ability to effectively communicate, collaborate, and work with others.

RQ is important in a wide range of settings, including intimate relationships, friendships, work, and social settings. It can be an important factor in success in many areas of life, as it helps build strong, positive relationships with others, and effectively navigate social situations.

An example found in employment could be that a person applies for a role in a new company and sends their application and resumé to the Human Resources department. On paper, they have all the requisite skills, background and education. They interview well, seem pleasant enough and are offered the role. Weeks later it becomes evident that they lack even basic interpersonal skills (RQ), which causes issues in the team and business overall, and now you wish you hadn't employed them!

The importance of RQ is thankfully entering the realm of the C-suite with some emerging businesses creating a new role: the CRO – Chief Relationship Officer – a role which can be both inward-facing (ensuring internal relationships are functioning well) as well as outward-facing (relating to customers and their needs).

The good news is that our RQ is not fixed and with appropriate education, practice and awareness, we can raise it to vastly improve all aspects of our interpersonal relationships.

Finally, I want to introduce you to one last 'intelligence': Spiritual Intelligence, or SQ. No, this is not some woo-woo, New Age, incense-burning concept (I like incense by the way!). For me, it is built solidly on an emotionally intelligent base and without one, it is not possible to extend into this realm.

SQ is becoming more mainstream, having been adopted and adapted by several major corporations in their training programs. Author Tony Buzan in his book, *The Power of Spiritual Intelligence* defines SQ simply as "Awareness of the world and your place in it." Once again, we see our relationship with the world around us, defined by our self-awareness.

The benefits of SQ are variously described by practitioners as offering greater fulfilment, helping others, improving society, living in harmony, maintaining inner peace – I'm sure you get the picture. What's important to convey here is that people with high SQ are becoming valued by society. Leaders of social conscience campaign groups who genuinely care what is happening to other human beings in some remote part of the world, whether it be Amnesty International or groups like Medicin San Frontieres, typically exhibit high SQ. In recent years and due to the pervasiveness of the Internet, we've seen the emergence of various social justice groups such as Avaaz and GetUp, supporting an increase in our ability to band together to make a difference and combine our SQ capacities.

Like EQ, the good news is that SQ can also be learned. As an example, I remember reading a definition, like the SQ '10 Commandments', and one that struck me was to leave any place in better condition than when you found it. For example, if we walk through a nature area and find any rubbish, we always attempt to leave it in better condition than when we arrived, so we collect it for disposal. However, sometimes finding large items like an entire mattress, for example, has its limits!

Initially, this might feel like a drag, however, on repeating this, our sense has changed from wanting others to think good of us (there's no one around anyway), to feeling good about ourselves and our place in the world, and that we have positively contributed in some small way.

To summarise, if you're looking for a job, IQ will get you in the door, EQ will keep you there, RQ will help you build strong relationships, PQ will help you manage your day-to-day stresses and SQ will support you in your quest to become a positive and modelled leader.

There is a mountain of books and information on the Internet about PQ, IQ, EQ, RQ and SQ, and I recommend that you acquaint yourself with some resources and read widely as to how you can create rich environments that support and promote these intelligences in your home, family, work or business. Your children, especially boys, can be supported in their learning and development with these intelligences in mind.

Key Points:

- *There are five generally accepted intelligences – PQ, IQ, EQ, RQ and SQ*

- *Each intelligence can be supported in its development, especially PQ, EQ, RQ and SQ*

- *Parents can create rich environments to support their child's development*

- *Emotional literacy can be learned, as can the nuance of feeling.*

7. MATURING

Warriors are not what you think of as warriors. The warrior is not someone who fights, because no one has the right to take another life. The warrior, for us, is one who sacrifices himself for the good of others. His task is to take care of the elderly, the defenceless, those who cannot provide for themselves, and above all, the children, the future of all humanity.
— **Chief Sitting Bull**

The process of reaching maturity is very complex and we often meet people whose psychological age hasn't reached their physical age. Regarding men, as sad as it is, a common complaint I hear from women is that they look after the kids they birthed, and the other child is their male partner. The 'man of the house' may not know how to look after himself at all, having never been taught to cook, clean, iron, use a washing machine or generally take care of himself, let alone a family. His own father's absence may have resulted in him becoming overly dependent on his mother, and all he might know how to do is work and bring in an income, but not know how to be an effective parent.

To many potential partners, a man who cannot perform even the most basic functions of self-care might be seen as 'chick-proof' and 'domestically-challenged'. After all, if a man cannot take care of himself, how can he take care of a partner and a future family? How can this be so prevalent? Why isn't this seen in indigenous cultures? What can we do differently?

If our parents are not willing to let us grow and take responsibility for day-to-day tasks, and don't provide learning opportunities to do so, we never grow up, psychologically speaking. It is vitally important that parents look for the right timing and opportunity to encourage their sons to take on more tasks, and this can be seen as an opportunity for the acquisition of further life skills.

Using Lashlie's adolescent bridge metaphor again, mothers can recognise when their son is ready for their adolescent journey, let him go and meet him on the other side, and the son can't do this with his mother leading him, or having her in tow. He needs to be unfettered, untethered and cut loose from her apron strings.

In Johnson's book, *HE: Understanding Masculine Psychology*, the myth of Parsifal and the Holy Grail provides a stark reminder of how, as men, we can be blinded and wounded (more on this in Chapter 17) by our 'mother complex', which ultimately prevents us from finding our own Holy Grail. In the myth, Parsifal decides to leave home to find Camelot and King Arthur, and become a knight, so he is sent on his way by his mother wearing a homespun tunic that she made for him. She also advises that if he ever finds himself in someone's house, out of respect, he must not ask questions, since it is bad manners to do so.

Sure enough, where the other knights have failed, young Parsifal finds the Grail Castle, the drawbridge lowers, he enters the castle and sees the Holy Grail, yet because he is 'blinded by his mother's homespun' or in other words, has not matured through his mother-separation stage or healed his 'mother wound', he doesn't ask the very question that will save the kingdom and heal the wounded King and the land, even though he knows the question to ask!

Johnson likens this to a man's quest. Often in late adolescence we find ourselves in the Grail Castle yet don't realise we have the opportunity to ask the very question that will irrevocably heal our wound, for life. Johnson also suggests (and this has been my experience) that it's not until much later in life that a man may get a second opportunity to enter the Grail Castle again, and hopefully, the man has developed the psychological maturity this time to ask the question, heal the King (himself) and the land (his psyche).

How could this maturing process be different for boys?

Firstly, Indigenous cultures that still maintain some semblance of their traditions, know that both boys and girls require different processes and skills to reach the level of culturally-related maturity required for their very survival. For boys, imagine a culture that didn't get the maturing process correct, such that the boys were not deliberately grown into competent hunters and defenders. If the next generation is weakened and that continues to the next generation in an ever-weakened state, then the tribe will never recover, hunting and warrior skills will diminish and ultimately, the very survival of the entire culture will be under threat.

By definition, these processes were honed over thousands of years to ensure the survival of the tribe, each member having a place and a role with the merging synergies that ensured the tribe's overall survival. We will explore this later in Chapter 18, regarding *rites of passage*, which formalise a process for helping boys mature, and also an opportunity for men to do a similar journey, as it's never too late.

For now, we need to understand especially what parents can do to assist in the process, day-to-day, and it starts with understanding that to not provide our sons with basic life skills, is to set them up to find a partner who will *mother* them. If they then have children, that mother will continue to mother her children and her partner, any sons in that relationship will become mother-dependent, and so the cycle perpetuates. Sadly, some modern cultures have almost institutionalised a mother's role to do everything for their sons, who then grow into very codependent men.

To return to my earlier comment about women complaining that their partners are another child they have to look after, this is a sign that their partner was never provided with the opportunity to cut their apron strings, and it seems to be the norm rather than the exception.

Let's look at the typical maturing process from babies, to boys, to men, to older men.

From birth, there is no doubt that any child needs their mother or someone in a mothering role (and yes, it can be a father in that primary parenting role too). There's so much recent research to support the early nurturing years with *attachment parenting*, breastfeeding, co-sleeping, hugging, skin brushing, baby massage, music, love! etc. that I'm at a loss to understand why more prospective parents are not educated about the substantial benefits.

From zero to about 2 years of age, children are very dependent on their primary caregiver for just about everything. As they reach 2 to 3 (or what most parents know as 'the terrible 2's') something changes, and children begin to understand they can now do things for themselves. They can stand, sit, play, get from A to B, communicate with language, express specific emotions, and a whole host of other things that don't require their parent's help. This is an age of understanding that they have *will*, and is a time of them learning to assert it!

Yes, the embarrassment of your child writhing on the floor like an upended cockroach with a voice level to wake the dead, coupled with the location being the well-placed sweet treats area at the checkout of the supermarket, is not the ideal place (clever kids!), and it's normal to hope that at this moment the floor would open up and swallow you, or that you'll wake from a bad dream. The good news is that any parent in the immediate vicinity knows exactly how you feel, and those that aren't parents will remember this day when it's their turn. How you respond at this moment is of paramount importance, as tantrums are simply little people's way of flexing their emotional muscle, to see what they can accomplish, how solid are *your* boundaries and how much patience do you have?

Any parent who experiences their child's first tantrum will firstly, be shocked that their cuddly, butter-wouldn't-melt, innocent child has just been possessed by some foreign entity and is capable of such outright emotional expression, then secondly, often not know how to deal with it. Robin Grille, the author of *Heart To Heart Parenting*, a family educator and father, said in one of his talks that the most important advice was to learn to develop the patience and skill to allow the tantrum to take its own course and ..... b r e a t h e ....!

At a parenting event I attended run by Steve Biddulph, he asked who in the audience had ever lost it with their kids? From about

50% of the room, a sea of sheepish hands was slowly raised, including mine and Steve's. In true Biddulph-style, he looked at the others who were probably feeling a tad smug by this stage and quipped, "And the rest of you haven't spent enough time with your kids!"

What was important about this experience is that no one is perfect. Kids stretch us to the limit on regular occasions, and if we can maintain any sense of self-awareness (high EQ?), we can move through this stage with both us and our children relatively unscathed. If we as parents are prepared to hold firm and consistent boundaries, have a partner who supports and reinforces this consistency, and the communication channels are open between the parents to compare notes, then children finally understand that they cannot control their world through emotional means.

If a child is not guided well through this stage, they can become the four- to five-year-old who is known for 'tantrums', and will often be excluded and isolated from group play, since the other kids don't wish (or perhaps don't know how to) deal with a peer that's losing their temper when they don't get their own way. Definitely not socially attractive!

If left unchecked, as the child grows into a teenager and then an adult, the result is a person who manipulates their world and people around them, by using emotions such as sulking, anger, 'the silent treatment', withdrawing, gaslighting, ghosting etc. That's when you know you're dealing with a five-year-old in an adult's body, and the best way to navigate this is to see them simply as that five-year-old.

This often happens as a result of the actual five-year-old not getting the attention and guidance required to move them through this stage, whether it's due to lack of parental bonding and contact, younger siblings being born so the attention goes to them, or simply that the parents don't have the necessary skills, education and awareness required to navigate through this minefield. The good news is that nowadays, there's so much help available in the form of books, online material and support groups, that one simply has to be motivated to seek it out. Sadly, many are not.

From about the age of five, children are in a stage of wonderment. Parents who get to spend time with their children from this age generally enjoy their role, as boundaries are relatively established, and the child is yearning to learn and develop independence.

There's also something profound about seven-year cycles in our lives.

Our first seven years form our character, we learn to talk, express ourselves and relate. When my first son was approaching his seventh birthday, we made a big fuss about it, explaining it was a major milestone in his life, and that he would be granted new freedoms and responsibilities. There would also be some memorable event that would mark his movement into 'big boy' territory! He chose a day at a major fun park that had him completely exhausted by the end of it, however a day that he still remembers.

Our second son received from me a very personal message, framed so that he can keep it, as a memory of that important milestone. I cannot emphasise enough how important it is for our children to feel seen, heard, acknowledged, respected and loved, at all stages of their lives.

Just as it is important to have rites of passage during the teenage years, I felt it was important for them both to know that 7 was a major moment, plus it provided an opportunity to plant the seed that 14 would be the next big transition.

From 7 to 14 a boy starts to become aware of the world outside of himself. He starts to develop his ego, the identity he will need to navigate life and find his place in the world. During this time boys who establish an interest in reading can devour exciting books on fantasy worlds, detective stories, superheroes and a whole host of masculine themes. Action movies (think Marvel or DC) are popular, shoot-em-up games and consoles are their regular form of entertainment, and also their social network. Their language is influenced by the shows they watch, the music they listen to and school-yard conversations.

Then boys reach adolescence.

Recent science has discovered that as children, our brains make many connections (synapses) between brain cells, then during puberty, the brain starts to lose these unused connections, known as *brain pruning*, while allowing others to strengthen. Over a few years, the number of synapses reduces dramatically, often by as much as 60%, while new sections are made and rewired. This can continue into their late 20s as their adult brain emerges and the frontal cortex matures.

In another presentation I attended by Steve Biddulph, he explained that at the pruning stage, a parent would find engaging with teenagers easier if we subtracted 12 from their chronological age. For example, a 14yo would be seen as a 2yo in that the 2yo tantrum stage of expression and emotional counter-dependence is very similar to a 14yo asserting that you as a parent know nothing, the world is all messed up and life sucks.

In regard to boundaries for boys during these years, Lashlie uses a fabulous metaphor of an electric fence. She advises that in school years 7 & 8 (typically 11yo-13yo), you imagine a fence that has a mild current running through it, like on a farm. You know it's there, and if you choose to touch it, it'll give you a reminding and unpleasant jolt.

In years 9 & 10 (14yo-16yo), the electricity through the fence has to be the equivalent to the National Grid! Nothing gets past it, any contact with it lets the boy know it means business, and it is certainly not to be messed with.

In year 11 (16yo-17yo), the electric current is reduced back to year 8 levels, so the boy knows it's still there and will provide a tingling reminder.

In year 12 (around 18yo), it turns into a white picket fence with several exits, each of which the boy-becoming-man can explore as he decides whether he will head to university, try to find a job, go travelling or move out of home.

Personally, I really liked this metaphor since it reminded me of my own years in high-school and the stages I traversed, albeit at the time completely unaware I was in any process, but my father surely let me know the electric fence was there.

At the time or writing, my eldest son is transitioning into a fine young man, and I've felt relief by seeing the National Grid turn into the white picket fence at about 17 years of age. To witness his change in focus from inward (all about 'me') to outward (about 'we') especially regarding his work and social group, has been a delight and I can see he's on a solid trajectory to becoming a healthy and functional man. His younger sibling, by six years, seems to have learned much from his trailblazing elder brother. Time will tell.

The years 14 to 21, therefore, are about *identity*, how boys fit in, building their social networks and hobbies, team sports, searching for independence, physical changes, dating, and a dawning realisation that soon, they might have to stand on their own two feet and head out into the big wide world as an adult.

Our society already has a special place for 21st birthdays, with a *key* as a common theme used to symbolise that the child has now reached a level of maturity, that they are bestowed with a key to the home, a sure sign they've finally matured and reached adulthood. For those that make it relatively unscathed, the adventure of adulthood awaits. Unfortunately, some boys don't do well during this transition and so we'll take a look in the next chapter at the statistics concerning men.

As mentioned in Chapter 4, Alison Armstrong's audio book *The Amazing Development Of Men*, captured my attention when she explained her model of the four phases of development, being Page, Knight, Prince and King, which I share here, in summary, to further enhance our understanding of how boys and men mature.

She asserts that up to 14 years of age, a boy is in his *Page* phase, learning the ropes, understanding how the world works and finding his place in the hierarchy of his immediate family, friendships and social groups. In olden times, this was the time of the apprenticeship, being with older men and learning a trade.

From 14 to 28, the *Knight* phase is the time when a boy grows into a man, perhaps establishes a relationship that might not lead to marriage or children, and 'storms castles, slays dragons and rescues damsels in distress'. In our modern world, this may emerge as risk-taking behaviour, drugs and alcohol, partying, one-night-stands, friends-with-benefits relationships (aka 'situationships'), tattoos and piercings, and exploration of his limits, hopefully without any major harm to himself or others.

It's common at the end of this phase, around 28-30 for a young man to suddenly hit the wall, ask "is this all there is?", and find himself in a state of *ennui* (pronounced 'ahn-WEE') and means a feeling of listlessness and dissatisfaction with life, and a lack of excitement. It's almost as if the previous fire-in-the-belly hero drive and ambition have quelled somewhat, and men I've coached at this stage and age, have reported remarkably similar experiences. This is an important time in a young man's life since it's the gateway to his next stage of maturing. (The feeling of ennui is discussed in more detail in Chapter 24, Seasons.)

Who is he? What does he value? What work will fulfil him? What kind of partner does he want? Will he get married one day? Will he become a father? Is he ready for the responsibility of family? Where might he find happiness?

As the famous DJ Avicii noted in one of his songs, *Wake Me Up*, "All this time I was finding myself, and I didn't know I was lost." (He tragically took his own life, aged 28.)

I've spoken with and supported men at this age of their transition, what astrologers also call The Saturn Return, and it can be a time of major upheaval. It's a necessary phase of further refinement and development, a time to self-assess and reflect on what's important, while setting a trajectory for his next stage of growth.

Following on from the *Knight* phase is that of the *Prince*. Typically, this occupies his 30-42 age period (of course, this can vary for the individual), where the young man might enter a long-term relationship (de-facto or marriage), secure his castle and settle into the responsibility of being a partner or husband, and consider becoming a father. It's also important for a Prince to ask himself whether he's a 'build for' or 'build with' type of Prince.

'Build for' Princes tend to work hard to build their castle, then invite their Princess into the finished work. 'Build with' Princes might do the same in terms of work effort, but they invite their Princess to work *with* them, in partnership, to build something together.

If a 'build with' Prince meets a 'build for' Princess, it can stress the relationship and it might not survive, since he may feel he's doing it all on his own and carrying a dream for both of them. If the opposite is true and a 'build for' Prince meets a 'build with' Princess, then he might feel constrained and overshadowed by his partner's eagerness to build with him, when he wants to do it all on his own.

Toward the end of the Prince stage a man typically feels he's finally 'made-it', can now feel somewhat secure in his future, perhaps has a stable job, good marriage, healthy relationship and growing children. Sadly, Armstrong notes this 'late Prince' phase only lasts a short time and precedes a man's transition into his midlife, which she sees as somewhat tragic, since the sense of peace often experienced at this time might be fleeting.

And then we enter midlife!

Whether a man's midlife passage is a transition, transformation or crisis, depends on many factors. Armstrong calls it *The Tunnel*, a place where values and beliefs that no longer serve are burned away or jettisoned, ready for the man to emerge as a King.

In John C Robinson's exceptional book, *Death Of A Hero, Birth Of The Soul*, he creates the story of Everyman, to show that while each of us men may think our journey through midlife is unique, it is in fact a well-known and documented path, that others have walked and lived to tell the tale. He asserts we must embrace the surfacing childhood wounds we haven't yet healed, so we may live our remaining life unfettered by them, and free to choose our path of service. Failure to do so can lead to living the life of an embittered and lonely old man.

Robert A Johnson's view is that our midlife is a repositioning of our internal centre of gravity, from our ego to something bigger than ourselves, a higher purpose, yet a challenging time to let go of our ego without hurting our physical body. He is of a similar view that this is a pivotal time in a man's life, to reinvigorate ourselves with new purpose and potency for our remaining years ahead.

A man who does this well, often with the support of other older and wise men, or Elders (see Chapter 25), who've successfully traversed their midlife, emerges into his *King* phase: solid, aware, focussed, self-assured and knowing he's out the other side. Kings need to know they can give and contribute, be appreciated by those around them and be acknowledged for their growth and contribution. They also hope that if they have a female partner, she has done her own Queen work, to meet him as an equal so they may reign together into older age. A relationship can end if the King emerges from his tunnel, only to find his partner is unable to meet him as his Queen, or perhaps has remained as a mothering figure whose focus is still on the children and no longer on the relationship. This can create havoc in an empty-nest situation, with two adults who realise that they don't know each other, and have lost connection and sight of why they came together in the first place.

Kings now know what they know, however, they can often be so enthused by their liberation that they want everyone around them to know what they now know too! Sometimes this can be a challenge and might even be experienced by those around them as preaching and telling others what to do and how to live their lives. Thankfully, some Kings mature further into King-Elders who know what they know, yet sit back, observing, waiting for those who come within their orbit to seek their counsel. King-Elders are more than willing to share their wisdom with those who seek it yet might also answer a question with a deeper question, on which the man can reflect. King-Elders are truly amazing men to be around and have a deep and palpable presence.

If you're a younger man reading this, yet to traverse your mid-life passage, find a King-Elder in your orbit, observe them and see what characteristics you admire and would like to model, to help you with this transition, then ask if they'd be open to mentoring you. You'll be very happy you did.

We will come back to explore the seasons of a man's life and Eldership itself, in the final chapters of this book.

Key Points:

◆ *Parents need to provide basic life skills education for their sons*

◆ *Emotional maturity and resilience come from experiencing adversity*

◆ *Maturing is a process with well-defined steps or stages, and many have written about it*

◆ *Men in their midlife can reach out to older men to support them through challenging times.*

8. STATISTICS

The corporate world dares to say to young men, knowing how much young men want to be men, that the only requirement for manhood is to become an alcoholic. That's disgusting. It's a tiny indication of the ammunition aimed at men who try to learn to talk or to feel.

– Robert Bly

I chose this albeit dated quotation from Robert Bly because after releasing his book, *Iron John* in 1990, the book resided on the New York Times best-seller list for 62 weeks and provided a platform for us men to take a good look at ourselves.

While the focus might have broadened from alcohol to additional substances, gambling, social media and pornography, Bly is the man who identified issues in our society primarily driven by a lack of fathering, missing rites of passage and a culture that preys on the half-state of boy-men who never really mature. The sons of these men then lack an immediate role model, and so the cycle continues when they become fathers.

Bly's specific mention of alcohol as a way of numbing feelings is pertinent to the previous discussion regarding learning that feelings are not only a part of life, but they are also a necessary expression and something to be cherished, not squashed down or numbed with various substances, whether legal of illegal.

What are the statistics regarding indicators of men's health? If you've listened to the radio, watched the news, read newspapers, scanned social media or immersed yourself in any books specifically about men, you might be confused since what you've read or heard may be contradictory.

I decided to do my own research, firstly via the Australian Bureau of Statistics (ABS), to better understand what facts are available, and supplement this research with other related information. I offer the information below as an extract of some very detailed statistics specifically about men, with an occasional reference to women as a comparison.

In a book of this nature, it's not possible to do this for every country, so I encourage the reader if you're from another country, find the statistics relating to your country as there are many high-quality sources on the Internet.

Please bear in mind this information extracted from the ABS is only as accurate as the collection methods involved, and only for Australia:

- In Australia by mid-2024, of the 44,399 people in jail around the country, 40,967 (92%) were men. This number grew from 27,078 in 2011, an increase of 50% in just over a decade. Of the men in jail 60% had been previously imprisoned

- The largest category of offence at 28% was 'acts of violence intended to cause injury'

- The second highest category at 18% was 'sexual assault and related offences', up from 12% in 2011

- Of the 7,352 prisoners held for 'sexual assault and related offences', 7,244 (98.5%) are men

- In 2023 there were 3,187 registered suicides of which 2,406 (75%) were male (almost 7 men per day), with the biggest group in the 40-44 age bracket, at 240 men. (Remember, these are sons, fathers, brothers, grandfathers, uncles, mates, work colleagues ... not just statistics!)

- In the last 30 years, the *standardised suicide rate* for males has reduced from 21.1 per 100,000 to 18.0, so gradual progress is being made, although with population increase, the actual numbers are rising

- Of the 96,180 total male deaths in 2023:

    - 10,343 (10.7%) were from heart attack and heart disease compared with 6,579 (6.8% for women), and the highest cause of death. This has decreased by 30% in the last decade, suggesting better health awareness relating to heart health and access to improving medical technology, such as portable AEDs (Automated External Defibrillator)

    - Dementia and Alzheimer's now rank #2 at 6,111 deaths (6.3%) and have risen by 7.6% in the last decade

    - Prostate cancer is currently ranked #6 at 3,726 deaths (3.8%)

- Self-harm ranked #11 at 2,406 (2.5%) but is the highest contributor for external factors outside of physical health

• Men are more than twice as likely as women to have substance use disorders, with alcohol disorders being three times more common than drug use. Young women are closing the gap on young men

• 1 out of every 7 men will experience depression at any given time.

Reading these grim and unsettling statistics makes me aware as a man, that being born male is very much an occupational hazard. Clearly, these rates of various forms of disease, incarceration, and death signify that there is much to do to increase the physical, emotional and mental health of men. While the previous chapters provide some foundational reasons why these results might be as they are, are we any closer to making the necessary changes to redress such issues? Surely, the first step in any process we put in place to tackle any situation is to admit we *have* a problem in the first place.

Men: We have a problem. The facts speak for themselves. Now let's get on with doing something about it since we are inherently good at fixing things, however not apparently ourselves.

Women: We need your help and not your judgements. We need it now and your sons need it urgently to ensure they don't become one of these statistics. Some boys are starting to believe they are the disposable gender.

Not that long ago, I was discussing men's issues with a female friend who retorted that as women, 'we're over the bleating hearts of men and wish they'd just step up and get on with it!' It got me thinking: what is 'stepping-up' and what is 'getting on with it'?

Does stepping up mean that we should suddenly drop our baggage and become more self-aware, more enlightened, emotionally available, better partners/husbands/lovers/fathers? And as for getting on with it, does this mean we're to magically undo our dysfunctional learning, so we can simply move on?

Believe me, I wish it were so, and that the resources were there to support such an approach.

There has been many a time in my journey where I wanted the pain of *unlearning* to go away, for someone to come along and 'make it better', to do it *for* me, especially during periods of loneliness and desperation to 'get it right' and simply wanting to belong. Yet that is not the way of this journey. Feelings of isolation seem to be the most prevalent amongst men, certainly in the groups and gatherings I've attended. It is very much a case of chicken-and-egg. On the one hand, we need to find someone to talk with, who we can learn to trust, and on the other hand, we need to find someone we can trust, who we can talk with. But if we don't know someone that well because of our isolation, we don't know whether we can trust them, so we do nothing, and the situation worsens.

I was alarmed at the statistics, particularly around jail, violence and the state of men's health in general. Evidently, we're not making headway, as these statistics would be reducing across the board if we were. Therefore, we have to broaden our approach and it must include women who can choose to support the boys and men in their lives by taking an active role, and being genuinely interested in understanding their issues.

There is now an emerging body of evidence from specialists such as Dr Bessel van der Kolk (*The Body Keeps The Score*), Dr Richard Schwartz (*No Bad Parts*) and Dr Gabor Maté (numerous books and *The Myth Of Normal* in particular), that our adult mental health, and our subsequent physical health and addictions, are tightly coupled with our upbringing and what Maté refers to as big 'T' and little 't' trauma experienced when we are young. No one escapes because how we are raised has shifted from a village environment, to many now living in impersonal cities, with *disconnection* and *loneliness* being major negative contributing factors affecting men's wellbeing.

Clearly, the statistics show that as a society, we're not doing well in regard to taking care of men's wellbeing, and while men can do more for themselves, women can also support the men in their lives by encouraging them to seek good, functional male company and to take care of their health – mental, emotional, physical and spiritual.

The Office For Women was established in 1974 and celebrated its 50th anniversary in November 2024. There have been many approaches and representations to our political leaders especially over the last 2 decades, to appoint a minister for Men's Health. Sadly, all to no avail as once again, such a move is seen as taking away funding from the plight of women and girls, making it an 'either/or' situation rather than an 'and'.

Instead, in May 2024, the Victorian state premier Jacinta Allan appointed Tim Richardson as the Parliamentary Secretary for Men's Behaviour Change, which, as you can probably imagine, received much criticism from many quarters, with men especially taking to social media and decrying this appointment, such as "You are demonising men when a very small % are offenders and almost all them are people you've already let out on bail or are known to police already." In other words, painting all men, once again, with one brush. Any death is a tragedy and a blight on the society around it, but my view is that moves such as this do little to heal the divide and even less to support the men who need it most.

Once again, the statistics speak for themselves.

Although the Australian Institute of Criminology (AIC) was quoted in a Washington Post article (www.washingtonpost.com/world/2024/05/30/australia-victoria-mens-behaviour-change-domestic-violence/), on the above parliameappointment, reporting that the *"Australian Institute of Criminology in April (2024) showed a 28 per cent increase in intimate partner homicides committed against women, compared to 2022-2023",* the same AIC webpage states, *"AIC Deputy Director Dr Rick Brown said that the 2022–23 homicide incident rate in Australia of 0.87 per 100,000 was 4% higher than the previous year.* **However, it still represented a 52% reduction in homicide incidents since the statistical program began in 1989–90."** (Emphasis added - www.aic.gov.au/media-centre/news/australia-sees-rise-female-intimate-partner-homicide-new-research-report/)

In fact, the Australian Institute of Health and Welfare (AIHW) reports the intimate partner homicide victimisation rate *decreased* for both females (from 0.95 to 0.32 per 100,000 – a 68% *reduction*) and males (from 0.36 to 0.04 per 100,000) between 1990-2023.

(www.aihw.gov.au/family-domestic-and-sexual-violence/responses-and-outcomes/domestic-homicide/)

We also know from the AIHW research that there are substantial contributing factors, such as:

- A history of sexual violence by the homicide offender
- The offender's mental and physical health, particularly depression and suicidal ideation
- The offender has experienced traumatic life events, including war, homelessness, incarceration, abuse and neglect as a child, and the death of significant family members
- Unforeseen separation between victim and offender (such as ending the relationship)
- The offender's jealousy and perception of violations of gendered norms (eg partner studying or working)
- Country of origin and other cultural influences

For some, one, or a combination of, the above can lead to catastrophic outcomes, and sadly, there is no silver bullet other than continued awareness and acknowledgement of who the at-risk populations are.

If a person is appointed for 'men's behaviour change', or any endeavour for societal change, those we are asking to change need to know if the change is happening and if it's in the direction we want, at the rate we need. Positive feedback is a well-known mechanism for supporting change, so when the media fails to report any progress in this area, it disenfranchises the very cohort to whom the requirement for change is being directed. It is, therefore, complicit in ongoing vilification by withholding the very information that would encourage more men to pay attention and support change.

As I've previously stated, any homicide (domestic or otherwise) is a tragedy that should never happen and has a huge local and societal impact, yet for the media to cherry-pick information to support a narrative that fails to address the very issue it purports to support, shows it is willingly ignoring any progress that's being made, by failing to report in a balanced way.

In the following chapters, we will look more deeply at some of the important areas referred to in these statistics, explore reasons why they are what they are, and in doing so, consider some solutions.

Key Points:

◆ *Being male is an occupational hazard*

◆ *Violence is on the increase as are addictions*

◆ *Men need to be honest about the state of men's health and make a concerted effort to address the decline*

◆ *Health programs for men must be tailored for men, as generic solutions are not the answer*

◆ *Women can do much to support the males in their lives by encouraging them to seek good male company, and regular medical and mental health reviews.*

9. HEALTH

When The Dalai Lama was asked, "What thing about humanity surprises you the most?" he answered:

MAN, because he sacrifices his health in order to make money, then he sacrifices his money to recuperate his health, and then he is so anxious about the future that he doesn't enjoy the present, and as a result he doesn't live in the present or the future, and he lives as if he's never going to die and then he dies having never really lived.

If you search the Internet about men's health, there is much information available from a range of sources. If you're an Australian man, you can expect, on average, to live to 81.1 years of age, compared to women who can expect to live to 85.1 (as of 2024). According to health statistics, men die in greater numbers than women from almost every non-sex-specific health problem. For every two women who die, three men die, and it is only in the over-65 age group that women catch up since so many men never reach retirement age in the first place!

If we look at the funding for women's health and compare that with men's health for the last four federal budgets (2022-2026), the picture is dire:

Funding Allocated to Women's and Men's Health (M$)

Budget Period	Women's Health	Men's Health
2022-2023	330.6	-
2023-2024	69.1	10.9
2024-2025	16.7	11.6
2025-2026	792.9	-
Total	1,345.0	22.5

(www.amhf.org.au/federal_budget_confirms _men_s_health_is_not_a_national_priority/)

We men are often viewed as being resistant to seeking help, which is somewhat true, but is this a symptom of another cause?

If men's health funding and, therefore, social awareness is in such dire need of improvement, then men are not being subjected to the education process that a well-funded men's health campaign might have. Without the awareness, men suffer in silence, so there is no wider perceived need for men's health. We have another classic chicken-and-egg scenario.

As an example, 'Pink Ribbon Day' and all the social awareness around breast cancer for women are one such area. Contrast this to education regarding prostate cancer, especially when more men die each year of prostate cancer than women die of breast cancer. It can be argued that breast cancer affects women often at a younger age while prostate cancer is viewed as an 'old man's' disease, so the focus goes more to women. However, when the imbalance of funding is 60 to 1 across a whole range of health sectors, one would have to ask, "Why is this happening?"

The prevalence of heart disease is by far the greatest risk to men, with the primary issue being the thickening of the arterial walls, which reduces blood supply to the heart. Ageing, smoking, stress, diabetes and high blood pressure are major contributing factors, along with hereditary factors. According to the World Health Organisation, heart disease is the most common cause of death in Western countries. When coupled with deaths from throat/lung cancer, stroke, respiratory disease, prostate cancer, dementia, colon cancer, blood disorders (such as leukaemia), diabetes and suicide, no wonder many men don't live long lives with two out of five men die prematurely (before age 75) from preventable conditions.

Men also work in higher-risk areas such as mining, construction, and logging, as well as the long hours associated with corporate life. Men also attach a great deal of self-esteem to their work. Rising male unemployment results in a rise in health-related issues. Social conditioning that encourages men to front-up, shut-up, put-up, man-up, and get-on-with-it-without-complaining, adds to the overall poor state of men's health, so the outcome should not be all that surprising.

Referring to the conditioning the majority of boys receive, being brought up to act tough and not show emotions or feelings, carries through into their adult life as a man. It is well documented that many men don't seek the help of a medical professional until the condition they are experiencing interferes with some aspect of their life, such as work, or they become debilitated enough that family members make medical appointments for them, out of concern.

When men suffer from depression, they can often be so resistant to seeking help that the entire family is affected. Depressed men are twice as likely as women to turn to alcohol, drugs or gambling as a coping mechanism, which exacerbates their depression.

Men are also considered by science to be the genetically weaker species. Recent research has suggested that the 'X' chromosome, of which women have two (X-X) and men only have one (X-Y), carries important functions that contribute to overall immunity. Maybe the X-X combination improves women's immunity, which is then passed on to their children through birth and breast-feeding. This makes it even more important for men to ensure we eat well and take care of our body and its immune system, as stress causes the release of the hormone *cortisol*, now known to be a primary cause of depressed immunity.

As an anecdotal experience regarding my own health, I had never experienced acupuncture but had heard about a local practitioner who was reputedly very good at his craft. I decided to visit him for a 'tune-up' and see what he could offer. After the initial questions about lifestyle and the like, he asked if he could take my pulse. He did, with three fingers, which seemed strange, then rattled off the childhood illnesses I'd had, such as scarlet fever, measles, and chickenpox, all of which amazed me. He then asked if I usually became ill shortly after starting a holiday. I was just about to take a holiday and didn't wish to pass up an opportunity to stay well, so I answered a surprised yet emphatic "Yes, I do! How did you know?"

He replied that in Chinese medicine, the *liver is the emotional seat of the body* and that he could tell I had a propensity to store my emotions and stress in my liver, rather than express them. Then, when I went on holiday and relaxed, my liver released the emotional and physical toxins (because it now could), and so I would become mildly but uncomfortably ill, often with a chest infection or persistent head cold.

The acupuncturist advised that a few treatments would rebalance my *chi* (energy) and all would be well. I had weekly treatments for six weeks and for the first time in my life felt like I was actually on holiday from the day I got on the plane. And I didn't get ill at all! I truly believe the acupuncture helped me gradually release my stress prior to the holiday and in doing so, kept my immune system functioning at its peak. I've also never re-experienced being sick while on holiday as I now ensure I manage my stress, especially before taking leave.

If we refer back to Chapter 6 on Intelligence, physical intelligence (PQ) refers to how well we use and respect our bodies. Diet, exercise, stress management and rest are all aspects of PQ and men's health would benefit substantially from an increased awareness of all of these, especially while we're growing up. Unfortunately, fast-food culture is impinging on our requirement for nutritious food, which often costs much more than a burger and chips from the local fast-food chain.

For me, diet is a particular focus as I see many men eating poor food. During my early adult years my diet was mostly processed food, I didn't eat much fruit as I'd convinced myself I didn't like it and I also ate minimal vegetables. However, during the mid-1990s I started to become aware of organic and homegrown staples, so today my diet and that of my family, which includes two growing sons, has plenty of organic food. While I have read studies that claim the nutritional value of organic and non-organic food is the same, apart from wanting to minimise my ingestion of pesticides and herbicides, organic food tastes better, and if purchased from a local growers' market or co-op, the food was most likely only picked recently, so still full of life! Anyone who has picked a tomato from a vine or an apple from a tree and eaten it then and there, knows the difference between a tomato bought from a supermarket that's been in cold storage for months and one that's just been picked.

Since buying from farmers' markets and food co-ops, I've also become much more attuned to the cycles of nature, as various fruit and vegetables disappear and reappear with the seasons. Supermarkets are notorious for putting food into cold storage so that we can have whatever we want, all year round, and I question the true nutritional value of eating an apple that's 6 months old. While organic food may cost more, a recent poster I read summed it up nicely: *Organic food is not expensive when you consider the cost of medical bills.* Touché!

We are repeatedly advised of the need for regular exercise, and I do see more men understanding the benefits and committing to bike rides, mountain biking, running, walking, sport, gym and a whole host of other activities.

When it comes to stress management, our Emotional intelligence (EQ) plays a major part since an increased awareness of our internal state and our mental health, provides an early-warning system that things might be heading off the rails. Rest is one solution for stress management, however, I know from personal experience that I can be resting but still stressed, with issues I haven't yet resolved running around in my head on an endless loop to nowhere.

All of these facets can be improved, yet if a man is not willing to make the changes, then perhaps those around him, who care for him, can begin to invite the changes. If you're a woman and looking for ways to help the men in your life, buy some organic pasta for the family meal along with a homemade organic sauce (or make one as there are plenty of recipes now available on the Internet) and see how it lands. Suggest a walk or an outing, book a surprise holiday or other event that will lead to some time-out and rest, perhaps coupled with massage and nurturing. And turn off the digital devices!

Men really do love to be nurtured from a loving and caring place and I know from talking with men that a lack of physical contact, touch, hugs, connectedness and nurturing, all weigh on men's isolation. When physical intimacy does arrive, men are often confused and see it as an opportunity for sex. At a recent women's gathering I attended, men were invited to participate in a healing ceremony for both women and men. The facilitator asked the men in front of the women, 'how many men here have had sex with their partners, when all they really wanted was a cuddle?' Every man's hand in the room went up! The sudden intake of breath from the assembled women spoke volumes.

Ultimately there is often confusion between intimacy and sex, and it is very prevalent. Only open, honest and caring communication will solve it. And if it isn't working, get professional help. More on this later.

If a couple decides to embark on the parent journey and kids come along, it's very easy for men to focus on their jobs, to ensure they provide the best they can for their families. I've seen men working in some atrocious conditions and often wonder if their families have any idea of the work these men do, day in, day out, to ensure there's a roof over the family's head, food on the table and an occasional holiday. If I have to get up before dawn to catch an early flight, I find myself thinking about the truck driver I see delivering fuel to the service station at 5am, while the majority of us are sleeping, unaware, of the many shift workers who keep our cities and infrastructure running. I know women do shift work also, however the majority are men.

Men's health will only be improved when we dismantle the tough-guy stereotype and encourage men to take care of themselves across the entire range of health. Education also starts with our boys when they're young, so look for opportunities to be an agent of change. Diet (with much less refined sugar, preservatives and artificial colours), exercise (less screen time and more sports/exercise) and good quality sleep (which provides emotional resilience and more focus while learning) are three areas that are easy to start yet sometimes, difficult to maintain.

You can do this for the man in your life too, which will contribute to healthier relationships, which we explore next.

Key Points:

- *Men are affected more by common illnesses such as heart disease, diabetes, stress and blood pressure*

- *More men work in higher-risk jobs*

- *On average, men die younger than women with 2 out of 5 dying prematurely*

- *Diet, rest and nurture greatly assist men with their health*

- *Parents can educate their sones about good habits around diet, exercise and rest, which they will hopefully carry into adult life.*

10. RELATIONSHIPS

I, with a deeper instinct, choose a man who compels my strength, who makes enormous demands on me, who does not doubt my courage or my toughness, who does not believe me naive or innocent, who has the courage to treat me like a woman.

— Anaïs Nin

Ah, relationships!

My personal experience with them contains the highest of highs and the lowest of lows, and I believe are the most difficult, yet most rewarding, opportunities that we humans can experience. Anyone who has been in a long-term relationship and has also been a parent, will attest that relationships and parenthood often stretch us to breaking point, and sometimes even beyond. Add a self-employed business into the mix and you have a combination that requires an extraordinary amount of self-awareness and support to navigate. Sadly, many couples don't make it for the long haul.

A guru once noted that anyone can go live in a cave and attain Enlightenment, however, if you really want to know yourself, get married and have children. The famous Western spiritual teacher Ram Dass added that when you think you've reached Enlightenment, go live with your parents for a month!

I'll state this upfront since I firmly believe that the majority of contemporary men seek authentic relationships with themselves and their partners, yet time and time again, as a couple's relationship educator, I hear women complain about the men in their relationship. As stated in previous chapters, the most common complaint is a lack of maturity, in that the women feel that if they have children, their partner is another child they have to mother. The second complaint is that men are afraid of committing to relationships. The third is that when they do, they're 'emotionally unavailable'.

I know from speaking with women and mothers that they are quite capable of talking with other mothers and complaining about their partner's *lack* of just about anything: money, commitment, status, tenderness, bedroom prowess, care, emotional availability (always a favourite), housework, manners, and income. I have to say to any women reading this that when I hang out with men, I *rarely* hear about their wives or partners, and if they do mention anything, it'll usually be in passing, or a positive comment. If the men are fathers themselves, they'll often talk about their children.

As men, we're certainly capable of bringing up our misogynistic tendencies, just as women are capable of displaying misandry (which, if you're unfamiliar with this term means *a dislike of, contempt for, or ingrained prejudice against men*), especially if we haven't addressed any deep-seated issues toward the opposite sex. However, when men gather at men's groups, gatherings or specific events, what usually emerges is men seeking ways to get connected with themselves, to become better men, lovers, partners and fathers. There are often enough men at such gatherings who have resolved their issues that they will guide any man who has any misogynistic leanings, to get to the core problem.

So, what is it with relationships and men?

There is so much misunderstanding and a lack of awareness from women that the men they date were predominantly *made* by their mother-in-law-to-be, strongly influenced by their father's physical or emotional absence. Apologies if this is too stark a reality, however, it is true. While there is a misconception that 'good men' are not easy to find, there's also a denial of the role men and women have played in raising boys to be the men they are today. It's not easy for parents to raise a boy into a man, especially if the father is a boy-man himself, and emotionally or physically absent. However, mothers really do set the tone for the *feminine* aspect of their boys, and by feminine I don't mean gender, I mean the qualities that are associated with the feminine aspect that both women and men carry (more on that in Chapter 19). These would be qualities of empathy, relatedness, EQ (again), respect for life and the environment etc. Relationship skills are mostly learned from our mothers too.

Where is the father's and mother's teaching when a boy stabs another in a fight, or a man commits a crime, or an atrocity in war? There's no doubt parents can do much more to prepare and educate their sons for life ahead, and ensure they understand the requirement to be sensitive to others' needs, empathic, honest, authentic and caring. The extraordinary thing is that when men undergo their own inner journey to discover more of who they are, even the most hardened, deadened men find their Heart again, and express these qualities, indicating that they were never lost, simply buried under years of pretence and 'stiff upper lip-ness'.

And then there's the dreaded 'c' word – *commitment*.

What is commitment anyway and how does it develop in a relationship?

The word 'commit' comes from the Latin *committere*, which means *"to unite, connect, combine; to bring together."* In the dictionary it means to bind, to pledge, to entrust. So in a relationship, commitment means that we expect the other partner to keep their pledge of trust, as we will with them.

Firstly, a man who is unsure of himself, who is not connected *with* himself, who does not know himself and therefore exhibits low self-esteem, will naturally shy away from a relationship as it gets deeper, simply because, as it does, the very nature of a committed relationship requires peeling back the layers to a core of vulnerability. Exposing his vulnerable centre may lead to pain, and many men have suffered deep pain from a failed relationship where statistically, 80% of relationship endings are initiated by women. Also, if a man has never plumbed the depths of his psyche, he's sure as hell not going to expose any of this to a third party, unless perhaps to a professional therapist, so that he *knows who he is* before he lets anyone in a relationship see his vulnerable underbelly. The best way to avoid the possible pain of separation, again, is by not going there in the first place. To face such a possibility a man must have a large storehouse of self-worth, be clear in who he is and, therefore, develop a deep level of self-awareness.

Secondly, if a man does commit, does that mean he will set himself up to be 'changed' by his partner? Men often experience their male friends' behaviour change once they enter a committed relationship. In many cases, his male friendships end simply from disapproval by his partner, and rather than stand up for his mateship, the man will choose sex over friendship, which in turn ends up a poor choice as he loses what little of himself he had in the first place. In abandoning his often-hard-earned friendships sometimes built over years, he abandons himself and some very important needs.

Thirdly, what is his model for relationships? Does commitment mean staying shackled to a criticising partner, just like his father did, killing any spark of life and fun his dad used to have and leaving him impotent in so many areas? Or did his father leave his mother because the relationship was too dysfunctional and neither parent knew how to fix it, resulting in another 'broken' family? Or are his parents dynamic, emotionally healthy, independent, authentic people who work at their relationship and are a truly loving and committed couple? The last one, by the way, is possible, yet certainly the exception.

As a relationship coach, I have asked hundreds of couples, "Who wants your relationship to be like your parents'?" The extraordinary result so far is that *not one couple* has yet said 'Yes'. Think about this for a moment: we come into a relationship with a model we *don't* want, and we don't have an external model to emulate (Hollywood?), so we do what the large majority do and set-and-forget, then hope for the best. With research showing 70% of couples *never* talk about the quality of their relationship, is it any wonder almost 1 in 2 marriages (45%) in Australia end in divorce, with an average lifespan of just over 12 years?

Here's a tip for any single women reading this book: if you think the man you're dating is 'the one', spend some time with his parents, together, and witness the relationship between him and his parents, as well as his parents' relationship. These are his role models. It doesn't mean if they are a nightmare to be with that he *will* be, but it does mean that for the relationship to work, he and you may need to get some relationship education, so you and he can unlearn any unhealthy relationship models, and replace them with more functional ones.

Boy meets girl, girl likes boy, girl and boy enter into a sexual relationship, attachment starts, girl wants to get engaged, girl wants to get married as marriage creates security, and security is seen as a requisite for raising children. To one person, security might mean a sense of stability and reliability, whereas to another it may feel more like a constriction.

Ultimately, how commitment is perceived within a relationship will be different based on many factors, so what's important is to at least discuss what is *meant* by commitment. If a man perceives a committed relationship as constant complaints and criticisms, feeling tied-down, locked-in, minimal-freedom, under-control, sexually-manipulated, kid-screaming, and a sex-less existence, then wild horses aren't going to drag him there.

If on the other hand, the future relationship vision is one of togetherness, independence, interdependence, honesty (no matter what), open communication, friendship, mateship, commitment and trust, with no guarantees, then at least this is an ideal to aim for.

We may think that *love* is the foundation of relationships. However, my experience is that while love is a vital component, trust is the glue that binds the relationship together. Many couples have gone their separate ways even when love is present, because, for whatever reason, trust has been lost along the way.

Nothing damages a relationship more than a lack of (or broken) trust. Trust is like a bridge over a river. On one side of the river is person A and on the other is person B. Each time someone *does what they say they will do*, or stays within the *explicitly* agreed boundaries of the relationship, that person earns the right to lay down a plank. As the planks collect and extend, they eventually reach the centre, the bridge is completed, and a union is formed. Any violation of the trust bridge will result in the removal of a plank at the very least and, depending on the magnitude, the removal of all the planks from one side, leading to a complete or catastrophic collapse of the trust bridge. Once the bridge of trust has been damaged (for example, by infidelity), it's a tough road ahead to rebuild, and it takes full commitment from both partners to do so, but especially from the one who broke trust, as their half of the bridge is the half with the planks missing.

If two consenting adults agree that monogamy is the model on which their relationship is based, and one party violates this agreement, then this leads to a breakdown in trust, and understandably so. If the agreement is to not be monogamous, then the rules of the relationship *must* be discussed and agreed via explicit agreement.

Infidelity and extra-marital affairs are particularly difficult to recover from since a fundamental tenet of a relationship (and often only an implicit one) is *monogamy*. To have a conversation with a new partner about our individual expectations of the rules of engagement, rather than assuming (for example) that a relationship is to be monogamous, openly requires each partner to *promise* and *commit* to the agreement. In a wedding, this is often in the form of *wedding vows* in front of witnesses. This makes such an agreement more difficult to break, and if it is broken, there's no wriggle-room based on loose or incorrect assumptions. "Oh! I thought you meant …"

Polyamory is a term used to describe an intimate relationship where one person loves more than one other, and is defined as, "*the practice of engaging in multiple romantic (and typically sexual) relationships, with the consent of all the people involved*" although the 'love' may not necessarily be sexual. There are polyamory support groups that assist with helping people who wish to embark on this path, so I suggest if this is something of interest, then check out the Internet. From what I have researched, it's not a journey for the faint-hearted since it challenges all kinds of values, beliefs and jealousy (as would be expected), however, for some people, it can be both a challenging and liberating experience.

When it comes to relationships, my experience is that men simply want to know the truth and be allowed to process it in their own way and in their own time, and open, honest communication forms the basis of all successful relationships. Men may not like what we sometimes hear, but we do know the truth when we hear it and yes, we may go into our *caves* (see Chapter 15) for a while to sulk, rant, withdraw or rest. However, be assured that we're in there processing the heck out of what happened, trying to understand the nature of it, get a handle on our feelings, review our part or contribution to it and come out the other side as soon as possible.

My advice to women reading this is: don't have expectations to be involved in this process and you won't be disappointed. If you can see the man is struggling, invite a good male friend over, ensure there's beer in the fridge and go do something for yourself. Let them sort it. When he's ready to surface, you'll know and you might even get some form of dialogue and explanation, but don't push for it, insist on it, or look for explanations, as this might simply make a difficult situation, worse.

There's some contentious research about the very nature of the wiring of men's brains (generally speaking) in that the density of nerve fibres in the part that joins the two hemispheres, known as the 'corpus callosum', is less in men than women. The inference is that women find it much easier to switch between their hemispheres, from talking to emoting and back again, while a man takes longer to do this. It may explain why as men, we're often not as good at explaining what's going on in our heads, or might appear 'slow' to women in articulating what we're feeling.

Imagine a woman and a man in conversation. She's wanting to know what he's feeling, and he's working out (thinking) how to answer the question. He might be *thinking* about what he's *feeling* (strange, I know, and that's how I used to function), then, just as he makes the neurological step to cross the chasm, he's interrupted with another question from possibly an exasperated partner ("What's taking so long?") and the process starts all over again!

I know some men who've educated their female partner that when a question is asked of them … wait … and keep waiting until the man can find his way to his response. This may take several minutes, an hour, or a whole day. Don't break the possibly awkward silence, as difficult as that may be, and instead, create the *space* for the man to process his thoughts. Advice for the man is to also claim that space by having this discussion about how you roll and what works best for you.

If as a man you find you're unable to think clearly, it's possible you are experiencing what's known as *diffuse physiological arousal* (DPA), also known as *emotional flooding*. This is a physical response to receiving ongoing complaints and criticisms, where the body kicks into the fight-flight response, cortisol floods the bloodstream and we can feel hot, sweaty-palmed, with increased heart rate and respiration, and brain fog.

Our partners might perceive this as stonewalling since we're not responding in a way that leads to a resolution. The solution when this happens is to communicate with our partners that we're *flooding*, find a way to change our emotional state (go for a walk, read a book, watch TV etc), and then come back to the conversation after 30-min or so to continue in a much calmer state. This does, however, require clear communication that this is a temporary time-out and a firm commitment from the man to continue the discussion at an agreed time. This is not a get-out-of-jail card to be used to 'escape' and never revisit the issue, as this will damage the relationship and, you guessed it, further diminish trust.

One aspect of social media I find particularly counterproductive to all of us enjoying healthy relationships is the posting of what I call, "Look at me and my perfect life" posts. In these, successful (often business) people parade photos of themselves in high-rise hotels, on exotic islands, or jet-boats, yachts or aircraft, holding a cocktail, perhaps with their 'perfect' partner.

For those who might be struggling in their relationships, this abnormal representation (and often a façade), broadcasts to others who see posts like this, that there must be something wrong *with them*, so it triggers their lack of self-worth, generates discontent, and discourages reaching out for support since *everyone else is obviously happy so there must be something 'wrong' with me*!

Don't be fooled.

This collective dishonesty does a disservice to us all because it doesn't normalise that real, long-term, healthy relationships are challenging and hard work, and require much ongoing maintenance if they're to last.

Let me assure you that in our couple's relationship education work, we're continually surprised that what we see on the outside of seemingly healthy relationships, is commonly not the case, and behind the façade, they're struggling like everybody else, irrespective of the trappings of 'success'. Don't be put off by other's "Look at me!" and if you want more quality in your relationship, *seek an education.*

As Dr Susan Johnson, founder of Emotionally Focussed Therapy (EFT) who sadly died in April 2024 was one of the giants in couple's therapeutic work, noted, *"Isn't it ironic that people will educate themselves about everything, except the one thing that is most important to them, and that's how to have a healthy, loving relationship?"*

Wise words informed by years of helping couples all over the world, so education is the key to ensuring our relationships function well and can be maintained into the future.

I read an article recently that announced, *"There's no such thing as personal development!"* It caught my attention and got me thinking deeply about such a statement, and on further reading, explained that all our development comes from relating and, therefore, cannot be done in isolation. This made sense to me in that only by *relating to other people* can we get a handle on where we are in our development. We need others to mirror 'us' back to us, and while relationships can be challenging at times, they can be the most incredible journey to self-realisation, with research showing that men who are in healthy relationships, live happier, healthier lives overall, with increased longevity.

In the next chapter, we'll keep digging a little deeper and discuss the wonderful world of sexuality!

Key Points:

◆ *Many men are seeking connected, authentic relationships and need help understanding how to do this*

◆ *Mothers play an important role in how boys evolve in their understanding of relationships with women*

◆ *Boys model intimate relationships from how their parents relate to each other*

◆ *Trust is the basis on which all relationships are built*

◆ *Men need space to move from thinking to feeling*

◆ *Don't buy the 'my perfect life' social media stories*

◆ *Relationships can form a rich environment for the development of RQ and conversely, improving your RQ will enhance ALL your relationships*

11. SEXUALITY

A woman's highest calling is to lead a man to his soul, so as to unite him with Source. Her lowest calling is to seduce, separating man from his soul and leave him aimlessly wandering.

A man's highest calling is to protect woman, so she is free to walk the earth unharmed. Man's lowest calling is to ambush and force his way into the life of a woman.
– Cherokee Proverb

On reflection, in the first edition, this was what I would call a 'light' chapter and some feedback I received identified it as such: men wanted more! As so much has changed since then, I've expanded it considerably, so let's take a deeper dive into the world of men, relationships and sexuality overall.

One of life's taboo subjects, along with religion and money, is *sex*. I don't mean the stereotypical assumptions about men boasting of their conquests (which, by the way, I've rarely heard), or the building-site, wolf-whistling, immature expression. I'm referring to the basic biological act of union that couples engage in, which can take both parties to places of such vulnerability that it can indeed be scary and wonderful ... all at the same time.

Expressions of human sexuality cover an entire spectrum. Albert Kinsey's research in the USA, *Sexual Behaviour In the Human Male*, started in 1938 and released in 1948 (yes, 10 years!), then followed by the women's equivalent in 1953 (it took Kinsey years to convince his funders that women had a sexual identity and fantasies too). It was assumed that expressions of human sexuality conformed to a fairly defined and narrow, moral path, with those outside of this assumed to be a small deviant minority. Kinsey turned that notion on its head by showing that despite the establishment and influence of the puritanical religious foundations in the 1600s and the ongoing shaming of sexuality, the level of digression from what was considered 'normal' was far greater than expected, and more importantly, that there was no such thing as *normal* sexuality at all.

The 1960s followed, the contraceptive pill opened up an avenue for 'free love' and provided women with choice and reduced the risk of unwanted pregnancy, Woodstock defined a period of liberation, and yet as we entered the 70s and 80s, sexual conservatism seemed to return, perhaps as a backlash. AIDS and HIV arrived in 1981, and the world of human sexuality has not been the same since, with an estimated 40 *million people* currently living with HIV.

We have seen the emergence of the acceptance of different sexual orientations, although homosexuality is still illegal in some countries. As preferences change and we become less fixated on sameness, it's not uncommon to hear the term LGBTIQA+, which is an evolving acronym that stands for lesbian, gay, bisexual, transgender, intersex, queer/questioning, and asexual. There are also many other terms (such as non-binary and pansexual) that people use to describe their experiences of their gender, sexuality and physiological sex characteristics.

Today we have also seen the proliferation of pornography, where millions of daily search engine requests are classified as pornographic searches. Although there are conflicting research results available on the Internet, I think for this discussion, we can agree that pornography is ubiquitous. While there's no doubt that some pornography can be labelled as erotica and may have some educational or arousal value that a couple (for example) may enjoy, the sad part is that a lot of what is produced is 'low grade' and by that, I mean a representation of sexuality that does nothing to promote equality, respect, sacredness, connectedness or a loving exchange.

It also saddens me that teenage boys can quite happily play violent games, see violent movies and incorporate language (kill, destroy, take-out, smoke, frag, eliminate) in their day-to-day language, yet any reference to sexuality is usually met with parental embarrassment and hope that if ignored, the problem might just go away.

Unfortunately, so will the boy.

He'll seek his education elsewhere, usually at school from his mates who most likely know about as much or less than he does. If you remember in Chapter 5, I shared when my eldest son was in his last year of primary school, and we had a fascinating week where he wanted answers from me to significant questions he had about *sex*. It left no doubt as to the poor quality of school-yard conversations, and while I was truly grateful that we had such an open dialogue, it concerned me at the time as to the nature of some of his questions. It led me to conclude that older siblings of his school friends were feeding these younger kids with incorrect, dysfunctional and ultimately damaging information.

Teenage boys and girls are mostly drawing their sexual relationship points of reference from low-grade pornography, without any thought that what they're viewing might not be how sexual relationships actually are. Some surprising statistics I found via a Mashable report (www.mashable.com/article/pornhub-year-in-review-2024) reveal that approximately 38% of viewers of pornography are *female*, up from 24% in 2015 (a 58% increase). In both the Philippines and Argentina, *women who watch pornography exceed men* (59% to 41% and 51% to 49%, respectively). And if we were ever in doubt about the use of mobile phones to access pornography, they accounted for 90.5% of access, with desktop computers at 7.9% and tablets the remaining 1.6%.

What's not commonly known is that many of the most popular websites are owned by one company, which used to be called Mind Geek, now known as *Aylo*, a multinational pornographic conglomerate owned by a Canadian private equity firm, Ethical Capital Partners. (An interesting name, is it not?)

If the current generation of teenagers is losing their sexual compass by believing what they are seeing via pornography and that this is how sexual relationships 'should' be, what will happen to the next generation and their children? The only avenue we have is to not stick our heads in the sand, understand that pornography is pervasive, do our best to limit its influence on our young people and be honest in our discussions with our kids.

In a radio interview, Lashlie (*He'll Be OK*) commented that it's not *what* a boy sees, it's what he does afterwards. By that, she means that if the communication channels are open, then the boy will seek clarification, hopefully from you, as he may be confronted by what he sees, and question whether it aligns with his experience of his parent's relationship.

In a commentary by feminist law professor Catherine MacKinnon in 1984 entitled *Not A Moral Issue*, she concluded, "Central to the institution of male dominance, pornography cannot be reformed or suppressed or banned. It can only be changed." And this was before the emergence of the Internet. How prophetic.

The simple fact is that boys and girls will find pornography and so we must be prepared for the inevitable conversation, and surely, we hope that they will come to us and discuss it. The only avenue I can see to address this is through honest, confident conversation. The old days of hushed tones and an embarrassed dismissal, or comparisons with 'the birds and the bees', or the standard high school biology-based explanations, just aren't going to cut it with our young people.

I remember when a rite of sexual passage was plucking up the courage to buy a copy of Playboy or Penthouse from a newsagent, and obviously, not the local one near home! Or hanging around outside the pharmacy until a male was on duty so you could go in, buy condoms and get the hell out of there before your heart exploded in your chest. Today, access to pornography, online shopping for sex toys, and self-serve supermarket checkouts, have all but taken this away, and the pervasiveness of pornography speaks volumes since, without the demand, there wouldn't be the supply.

Regarding men and sex (as I mentioned in Chapter 9 about that weekend workshop for women), when the facilitator asked how many men in the room of 30 had had sex when all the man wanted was a cuddle, every man's hand went up, much to the shock of the women present. The dilemma for men is simple: we have been brought up to believe that the prelude to sex is one of the hunt and the chase, and that sex is a transactional and/or bargaining pursuit.

To quote Harris O'Malley from his July 2012 article, *It's OK To Want Sex* (www.doctornerdlove.com/its-ok-to-want-sex/), *"As far as I knew, sex was something of a transaction: guys bargained, cajoled, argued, c*  *onvinced, begged or otherwise persuaded women into performing some sex act – ideally some penis-in-vagina action – and women would give in. Sometimes reluctantly, sometimes with enthusiasm but rarely without some form of negotiation. The fact that men wanted sex was something of an inconvenience at best, something actually shameful at worst."*

It may sound like a generalisation, however, men do tend to have more active libidos, driven by the 1500-2000% more testosterone in men than women, which drives sexual appetite, especially in relationships that have a few years in them, and perhaps a child or two. The natural focus on children and the lack of focus from both parties on the relationship itself, creates distance, which results in a poor environment for any form of physical intimacy. So, on the one hand, the man might be yearning for some contact, while on the other he isn't emotionally connected with his partner.

This leads to the generally accepted idea that women need to feel *emotionally connected* with their partner to want to have sex, while a man needs to have sex, to open his Heart and feel emotionally connected.

What a dilemma!

The solution is for both to invest in the relationship itself and maintain emotional connection, so some level of *emotional intimacy* is required to keep the relationship healthy. My experience with couples has shown that when emotional intimacy is absent and not maintained, physical intimacy (not just sex but all the other physical aspects), also disappears, and men can deeply yearn for touch.

With an estimated 90% of couples dissatisfied with the quality of their sexual relationship, learning how to have open, honest and perhaps vulnerable conversations about what's working and what's not, is paramount to couples feeling their needs are being met. We can only navigate our sense of shame and embarrassment by talking about exactly that with our partners, which then leads to realising that such conversations become less awkward the more we have them.

Some ideas for this are *not* to discuss what might have worked (or not) in a sexual encounter, straight afterwards in the afterglow, but to open the conversation *the next day*, like a debrief: "Hey! When you/we did 'x' last night, I really loved it! What about you? How was it for you? What do you think I/we can do/change/add to make it even better?" Such a regular debrief starts to normalise the conversation, reducing any sense of shame and embarrassment. I know this because in my third major relationship, a 'post-match' analysis is part of our routine, often while walking the dog, and we've developed a wonderful matter-of-factness about it. Practice really does help.

It's also well known that the person with the *lowest libido* will control the nature and frequency of sex within the relationship, so it's vital to ensure both partner's needs are being met and openly communicated, otherwise, it can feed resentment, or interest in other activities, like pornography, 'happy ending' massages, prostitution or an affair, which result in a breakdown of connection.

I remember watching a female psychologist on TED Talk, speaking with an audience and declaring, "Men will have an affair to stay in a sexless marriage, while a woman will have an affair to prepare to leave the marriage."

I found this such an incredible insight, and it explained so much.

As a man, I can understand how a man can love his wife/partner, but in a sexless marriage, still wants to explore his unmet needs or fantasies via a baggage-free and almost anonymous 'one-night-stand'. Does he or doesn't he? He might have signed up for monogamy, but not celibacy.

The challenge happens when it becomes more than this, and complicated and conflicting emotions and feelings arise, which the man may find difficult to navigate, often leading to not dealing with them and resulting in living two, separate lives. If 'discovered', he's likely to lose his relationship, friendships, social circles (he will become 'that man' and a social pariah), access to his children and often suffer significant financial loss. The longer it goes, the more chance he has of being discovered, the harder it becomes for him to reconcile. I'm not condoning infidelity here, but I am explaining why we see this pattern play out in so many relationships.

If it's the woman having an affair, chances are she's already grieved the relationship and infidelity results from her exploring her sexuality in a newfound way, without strings attached, so she too can explore her unresolved needs, again perhaps with some level of anonymity with no sexual baggage or attachment.

When a sexual relationship becomes long-term, it's also normal for tastes to change, yet we face a conundrum only found in long-term relationships. Imagine that you're finding your sex life somewhat boring, and the same-old-same-old has become what some might call routine, or 'vanilla sex'. The conundrum is that one (or both!) of you might be feeling this, yet neither wants to break the silence on the subject. Underneath, one of you might wish to experience a fantasy with your partner, something a little 'edgy', but thinking, "*I can't go there because my partner will judge me and think I'm weird!*" We face the risk of hurtful rejection and/or judgment, so nothing changes. After a while, vanilla sex becomes so boring that it often leads to no sex at all, so the lack of knowledge of how to have vulnerable conversations becomes a self-fulfilling prophecy.

A healthier way is to have a gentle and invitational conversation that could go something like this, "*I really miss you and times past when we had a great sexual connection. I have so many erotic memories of our early days, and I know things have changed. I'm nervous, yet willing to have an open and honest conversation about what we can do to spice things up a bit. How about you? Can we plan a time to talk and explore what that might look like? I'm feeling excited just thinking about it!*"

No matter what setting you choose, it's important to create a safe and respectful space to have an open conversation, and it can begin with a pledge to each other that "*all your desires are welcome here.*" It doesn't mean that if one partner wants to do something the other doesn't, it happens anyway. That would not be a co-created experience. Both parties must be empowered to say 'no' and boundaries respected, and both must be open to alternatives, "*I'm not sure about 'x', but what about 'y'?*" It's often the 'charge' behind the unlived fantasy that drives the yearning itself.

If, for example, the fantasy is played out in a way you both agree, it may be that it's such a turn-on that it becomes another part of your sexual repertoire. That's a win, is it not? Or, if it turns out that the fantasy was better than the act itself, at least you tried, which often diminishes the yearning. Or, if it was a disappointing experience, it completely resolves the fantasy. Either way, nothing ventured, nothing gained!

Compromise is key.

Why would a man decide to have sex when he doesn't want to? As an example, I remember as the years moved on in my first relationship, sex became a rarer and rarer event. After being rejected for months and finally giving up looking for any interest from my partner, one night after a party and her consuming copious amounts of alcohol, she was obviously feeling frisky. I didn't feel like a drunken romp as I was still relatively sober, so for the first time, I politely declined. The result? I ended up in Sexual Siberia for longer than the first round, this time lasting many months. The lesson I learned from this was 'take it while it's on offer', irrespective of how I felt, because I never knew how long the next drought was going to be. Both sad and true.

Thankfully, I've moved on and matured substantially since that time, and as well as understanding more about myself, I've also increased my EQ and RQ, which has allowed me more mobility and an ability to communicate much more openly and effectively within my relationship. Learning to navigate discomfort, and being comfortable *in* the discomfort, has led me to be much more courageous in conversations. When matched by my partner, we've become far more adept at conversations I could never have imagined having, and the rewards of feeling connected, close and emotionally open to each other have paid huge dividends for us both. It's also kept our sexual relationship active and we now realise it truly is about the journey and not the destination, and we've evolved to explore pleasure for pleasure's sake.

For men, this is particularly important. If you ask someone, "What's the opposite of pain?" they will invariably answer, "Pleasure!" Yet most of us have forgotten that our pain is felt *in-body*, yet we seek pleasure *externally*, through material means – the new car, house, boat, trinket, 'retail therapy', social media or whatever gives us our dopamine hit. We seem to have forgotten that only when we feel our pain viscerally, can we heal it. So, for men, receiving pleasure with no agenda helps us get out of our heads and into our Hearts, helps us stay in our bodies and learn how to stay there. When invasive thoughts pull us out of our pleasure experience, we can use mindfulness to notice, park the thought, and refocus on the sensations we're feeling in our body, from touch, massage, stroking, or any other form of bodywork, erotic or otherwise.

I have personally travelled this path with my partner and we've both become so much better at *reading* our partner's bodily responses and cues, that we get as much pleasure out of being the giver, as the receiver.

The Cherokee proverb at the beginning of this chapter, for me, speaks to its relevance where we find ourselves, and more so for me as theirs is a matrilineal culture:

> "*A woman's highest calling is to lead a man to his soul, so as to*

unite him with Source. Her lowest calling is to seduce, separating man from his soul and leave him aimlessly wandering."

If a woman can guide a man to find his Heart in an undemanding way, she will be encouraging him to connect with his very Soul, support his link with that inner realm. His true Self will create the very environment needed for him to connect with his honesty and vulnerability, and understand his own needs, to be more functional in the relationship overall.

"A man's highest calling is to protect woman, so she is free to walk the earth unharmed. Man's lowest calling is to ambush and force his way into the life of a woman."

If a man can understand and be honest with himself about his own needs, take responsibility for them, remove this from his partner and connect with his own Heart, he will organically become the protector he was instinctively born to be. He will need the company of other good men who have walked their path and done this for themselves.

Win-win.

And so the empowerment cycle begins and continues to grow.

Sometimes, men who have not matured in their sexuality, manifest what's known as 'creep' behaviour and those who experience the opportunity to own this place within themselves, as painful and challenging as it is, liberate themselves from both the inner burden of always seeking someone to fill their void, and the outward burden of being seen as a predatory man.

I'm convinced that most women can sense a man a mile away who is stuck in this place, and if they so choose, play him like a fish. This leads to his increased sexual frustration and if he doesn't have the necessary EQ, or worse still, is under the influence of alcohol or other substances, his boundaries are blurred and he may not listen to or respect a woman's "NO!"

We then hear of a man's repressed sexual frustration getting out of control, coupled with violence, which can result in rape. This is one of the most tragic, harmful and traumatic situations a human can endure, often being scarred for life with an understandably deep mistrust of men. The man, if reported and convicted, will most likely end up in jail and on the sex-offenders register for life. We also know that some women and men are sexually invaded and don't report it due to a whole range of reasons, including shame, interrogation, and victim-shaming. We need to educate our boys that *consent* is an absolute necessity and that 'no' means "NO!"

I also believe that it's this lack of a functional sexual boundary in some men that perpetrates sexual abuse of children, who are far more easily manipulated and threatened. With the emergence of story after story of women and men discovering their own history of being sexually abused as children and then seeking retribution, I wonder how perpetrators of such abuse go about their daily lives, while a time bomb ticks away until one possible day, the police turn up at their home or workplace, sometimes in front of their family.

The Jimmy Saville revelations, which aired in the UK in 2009, have shocked an entire generation of UK adults who had grown up with *Jim'll Fix It*, and now other well-known personalities are being implicated. For me, the unfortunate aspect of this is that it tarnishes men in general, even though the estimated rate of men committing such abuse is less than 3% of the general male population.

When I hear of a convicted paedophile trying to start a new life who has served his time in prison, while we don't know whether he has been rehabilitated, he has paid the debt that society and his peers, the jury, imposed. We may not agree with it, however, our laws and judges set the sentence. So, when a paedophile is released and moves into a quiet country town to start a new life, to see the media get on the vigilante bandwagon to drive him out of town, simply sends a message to other abusers that their behaviour must remain secret, otherwise, they'll be lynched by the media too. It might make for sensational TV but it does nothing to address or solve the issue. What irks me is that based on the statistics, you can be assured that a percentage of those attempting to run the person out of town, are also committing abuse themselves.

A solution would be to create an environment where those who have committed acts of abuse and are truly regretful and seeking help, can in some way discuss and redress their behaviour. Don't get me wrong here; I'm in no way condoning their behaviour. What I am suggesting is a better process to allow people in this situation to *heal*, along with the people they have affected. The current model does little, if anything, to encourage them to reconcile their actions, and everything to stigmatise them for life, including jail time. Fear of being labelled for life, naturally forces the behaviour underground since there's no avenue for them to seek help or heal.

It's well known that the majority of sexual abusers were themselves sexually abused, indicating that their values and standards of what is socially acceptable behaviour, were malformed. Hence, the perpetuation of the same behaviour as an adult. Yes, they are responsible for their actions. Yes, they should not have acted improperly. Yes, they have undoubtedly and probably irreparably damaged another human being. The statistics, however, speak for themselves, with an estimated 1 in 4 girls and 1 in 7 boys affected by childhood sexual abuse.

Thankfully, the numbers seem to be declining as we, as a society, become more aware and implement child safety processes, and opportunistic groups where paedophiles can access children, are being exposed, yet we still have a long way to go. The longer we take to bring this situation to a more open and functional debate, the more children will be abused, the more abused and abusive men will continue to live in secrecy, and the more men, in general, will be perceived as predators. There has to be a better way, yet to seek a better way, we must decide to stop the lynch-mob mentality, otherwise, nothing will change.

'Dr Nerdlove', who we met at the start of this chapter, explored ways to improve our interpersonal relationships regarding sexuality. He introduced the concept of *enthusiastic consent*. The concept is that while 'no means no' and 'maybe likely means no', each can listen for an enthusiastic 'Yes!', rather than negotiating, cajoling or manipulating. Again, this requires a modicum of EQ, RQ and self-awareness. When both partners unequivocally give enthusiastic consent, there is no room for doubt. Both parties can enjoy an experience without one feeling pushed into it by the other. This topic of conversation could even be the beginning of an agreement for new couples on how to navigate this tricky area by discussing the terms of engagement. How refreshing this would be, and I'm sure it would reduce the incidence of cases where 'consent' was not clearly defined or understood.

Navigating sexuality can be a tricky and often difficult terrain, yet it doesn't have to be. I believe we owe it to our developing youth to bring it out of the closet, be honest about what's really happening, and work as a community to ensure the values and standards we espouse are being lived so they can be effectively modelled, and we can explore our sexuality without shame, embarrassment, guilt, judgement or self-consciousness.

For men, open, honest and mature conversations about sexuality, what it means to each of us, where we stand in relationship to it within ourselves and with sexual partners, the influence of pornography itself, and being open to discuss and explore alternative perspectives, is a path we might resist yet must explore. The alternative is what we have now, and with so much pervasive and evident sexual dissatisfaction, I don't see another choice.

In the next chapter, we'll explore *shame* and how it particularly affects men.

Key Points:

- *Discussing sexuality can be a difficult subject, best approached with honesty and confidence*

- *Do your best to keep the communications channels open so your children will come to you for advice, and not get it from the schoolyard or the Internet*

- *As a society, we need to do more to open the subject of sexual abuse and find more creative ways of solving a deep-seated and sensitive issue*

- *As a society we need to do more to open the subject of abuse and find more creative ways of solving a deep-seated issue*

- *Education about 'enthusiastic consent' will reduce confusion and improve relationships.*

12. SHAME

> *We do not have to be ashamed of what we are. As sentient beings we have wonderful backgrounds. These backgrounds may not be particularly enlightened or peaceful or intelligent. Nevertheless, we have soil good enough to cultivate; we can plant anything in it.*
>
> — *Chögyam Trungpa*

The origins of the word *shame* show that it is derived from feelings of guilt or disgrace. From an early age, most of us were shamed by our parents, family, relatives, teachers, or other carers, about a whole host of things: height, weight, skin colour, sexual curiosity, accent, clothes, body odour, birthmarks, glasses, and the list goes on. Shame also damages the development of our EQ and RQ, and therefore our ability to empathise with others, since shame encourages us to construct a sort of armour, to protect ourselves from the feelings elicited by shame.

Shame can linger in us for decades, quietly and surreptitiously affecting our interpersonal relationships and how we navigate the world, and due to its armouring nature, can greatly affect how we relate to our own children. The armour we put in place to protect our own 'inner child' can prevent us from empathising with our children, thereby creating an emotional distance, a wall, that gets in the way of true empathy.

The issue with shame when it is imposed on us, especially as children, is that we don't have enough maturity at that stage of life, for a sense of who we are. Then we are not equipped to decide whether the imposed shame is rational. Many a child has been shamed for something that was actually the carer's issue – 'we don't do that here', 'that's wrong', 'why would you say something like that in this house?', 'you're fat/ugly/skinny/short/no-hoper/useless/stupid …'.

The difference between shame and guilt is that guilt is felt as a result of an action (or inaction) regarding something that we do or don't do. Shame is about *who* we are and as a result, scars us much deeper since it affects us at our very level of *being*. Unlike other emotions that tend to be quickly expressed and let go, shame is very sticky, as it can linger for the remainder of our lives, and without any form of therapy, often does.

This is different to feeling *ashamed*. Many times in my life I've felt ashamed of my behaviour, not necessarily because someone has said something to me, or disapproved in any way (although that has happened), but mainly because I know I have demonstrated an action that is incongruent with who I believe I am. In these instances, the power of feeling ashamed galvanised my will to commit to never do again whatever it was I did, and subsequently modifying my behaviour. Sometimes we don't get it right a second time and ashamedness returns, however after a while, the message sinks in and we permanently modify our behaviour. If we're unable to do this for ourselves (which can be difficult), then therapy of any kind is an avenue we can pursue to get external help, but in heading down this path we must be honest with ourselves. In the end, behaviour only tells us *what* we are, not *who* we are, and the 'what' can be changed.

Shame, on the other hand, imposed by another's values and beliefs, relies and depends on self-doubt. It undermines much of our self-worth and is fed by the lack of it. If imposed at a young age, we may not even be aware of its existence. Adults carry shame into personal relationships and may not know that their values and judgements are being driven by unseen forces.

If you remember Chapter 2 on Stereotypes, shame seems to be an occupational hazard for men. The requirement to be reliable, unemotional, solid, fearless, invincible, confident, decisive, unfeeling, dedicated, tenacious, respectful, wise, determined, intelligent, independent, detached, ambitious, logical, active, career-minded, warrior-like, a hero, athletic, and powerful, leaves plenty of opportunity to not 'measure up.'

Add media depictions of men being stupid, idiotic, smelly, bumbling fools, or campaigns as mentioned in the previous chapter that tarnish all men with one brush, and is it any wonder that men impose self-shame for not making the grade, falling short, or feeling inadequate? We often hear, "size doesn't matter" and of course, it's in reference specifically to penis size. I see many debates on social media about this very topic. I believe that the whole 'size' thing is really questioning whether we measure up as men in general and that can be in a range of areas, not just in the bedroom.

"Man up!", "Grow a pair!", "Stop being a girl!", "Don't cry, be a man!", "Don't be a pussy!", and on it goes.

In the many men-centric groups I've found myself in, there is often an underlying and central issue that drives men in almost everything we do; a super-massive black hole at the centre of our being-ness that we know exists, yet are very afraid of facing. If a man is fortunate enough to touch it, taste it, experience it, be honest with it, then work hard as hell to own it and integrate it, then and only then can a true sense of freedom and purpose emerge.

At this core is a fundamental (and often total) *lack of self-worth*, usually layered with shame at being a man, which makes it doubly difficult to resolve. It may seem a self-evident truth however I'll state it anyway: *You can't give what you don't have.*

Lack of self-worth comes from never feeling that who we are is good enough and so we will try to compensate for this aching wound across all areas of our lives, whether it be the job we have, the house we live in, the car we drive, the partner we choose, the material things we collect, all of which simply add to our financial burden. They do nothing to connect with that central place, simply because outer world possessions do nothing to heal it. And never will. If we look around, we can see the effects of shame on men in so many ways, evidenced by the statistics in earlier chapters on health, depression and suicide.

Dealing with shame is like taking off the outer layer of an onion. It's the place to start for any man wishing to move beyond the place of 'look at me', doing everything he can to satiate this painful yet possibly unknown place, while at the same time fulfilling his role as primary bread-winner for a family.

The first step for any man is to be honest with himself. It sounds simple; yet finding the capacity for deep, radical and perhaps brutal honesty with one's self is not easily done, and underpinning the fear of doing so is a deeper fear of being rejected. That's why high-quality men's work is vitally important, as these environments present an opportunity for shame-filled men to listen to other men who have taken their own courageous steps, put a voice to their shame and healed it.

Each man's story is unique yet the themes are very similar, often stemming from being under-fathered, never feeling good enough, being told that to be a man in today's society is a 'bad' thing, and at the extremes, that men are predators, paedophiles and rapists.

Sir Bob Geldof once said, '*We've demonised men. Men really are sort of considered brutish and hairy, and unemotional, and aggressive, and loud, and smelly ... and this big hairy thing between their legs. That is seriously present in a lot of current thinking. This is a disgrace. This truly is a disgrace, where you view a man as a suspicious being. Men, in general, are a protector. We have seen a complete perversity, a complete change of what men are, and what they're supposed to be. We've almost lost our reason with regard to it.*'

For boys it's very important to avoid shaming situations, as shame stunts emotional and relational growth, leaving deep scars. This stunted growth prevents men from *feeling* when they grow older. Robert Bly believes that we can overcome this feeling of being inherently flawed, by revisiting our shame, which although overwhelming to us as boys, can be handled by us as men. In fact, revisiting and owning our shame and feeling the emotions around it, seems to be the only way we can integrate and heal.

More and more exposure is happening in the media about initiations (also known as *bastardisation* or *hazing*) in multiple establishments such as private schools and the armed forces. Invasive initiation events have created suffering in men and women, often for decades, as they begin to understand that their shame occurred in situations that were out of their control. The cruelty experienced in some of these incidents is appalling and the scarring not only visible, but completely understandable. The courage of those men and women who step forward and expose some of these terrible practices is to be commended, especially as their shame is often put on public display.

It's only by acknowledging our shame that we can do something about it. Bly suggests that we can relive any shameful situation by replaying it with adult awareness and reprogramming the incident, offering an alternate 'director's cut' ending that doesn't result in shame but in acknowledgement. For example, you may have a memory of being verbally abused at a sporting event by a parent/coach for not being good enough, which completely negated the months of effort you put in. An alternate ending might be that even though you had a bad game that day, your parent offered you some solace that we all have good and bad days, and the important thing was that you turned up, did your best, and in the end, that's all that matters.

This type of exercise is good to do in men's groups since the environment is usually conducive to getting positive feedback from other men, who can role-play whatever part is needed for the man to bounce off. Often, it's an overbearing or underachieving father, living through his son, berating and putting him down at every opportunity, or an absent father who, when he was around, only ever criticised and never praised.

Under the emotion of shame is often the *rage* of feeling helpless at the time of the event, and expression of this in the company of other men is also healthy, as it releases the underlying emotional energy in a constructive way, thereby providing an opportunity for healing.

I've sat with men as they've spoken from that deep, deep place of shame of being a man and I have to say that the acceptance, honouring, support and respect afforded another man by a conscious group of men holding a truly non-judgemental space, is an experience I will always remember, for within that sacred sharing are the seeds of hope for all of humanity.

To witness a man own such a wounded and burdensome aspect of himself, while not seeking absolution or approval, yet speaking simply to express, perhaps for the first time, the overwhelming and all-pervading pain and isolation that shame has imparted on his life, is truly breathtaking.

It is moments like these that give me a profound sense of hope that masculinity is returning in a new-formed way, as men find their voice, understand that we all carry similar yet individual burdens, and that there truly is light at the end of the tunnel.

There is now emerging evidence from psychiatrists and psychotherapists such as Dr James Gilligan (who was the medical director of a prison mental hospital), of a proposed a link between *shame*, the resulting *humiliation* and subsequent expression of *violence*. Most of his patients were classified as criminally insane and had committed murder. Gilligan started to notice a pattern of shame-humiliation-violence, and argues that we have not adequately considered shame and shaming as root causes of endemic violence. He claims we have been too preoccupied with focussing on guilt, both personally and within the criminal justice system of 'crime and punishment', which although necessary to address symptoms of violence, doesn't address the underlying systemic drivers.

From personal experience, I can confirm that finding and speaking from such a place within myself, generated extraordinary relief that can only flow from taking such a step. This has been shared by other men too. The result is so unburden-some that it's not until we put down our load of shame and realise that we don't have to carry it anymore, that the *gravity* of its effect on every aspect of our daily life becomes clear. To say it's a liberating feeling does not do it justice.

When you realise that the light at the end of the tunnel is the light of freedom, freedom to be yourself, freedom to not be ashamed of who you are as a human, or specifically as a man, your sense of your place and value to those around you, contributes greatly to your sense of worthiness.

As the eminent psychologist Dr C G Jung noted, "Shame is a soul-eating emotion", so if shame is eating away at your Soul, find a way to get the help you need to understand why it is within, and let it go.

As one of my mentors once noted, "You don't have to be acceptable, to be accepted."

Key Points:

◆ *Shame is a deep-seated emotion often imparted to us by our immediate carers*

◆ *Shame can be debilitating and pervade so much of our life that until we understand it within ourselves, we have no idea how much it influences us*

◆ *Society is getting better through education at preventing shameful experiences like 'initiations' and courageous people are stepping forward and sharing their painful past to stop it from happening to others*

◆ *There is growing evidence of a correlation between shame, humiliation and violence*

◆ *Under shame often sits rage and it's important in the healing process to express that rage, safely, in the company of a supportive therapist or other trusted men who understand.*

13. DIVORCE

Some people believe that holding on and hanging in there are signs of strength. However, there are times when it takes much more strength to know when to let go and then do it.
— **Ann Landers**

(Disclosure: I have been through two divorces, and both were challenging. My two sons were around for the second one at the ages of 13 & 7, making it even more difficult, yet finally, liberating for both the mother of my children and me. My notion of not wanting my children to 'come from a broken home' changed during that time, as my two sons were observing and modelling an unhealthy relationship, and the question I asked myself was, "What type of future relationship are they going to create?"

Separating and divorcing, being in the relationship wilderness for a while, allowed me to 'regather' myself. This was to become a major turning point and buoyed my hope of finding someone with whom I could build and have a healthy, loving relationship. Although this was a major and fear-filled step, it paid dividends in the end. More on that later!)

Divorce can be one of the most stressful things we experience and from surveys of the top 10 stressors in life, with number one being death of a spouse, divorce comes in at number 2! Let's take a look at some of the divorce statistics in Australia, so we can get an idea of the magnitude of the issue.

Approximately 40% of heterosexual divorces in Australia are initiated by female partners, 30% by mutual agreement and 30% are initiated by the husband. With 5.5 marriages and 2.3 divorces per 1,000 population in 2023, this is about the same as 2010-2011 rates, although 2021 rates were 13.6% higher than in 2020 and possibly influenced by COVID and associated lockdowns.

The average time to divorce has remained relatively steady over the last decade at just over 12 years, and the median age at divorce was 46 years old for males and 43 years old for females. This has also remained relatively consistent over recent years.

If we look at the age groupings of divorce in the *40-44 age group*, the rate is up from an average of 2.2/1,000 to a whopping 10.3 for men and 10.4 for women! That's an almost 500% increase on the average rate. Could this be an indication of turbulent times in a man's midlife passage and not knowing how to navigate a deeply transformational process?

The divorce rate also means that 1 in 7 families are one-parent families, so that's 1 million of them with 80% being single mothers. Over 20% of children aged between 0 – 17 years old don't have regular contact with the remote parent and in 80% of these, it is the *father* that lives away from the family. Where one parent lives away from the family, 25% of them see the other parent less than once a year, or sadly, never.

Divorce and/or separation bring with it a large social and financial impact, estimated to cost the Australian economy $4B/yr. It also brings with it a personal cost for the children involved, who often see the breakdown of their parent's relationship without a mature understanding of why it's happening.

Based on these statistics, I think we can agree that we have a relationship problem!

With the dramatic increase in divorce in the 40-44 age group, what has midlife and a man's journey got to do with it?

Robert A Johnson was the author of many books and has been a leading light for me in my journey through life. When I was 44 years old and reading his book, *WE: The Psychology Of Romantic Love*, there, on a single page, was a man's 'midlife crisis', in stark black and white, so simply and eloquently explained that I felt such anger rising in me. I couldn't help but wonder why such crucial information that explained a well-known but misunderstood phenomenon, was buried in a non-mainstream book, and not plastered on every bus, billboard and the back of every public toilet door! Had I known what Johnson was describing before I reached my forties, it would have given me valuable insight into the processes unfolding within myself, well ahead of time.

In a nutshell, Johnson's explanation goes something like this:

> Man meets woman, falls in love and gets married (or lives in a de-facto relationship). Man puts wife on a pedestal as she fulfils his 'missing half', his feminine aspect (and by that I mean his 'harp' as mentioned earlier in the sword-harp analogy, in Chapter 6).

At 40-ish, man sees wife has changed, most likely has had children, and perhaps isn't the Goddess image the man initially created, when he put her on a pedestal all those years ago.

Man begins to withdraw his *projected* Goddess image and redirects it onto a younger woman, often someone at work or met through work (since he typically spends so much time there).

New girlfriend sees older man as stable, powerful, mature and successful, but is unknowingly seeing him as a *father figure* to complete her own masculine (sword) aspect, so she too has entered into a *projected*-image relationship.

Man makes her his new Goddess and has an affair.

Wife divorces man and takes ½ (or more) of family assets.

Man doesn't initially care so much because he's getting regular and exciting sex from his new Goddess, where everything is new. He feels *renewed*. This feeds his unhealthy mid-life ego.

Several months later, girlfriend realises it isn't going to work, as the generation gap is too great, so girlfriend dumps man.

While this is certainly a broad generalisation, when I read this, I knew of several relationships where this exact pattern had played itself out.

The bi-directional projections, the man's Goddess-image and the woman's God-image, both dissolved over time, and if no learning is gained from this, it will most likely be repeated with different partners.

Often, the man attempts to return to his family only to find his wife has moved on, possibly now with a new lover. He moves into an apartment or caravan, pays child support and/or school fees for children he might only see every other weekend, pays mortgage payments for a house he doesn't live in, with another man possibly living in his house, sleeping in his bed with his ex-wife and bringing up his children. Usually, by this stage, it's too late. The damage to the original relationship has been done and the man's future looks bleak indeed.

In *What Men Don't Talk About* by Maggie Hamilton, one of the tragedies of events such as this was that Maggie had interviewed men who had found themselves living in a caravan park and working three jobs, just to meet financial commitments. The Australian Family Law Court has not been generous to men who have gone down this path, and are often burdened both financially and emotionally. It's almost as if the man awakens from a daze, grows through his mid-life transition, looks back and wonders "What the hell was I thinking?"

The despair felt at such a time can be totally overwhelming, leaving the man feeling depressed, isolated and very much alone, which can lead to self-medication via substance abuse, and in extreme cases, to suicide or murder-suicide.

In a recent example, a man who had had an affair and returned to his family shared with me that the experience, although exhilarating, was not worth the ensuing pain of having to rebuild trust. Years after the event he was regularly being reminded of his infidelity, as his partner ensured he 'paid', ongoing, for his actions and it seemed no amount of apology or atonement was ever going to be enough. This continued to feed the man's lack of self-worth and 'keep him in line'.

The saddest part is that there is a solution, and that is for men to do (as Johnson puts it), the 'inner' work. By that he means for men to look inside to understand what it is we are seeking to complete us, for as long as we look to another to do this, we are never whole and we'll be on the lookout for the next 'fix'.

The solution to owning our own 'feminine' aspect is to simply do something that completes that aspect *in us*, in endeavours that demand we bring forth our creative expression. We need to find activities that acknowledge and nurture our creative side, so that we can discover the Goddess aspect within ourselves as men (more on this in Chapter 19), so that we don't continue looking and expecting someone else (our partner) to do that for us, whether it is learning a musical instrument, drama, painting, sculpture, writing, woodwork, gardening or whatever else is calling us from our yet unlived potential.

If we honour this within ourselves, we do two things: firstly, we begin to own the projection that got us into trouble in the first place and secondly, we set a course to make ourselves more psychologically whole, which leads us into a far greater appreciation of who we are and more able to relate to others.

Not only does this commence the withdrawal of the projected image we've put on our partners with the expectation to complete us, but it also expands our EQ and RQ, as any pursuit in the Arts, if done with purpose, will open up our *feeling function* and make us more emotionally intelligent and relationally available. We can then hopefully see our partner for the person they are, their imperfections and humanity, the mother of our children, another human being travelling through life in partnership with us.

As a relationship educator, what I have learned is that *emotional intimacy* is the foundation of all intimate relationships and by that, I mean the ability of both people in the relationship to maintain an open-hearted and emotionally-available context. 'Into-me-see' is a good way of understanding what intimacy is and this is a vitally important component of any partnership.

As mentioned in Chapter 11, men generally want sex to feel connected with their partners. What man hasn't felt the warmth of the post-orgasmic afterglow, that time when we feel our Heart has completely opened and the depth of the bond we then feel with our partner, which flows from that, albeit sometimes temporarily? Women on the other hand generally need to feel connected first, to even consider sex, and therein lies the disparity. So, for women, *emotional connection* and how they feel toward their partner, sets the foundation on which physical intimacy rests.

If the relationship lacks emotional intimacy, spontaneity and passion (which are often the catalysts for men seeking sex elsewhere), both parties need to be open and communicate their needs. If covert and overt manipulations start to flavour and tarnish the relationship, it can lead to a Mexican stand-off, which further stresses the relationship.

Talk with any couple who've been together for more than 10 years and have children, and they'll relate to this. The lack of emotional and physical intimacy creates disconnection, which leads to disharmony. The man might need sex or at least the physical intimacy aspects of a committed relationship. His partner might not, yet if he satiates his need through pornography, an affair or prostitution and is 'discovered', he risks being shamed. If his social circle finds out through gossip, he's now further shamed and isolated. When situations like this cannot be adequately or openly discussed within a relationship, it makes the situation more untenable, as nothing changes.

All these factors contribute to the reduction in quality and breakdown of relationships, which can become 'flatlined', where neither party is getting what they need, presenting lessening opportunities for connection, potentially stressing the relationship to such a degree that one partner decides to call it quits.

If any form of domestic violence, or what's become known as *coercive control*, and in more recent times *narcissism* find their way into the relationship, this is a further symptom of deep, underlying personal issues, and can lead to some tragic outcomes. I know of men and women who've been on the receiving end of all three, and the outcomes have not been pretty, especially if children are involved. These cases often end up in the Family Court system for years and at unimaginable emotional and financial expense.

There's no doubt that some relationships reach the point where separation is the best option, since an acrimonious or violent environment is not good for anyone, especially children. However, I'm convinced that if men and women truthfully discussed that there may be a mismatch in perceptions, needs and expectations, and sought help through effective coaching or therapy, or invested in their relationship to understand how to 'do' relationships well, the divorce rates would be much less, kids (especially boys) would be fathered, and society at large would be much improved. Couples can also seek support with Tantric education and weekend retreats on how to bring pleasure back into their relationship, and other ways to reignite the 'spark'.

When relationships do break down, women usually flock around the female partner to console, support and provide encouragement. If kids are involved, other mothers who are generally part of the school social circle will step in with playdates, drop-offs and pick-ups, to show their friend that they care, understand and can be relied on for support during this difficult time.

In contrast, a man who has not had or taken the opportunity to build a social network centred around his kids, is left to fend for himself, is seen as somewhat of a social pariah and to be avoided at all costs.

In my last divorce, I had been on my son's primary school Board for 5 years. It was a small school with some 50 families at the time, so I knew most of them, as well as all the school staff. When we separated, I became the 'invisible man', while my wife had all the support of the mothers' school social network. In the first year, the only person who asked how I was doing was the mother of one of my son's friends, who happened to be a clinical psychologist. Thankfully, I had a solid network of quality men outside of the school scene I'd learned to trust and could turn to for support in navigating such a difficult time. I never recovered any of the school relationships or friendships forged during those 5 years.

Often, other fathers in, or orbiting, the school community might not even know the father, nor his situation, leading to further isolation. If the man has 'transgressed' via inappropriate behaviour such as an affair, for example, then not only does he have to deal with the isolation but also the judgement of the other mothers.

I remember one situation where an active and hands-on father at the school descended into a period of deep depression, but I and others had no idea, since he isolated himself. Over time, this and other mental health issues became too much for his spouse, as he was negatively affecting her and their children, so she initiated a divorce. This made his situation worse, and he spiralled further. One day, a mother I knew bumped into him, spoke briefly, and then contacted me as she knew I operated in this 'men's space', sharing that he wasn't coping. I reached out via text and enquired as to his state and to let him know he could reach out anytime. He responded with a simple "Thanks" and I checked in every few weeks via text. It was some 2 years later, after the dust had settled and he'd emerged out the other side of his depression and divorce, that I bumped into him while shopping. We shook hands, he looked deep into me and shared that although he and I never spoke during that time, the text messages were enough for him to know *that someone cared*. He was evidently grateful that I'd had taken the time to keep in touch. Had that mother not reached out to me, who knows what the consequences might have been?

Next time you hear of someone in your social circle who is facing separation or divorce, spare a thought for the man and even better, if you're a woman who knows him to some degree, let him know that you care about him too (if you do), even if you don't know him that well. You will show the man that you recognise he too might be in emotional pain. You may ignite a little ray of hope in the man that someone has noticed and cares enough to show support, which might avert a depressive state or even thoughts about suicide.

A woman in this role can also suggest the man seek the company of other good men in the community that she may know, or recommend a men's group, Men's Shed or other avenues for support, such as counselling or therapy.

When it comes to divorce, men need to know that someone cares about them even if it's someone they don't know well, especially if the situation involves their children, since most men I have met in this situation face a multidimensional calamity: the end of their relationship, the painful separation from their children that they so dearly love, the ending of the couple's social circle, the loss of friendships and in-law relationships, and the fear of loneliness and an uncertain future.

Perhaps, as noted in the introduction to this chapter, divorce is the second most stressful event in life, and we now have some notion as to the causes, implications and some of the possible solutions, such as *relationship education*. Maybe it's something that we need to teach in schools!

Key Points:

- *50% of marriages and de facto relationships don't survive, and the majority of separations are initiated by the female partner*

- *Divorce is a painful process for both parties, their children, family and friends*

- *Women generally have a social network to help them through such times, whereas men do not*

- *Separation can lead to deep emotional pain for men, resulting in a deep sense of failure, depression and isolation*

- *Men often turn to alcohol or other substances to cope with the emotional state of relationship breakdown and separation.*

14. DEPRESSION & SUICIDE

Men can be around each other for years and never know the other man's true situation. Often when a man has suicided, his friends say they had no idea that he was unhappy. When a man has huge problems in his marriage, or has a child with cancer, a parent with dementia, or frightening health problems of his own, he may never speak of this to even closest friends. If he does mention something so intensely personal, his friends may not know how to respond, and either ignore him or make a dumb joke that discounts his feelings, so that he does not try again."

– **Steve Biddulph**

Wikipedia defines depression as, "a state of low mood and aversion to activity, which can have a negative effect on a person's thoughts, behaviour, feelings, world view and physical well-being."

As we learned in Chapter 8 on Statistics, depression and suicide are major issues for men and perhaps now we have some understanding of the situations that create such a difficult and desperate environment.

The highest rate of depression in men is between 35-44 years of age, at 4% of the population. For women it is 8% in the same age group and in fact, depression in women is often more than double that of men, however as men typically don't seek help, depression is often under-reported and tends to be a longer-term issue for men.

Ultimately, depression is a mental illness that affects a person in varying ways, such as tiredness, difficulty sleeping, moodiness, and a general lack of interest in life. If left untreated, depression can become disabling, preventing a person from fulfilling the functions they would normally do. As we've noted earlier in this book, men often have difficulty articulating what they're feeling and depressed men often suffer in silence, believing that somehow, they're weak, or have failed.

Feelings of shame from not being able to fulfil their role also contribute to depression's debilitating and pervasive condition. These feelings compound the sense of lack of purpose, and result in a man losing connection with himself, family, friends and colleagues. If left untreated it can have a serious impact on the whole family environment and, in severe cases, lead to suicide.

There are different types of depression that have been categorised by various health departments. The Black Dog Institute, created in Australia, is an organisation specifically chartered with assisting mental-health sufferers and has extensive experience in supporting multiple treatment regimes. They categorise depression into three major areas:

- Melancholic depression
- Non-melancholic depression

- Psychotic depression

Melancholic depression is the most uncommon, affecting less than 5% of people who experience depression. Its characteristics include a lack of pleasure, difficulty being 'cheered up', low energy, poor concentration, and lethargic or agitated movement. As it usually has a *biological basis*, it does not usually heal itself and responds best to various treatments including medication.

Non-melancholic depression is the most common being related to *psychological* factors, unlike melancholic which is primarily physical. It can spontaneously disappear as it is often linked to stressful events, which once resolved, tend to lift the depression. It can however be difficult to diagnose since it has a lack of defining characteristics, which include a depressed mood or a lack of sociability. Due to its psychological nature, it does usually respond well to counselling and therapy.

The last classification of psychotic depression, is less common than melancholic depression and often presents itself as a combination of both physical and psychological factors, including severely depressed mood, more severe physical melancholic characteristics such as lethargy, agitation, delusions, and hallucinations or deep feelings of guilt. It does not usually disappear of its own accord, often requires hospitalisation, and responds best to medication.

Any depression that doesn't present within the above three categories is called *atypical* depression and is a category created to cover depression that does not clearly fit. For example, appetite loss is a common factor, yet some depressed people eat excessively when depressed. As well as weight gain, other factors include excessive sleeping, feelings of heavy limbs, sensitivity to feelings of rejection, while happy occasions can cheer up the person.

Treatment is best approached by an assessment, preferably by professionals such as psychologists, psychiatrists or counsellors. BeyondBlue and The Black Dog Institute are examples of local organisations that provide resources such as national listings of health practitioners who have expertise in assessing and treating depression, as well as Help Line contact details, so they are worth reviewing.

There are three major recognised categories for treatment: psychological, physical, and self-help and alternative therapies. It may be a combination of these that produces the best outcomes.

Psychological treatments can include psychologists, psychiatrists, counsellors, psychotherapists, and a range of modalities such as cognitive, narrative and psychotherapies.

Physical treatments such as medication, electroconvulsive therapy (ECT) and repetitive transcranial magnetic stimulation (rTMS) can also help.

Self-help and alternative therapies can include exercise, meditation, mindfulness techniques, breathwork and natural supplements.

This page from the Black Dog Institute is an excellent resource on depression and treatment options: www.blackdoginstitute.org.au/resources-support/depression/treatment/

Many men suffer depression *alone* for reasons mentioned in this and earlier chapters, and primarily it is an ingrained 'don't complain' attitude that pervades most men. I'm sure it stems from the stiff- upper-lip Victorian days when men were taught to grin and bear it, yet this attitude has not served men or society at large.

It is well known that *aloneness* and *loneliness* contribute significantly to depressive states, so seeking the company of others will help in navigating depressive moods. Pets, particularly the unconditional love of a dog, can help too. If you're a man reading this and you suspect you experience depression, then I implore you to seek help, even if it's finding a local men's group. They provide a forum for men to be with other men and understand that these issues are not unique. Depression is pervasive and common, and with the support of other men you might just find a way to understand what's really happening. By hearing how other men have acknowledged their depression and what worked for them, you might well discover some hope and realise that you are not as alone as you thought. Plus, the peer support will assist you in breaking the depressive cycle and bring you back into a sense of balance.

If you're a woman reading this and you're aware of or suspect a man in your life may be experiencing depression, then perhaps try to find a way to encourage him to seek help. You may just save his life.

Unfortunately, the use of antidepressants is on the rise, with around 1 in 7 Australians taking them daily, ranking us second to Iceland for OECD countries. Stopping them is no easy task either. "We know from systematic reviews of studies … withdrawal symptoms occur to at least half of people who try to stop their antidepressant," says Mark Horowitz, an Australian researcher at University College London. "Up to a quarter will experience severe withdrawal effects." (www.www.abc.net.au/news/2022-02-22/australians-coming-off-antidepressants/100847462/) Sadly,

withdrawal symptoms when coming off antidepressants can be mistaken for recurrence of the initial problem, so that can make diagnosis difficult too.

Depression affects many people, and thankfully, the importance of mental health is receiving more attention across society, with general practitioners (GPs) often the first line of contact for those affected. If you're experiencing depression, start perhaps with your GP to explore options.

An unfortunate outcome of untreated depression is suicide. Relationship breakdown, financial collapse, retrenchment coupled with periods of unemployment, being overwhelmed, substance abuse or addiction, and many other factors can lead a man to the edge. What tips a man over that edge, to take his own life and, in extreme cases, the life of others such as his wife and children, can only be seen as a last desperate and catastrophic act, a tragedy that impacts everyone who comes into contact with it.

It is often assumed that men are ill-equipped to deal with strong feelings, whereas research shows that it is a lack of social support services and education, that compound feelings of isolation and trauma.

As per the opening quotation for this section, it is not uncommon for a man to take his life yet those around him had no idea he was battling such demons. At one stage in my life, suicide appeared as a viable option. A business collapse in 1991 in the 'recession Australia had to have', resulted in the catastrophic loss of my 17-year relationship, family home and life savings, which left me in a terrible state and completely shattered my already minimal self-worth. I vividly remember considering my options, yet thankfully at the time, I didn't have the capacity to act. I also believed I couldn't reach out to family or friends as my sense of failure left me feeling completely alone, embarrassed, a total 'failure' and deeply ashamed.

Suicide as an option was purely and simply one way I considered to remove the pain I was experiencing. At that time, I had little sense of myself, minimal emotional intelligence and was immobile in my feelings. When these very strong feelings of failure emerged, I didn't have the necessary emotional resilience or a storehouse of self-worth to carry me through. That's when I stumbled into therapy and over the ensuing years began to understand the unconscious forces that drove me to such failure.

At current levels, over 2,400 men take their own lives every year. That's almost 7 men every day, so somewhere in Australia, on average, a man takes his own life every 4 hours. That's a grandfather, father, son, brother, uncle, husband, friend, work colleague. It is also estimated that there are approximately 140 unsuccessful attempts *every single day*.

Please pause here for a moment to think about that and ponder how that might affect you, if it was someone you knew. I have known several men who've taken this drastic step, and I'm always left with feelings of profound grief and sadness for the immediate family. The scars on those left behind can be debilitating and long-lasting, with 'suicide grief' being far more complex than the grief experienced through the loss of a loved one from other forms of death. Apart from the sudden and tragic loss, questions naturally arise such as 'why?' and 'what could I have done differently?', so it often requires specialist grief counselling.

Remember suicide is the leading cause of death in men under 50 and that almost 80% of suicides are male, which is indicative of a deep and systemic problem in men's ability to navigate the complexities of life. More men take their own life than are killed in traffic accidents or by skin cancers. If there were a series of pointers that identified a failure in the way our boys are raised toward manhood, this would have to be it.

The facilitators of a men's weekend workshop that has been running for over 20 years, start the event with a fascinating and interesting exercise. The men are asked to stand in front of a grid marked out on the floor with each square about 30cm (12") on each side. The grid is 8 x 8 squares so it looks a bit like a human-sized chessboard. The men are told that *there is only one way through the 'maze'* and that they have to find the starting square, or entrance, on the edge at which they are standing. The men take turns to step on the various squares. If they step into the 'wrong' square they will hear a loud 'beep' from the facilitator who holds the map.

Eventually, the group of men identify the starting square along the entrance edge, but then they have to find the next square, which is either to their left or right, diagonally ahead, or straight ahead, giving them a choice of five 'future' squares. If they guess incorrectly and step into the wrong square, the man will hear a 'beep' and he then has to back out of the grid *the way he came in* so that another man can start at the entrance square. Of course, if the previous man has managed to get some way through the grid and has to back out, then the new man has to remember the sequence of squares. There can only be one man on the grid at a time, until the maze is solved, then men can follow each other. When all the men have walked the path correctly, the exercise is over.

I've experienced this event three times now and the first time was a real challenge as we men fumbled our way through the maze until we finally got smart and worked out a way that supported each man's journey. And this was the key to the exercise!

Afterward, the facilitator explained the grid is a bit like life for a man. If the path was a straight line of squares from entrance to exit, it'd be easy, but life isn't like that and some squares are close to the edge, on the edge, or as in life, off the edge.

The 'beep' notifying us of a failed step, is parents, relationships, community and society at large, letting us know that we've stepped on the wrong square and transgressed in some way. In life, the message is simply that you *have* transgressed, you've made a mistake, cocked up, made a poor decision, and perhaps don't know *why*. So as men, we take one blind step after another in the hope of not stepping on a square that'll lead us into painful territory. Often, one poor decision leads to another and before we know it, we've fallen off the edge.

I found the exercise very meaningful since it parallels how most men navigate life, with little guidance, leadership, mentorship or eldership, and the feedback system is often unforgiving and can be as extreme as removal from society through incarceration. Introduce drugs, both legal and illegal, and we create a potent cocktail, the results of which are seen on the nightly news. As the Australian group Skyhooks noted in the lyrics of their song, *Horror Movie*, "Horror movie it's the six-thirty news, shockin' me right outa my brain."

Suicide is an avoidable tragedy. We have a serious national issue that is all too slowly receiving the attention it desperately needs, and even with funding and education being recognised as primary drivers, little progress is being made as we're not addressing root causes.

The rates of male suicide from 2000-2013 hovered between 1,600 and just under 2,000 per year, however, in 2014 the number unexpectedly jumped to 2,221 and has since remained above 2,000, peaking in 2019 at 2,546. Preliminary estimates for 2023 sit at 2,419:

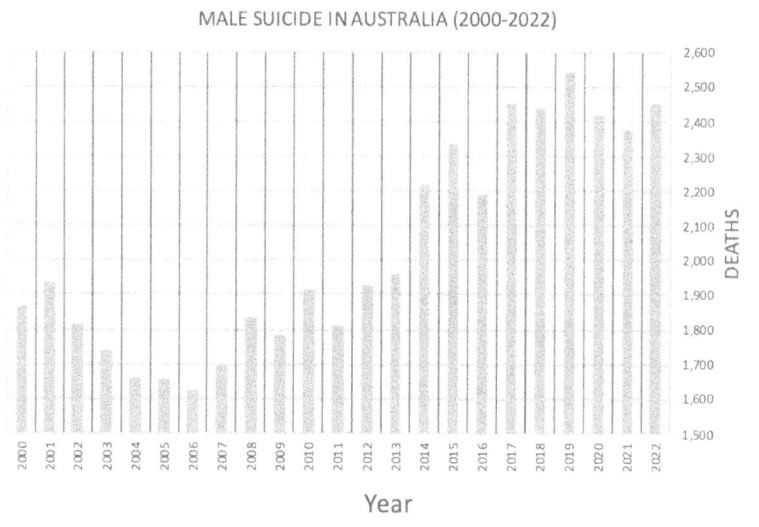

Suicide death rates in Australia from 2000 to 2022

Of course, as the population increases so does the number of deaths, so suicide is often reported as a *standardised value*, being the number of suicides per 100,000 of population. Over the same period, the 'age-standardised' rate for male suicide has hovered from a low of 16.2 (2006) to a high of 20.1 (2019).

To provide some international context and while it's not practical to list the standardised rate for all countries, I located a World Population Review website (www.worldpopulationreview.com/country-rankings/suicide-rate-by-country/)

that separated male and female suicide across all countries, then chose a few with similar cultures (such as Canada, New Zealand, Europe and Scandinavia), to arrive at the summary below for the latest year of consolidation, which was 2021:

Country	Rate / 100k
Australia	**19.8**
Austria	22.3
Canada	19.4
Denmark	16.3
Finland	24.0
France	22.0
Ireland	13.7
Netherlands	15.2
New Zealand	17.0
Norway	16.4
Portugal	18.3
Spain	11.9
United Kingdom	13.2
United States	24.1

Greenland	87.0
Lebanon	1.2

Standardised male suicide rate per 100,000 population for 1012

As you can see, of the 14 countries I chose, Australia is at the high end, at 19.8. You can also see that below these 14 are the highest and lowest rates, 87 (what's going on in Greenland?) and 1.2 for Lebanon.

If you're reading this from another country not listed and you're interested in your country's statistics, you can easily find these via the Internet. In the USA, for example, the 24.1/100,000 rate equates to approximately 40,000 men per year! That's one death every 13 minutes with more than half taking their own life via a firearm.

What these numbers show is that across the Western world, male suicide is an issue, irrespective of country. This indicates that while culture may have *some* impact, there are underlying systemic issues that affect men in this way, and I believe the understanding of our inner journey, as explained in this book, and what happens if we don't explore, speaks to more a universal issue and explanation.

It makes complete sense that a man who explores his inner landscape with guidance and support, and knows more about his unresolved trauma and wounds (Chapter 17), is much less likely to consider taking his own life, once *the pain of unknowing* is replaced with *self-compassion.*

What is surprising is that even though the ratio between male and female suicide averages 4:1, the rates follow similar trends in that when one goes up, so does the other, although the female rate in Australia between 2000-2023 had a low of 4.3/100,000 (437 women) in 2004, to a high of 6.7 in 2017 (838), perhaps indicating the impact of other societal factors such as the Global Financial Crisis.

What is evident and disturbing is that since 2006, suicide rates are on the rise for men, indicating that there is a dire need for increased funding and suicide helplines specifically for men, and a deeper understanding of the cause-vs-symptom influences.

There is also believed to be a hidden suicide rate whereby young men, often driving alone, lose their lives wrapped around a tree or drive into an oncoming truck, and it is believed that these are often successful suicide attempts recorded as road statistics, thereby reducing the true suicide rate for young men. It is estimated that the true rate is closer to 3,000 deaths per year or more than 8 deaths per day.

Depression and suicide are deep-seated issues for men with one often leading to the other. The important need for men to support other men who are experiencing such conditions cannot be overemphasised, and we can support the men in our lives to seek the help they need.

In the next few chapters, we'll explore some ways that we, as individual men and women, parents, mothers and fathers, can affect these statistics, but first, we will go to a place that is little understood by both men and women alike.

The 'Man Cave'!

Key Points:

♦ *Depression affects many men who suffer in silence*

♦ *Depression can be treated by various modalities, once a man seeks help*

♦ *Suicide is the largest cause of death in men under 50*

♦ *The suicide rate has been steadily increasing since 2006*

♦ *Seven men suicide every day and an estimated 140 attempts*

♦ *We need much more funding for awareness campaigns and education, as the causative factors influencing depression and suicide are still not being adequately communicated.*

15. THE MAN CAVE

Immersing myself in the world of men and boys has proved life-changing. I now know that men have the same emotional breadth as women, that they can be just as articulate, tender, thoughtful and wise, that they love their children passionately, and that they too want relationships that lift their Hearts and feed their souls. The thing is that men communicate in different ways to women. They have different perspectives, different ways of showing they care. When we women can understand and celebrate these differences life will be far richer, far more meaningful.
– **Maggie Hamilton** (in private dialogue, author of *What's Happening To Our Boys* & *What Men Don't Talk About*)

I've opened this chapter with a quote from Maggie Hamilton since her experience of men is probably atypical. Maggie intended to write a book about men by interviewing a few she knew, but as she immersed herself in this world, her research grew and included hundreds of males ranging from 4 to 80 years old!

Her book, *What Men Don't Talk About*, was for me both insightful and tragic. It explores the world of masculinity with remarkable objectivity and respect. I remember reading sections about men's lives that left me aghast that their world was so full of suffering and isolation. Maggie does make mention that men communicate in different ways to women.

Lashlie (*He'll Be OK*), interviewed 180 classrooms in New Zealand's *The Good Man Project*, and her conclusion about communication was the same. Men often communicate without words, sometimes with a simple yet meaningful look, capable of conveying an entire paragraph! She commented that the pragmatism of men, especially adolescents approaching manhood, was one of their most endearing qualities. For example, when a boy was interviewed and asked what a major advantage was of being in an all-boys school, he answered that he had more time for a morning sleep-in. Curious and not seeing the link, Maggie enquired further. "*Well, being in an all-boys school means I don't have to shower and put gel in my hair!*"

How do we, as men, avoid the often-burdensome requirement to engage in drawn-out and sometimes painful communication with others, especially our partners? To get some 'quiet time' we go to our Man Cave.

The Man Cave has been the subject of much conjecture, derision and even ridicule. There are various definitions to be found on the Internet and I particularly liked this one from The Official (yes, there is one!) at www.mancavesite.org:

man cave [*man-keyv*] *noun:* A Man Cave is a room or space (as in a basement) designed according to the taste of the man of the house to be used as his personal area for hobbies and leisure activities.

It is generally a place where a man can go into his own space, away from the family and what one site described as 'free of female sensibilities.' By this they mean a place where the rules are not set by the woman of the house, but by the man-cave owner himself. A place to be quiet, read, potter, attend to a hobby, watch films or just about anything else a man might do. The site mentioned above even has competitions for the 'Man Cave Of The Year' with photos and hints on how to Do It Yourself!

If decorated, it is always done by the man since any female influence such as furnishings defeats the very purpose of the man cave, which is intended to be a female-influence-free habitat. It can be a place for solitude or mateship, depending on the man's requirements. I'm not sure what women think of such places, which are probably more tolerated than understood, however they fulfil a basic need for men to get some time away from their normal routines and pressures of daily life.

In Australia, an emerging phenomenon is 'Men's Sheds' that are springing up as community-based sheds, garages or buildings where men go to hang out with other men. Women may think that such a place is a den of misogyny where lives are compared, alcohol is consumed and nothing much happens.

Not so.

Men's Sheds provide a venue for men (and in some, women) to congregate and do a whole range of things, whether it's making, restoring or repairing furniture, making things for children's charities, fixing bikes and mowers, or simply providing a place where fathers and sons can work together so the sons can learn skills from other men. The sheds are usually apolitical and non-denominational.

There is even an Australian Men's Shed Association with the first shed opening in 1993 in Goolwa, South Australia. As the idea took hold, the AMSA was established in 2007, and now provides advice on where to find a Shed, insurance coverage, legal requirements, how to start a shed, events and conferences, and a forum for discussion of topics such as depression. As of 2024, there were over 1,200 registered Sheds in Australia (or as the site proudly proclaims, "that's more Men's Sheds than Macca's restaurants!"), which leads the world by far in this area. While AMSA is federally funded, sheds can be supported by councils, individuals and even community programs.

Men's Sheds provide a much-needed place for men who don't want to sit in their own cave and want to be with other men to simply be, help out or find someone to talk to who they might know and trust. It is estimated that more than 50,000 men participate nationally in men's sheds. Some Sheds have a coordinator who often has social skills training and can identify a man who might need an ear, or is heading for a troublesome mental health time.

It has certainly been my experience that when a man is sitting on some unexpressed emotion, other more perceptive men can often see through the "I'm OK" façade and will gently but firmly challenge the man to get real and connect with his underlying feelings, eventually leading to some conversation, expression and perhaps resolution. For that to happen, we have to knock and be invited into the man's 'inner man cave'.

Let me explain.

In my coaching I educate men about what are known as level 1, 2 and 3 conversations.

Level 1 goes something like this:

> "How are you doing?"
>
> "I'm good."

And that's it, especially for a man who doesn't want, or feel safe, to go any deeper.

A perceptive listener might then follow up with:

> "Well, you don't look/sound/feel good. I'm worried about you. Are you really ok?"
>
> "Mmmm ... not really. There's some trouble at work and maybe some impending layoffs, and I'm worried I might lose my job!"

If we're prepared to go to level 3, we can express empathy and support:

> "That must be worrying for you. I've been in that same situation and I remember it was tough. Is there anything I can offer that might help you with your anxiety?"
>
> "Errr ... I guess. I hadn't really thought about it until now. How did you get through it?

And then a supportive conversation can begin because we've gently knocked and been 'invited in' to the man's inner man cave.

Gaining access can be a challenge and any woman reading this who has spent any length of time with men in a relationship will know when the "Do Not Disturb" sign is up. While this may not be applicable to all men, those I've shared it with have nodded in agreement and for them, they know this place. It is often represented by a 'mood' that clearly states, *I don't wish to talk, explore my feelings or get into any deep and meaningful (D&M) conversation. I simply wish to be left alone to internally process whatever it is that's going on inside of me.*

At a men's gathering I attended, in one of the many wonderful workshops that were being offered, the subject of the internal man cave came up and after various discussions and points of view, we concluded that there are actually *two* inner man caves.

The first is the entrance cave, discussed above, which has a door, usually left open, where the man might go for some internal solitude. Outwardly he may seem distant, not present, distracted, as he chews his cud and mulls over whatever it is that's troubling him. Sometimes he may retreat to his physical man cave to distract himself, since we men aren't usually good at sitting with uncomfortable feelings unless we've done so many times before.

The message here is, "I'm troubled, I'm thinking about stuff and trying to work out what to do next, so just leave me be for a while, let me know you care (an occasional cup of tea?), try to keep the kids under control, and most probably it isn't about something you've done."

The advice to women here is to (in the immortal words of The Beatles) 'Let It Be!' and show you're there if needed. Do your best to not engage or pry by asking probing questions.

The other internal 'man cave' is the one at the back of the open-door ante-cave, with a big steel door and painted with a skull and crossbones. The message here is blunt: "Leave me alone 'cos I'm really pissed off or hurting and I've retreated so I don't do any harm to anyone or myself. You'll know when I'm ready to talk because if or when I can find the words, I'll probably share them with you."

Even if this form of expression is viewed as lacking in emotional intelligence, it'll be an inkling into that inner chamber of the man cave. While the first ante-cave might have a metaphorical lounge, remote control, good book, fridge or movie, with the man still functioning but in some perhaps reduced capacity, this inner cave is bereft of furniture and set up specifically for pacing, since we do our best thinking on our metaphorical feet.

An aware man who has explored his emotional landscape and developed the skills to navigate this place might even go for an actual walk, to put some distance between himself and the situation, and to get some 'air' that will allow perhaps just a hint of perspective. Be prepared though, that when he returns, the man might have something to say – but don't have any expectations.

Women can help enormously here by identifying firstly that the man has retreated either emotionally or physically, and the prevailing mood indicates the nature of that retreat. If I can provide any salient advice, it is to *let the man do what he knows how to do*, and that is 'process'. Women tend to think that just because a man isn't talking about something, we've moved on in the hope it'll go away. Yes, that does happen, however, men mostly simply need *time* and the opportunity afforded by *silence* and isolation to get themselves back on an even keel. Remember from earlier in this book that we've not been raised to identify our feelings, let alone talk about them. Women generally have such a social structure about them for most of their lives, so they process externally with words, while men process internally with thoughts.

Perhaps some men who withdraw from very painful experiences by entering deeper into this cave, lose their way, since really, the only way out is the way we came in, baggage and all. However, we cannot exit in the same condition we entered. There is no point leaving the cave if nothing has changed. We're well aware of the pain that we're carrying, and dealing with the outside world on top of this can feel unbearable.

When coupled with a lack of emotional mobility, or convincing ourselves that we don't need help, or we are unable to see a solution or a way out of the situation, we can easily get 'stuck'. It may even be that an aspect of male depression and the feelings of aloneness and isolation, find their seeds in the deep, dark recesses of this inner, reclusive man cave. One thing I know for certain is that such deep introspection can provide extraordinary insights. However, I'm also convinced that some men get lost in this place and unwittingly decide to throw away the key … and never emerge. When this happens, what potential are we losing in these men who are unable to find their way back to relate with the outside world?

If a man chooses to develop his inner sense of who he *really* is, where he stands and what he stands for in this world, what are his foibles and strengths and how best to navigate his way through life, he can move mountains. I've experienced many a man, including myself, dig to the deepest, darkest recesses of our being-ness and create remarkable transformations in so many aspects of our own lives, and consequently others around us.

It simply takes the time it takes, and we need to do it our way. We can, of course, be supported by those around us who love us, understand how we deal with difficult situations, and perhaps have compassion and respect our need for some 'man-cave' processing time and privacy.

One woman I know who has had almost three decades of helping men in this way is Diane McCann, a co-facilitator of workshops for both men and women. Having seen many men bare their souls and emerge from their cave, sometimes after years of pain, I asked Diane to share her experience of men.

"Men are divine, wonderful beings, they want the same things women want except they have never been shown or told a) what we need or b) how to best give it to us. Men are in a more difficult place than women because of women's natural inclination toward intimacy with their friends and many men have no one close they can confide in. So, men need our respect, our love and our hands reaching out to bridge the gap so that we all might find equality and stop the war that has been going on for way too long. Here's to peace between the sexes, understanding between us that allows the divinity in each of us to shine through."
– **Diane McCann** (Co-creator and co-facilitator of *The Goddess Within* and *Man's Inner Journey*)

Wise words from a wise Elder.

Hopefully, this exploration of the various levels of the man cave has provided you with some deeper insights into what they are, an understanding of their purpose, and how to navigate them!

Key Points:

◆ *The 'Man Cave' can be a real place such as a garage, shed or den where a man can go to get some time-out and relax*

◆ *Men's Sheds are a way for men to socialise with other men and seek camaraderie, as well as build a functional social network of like-minded men*

◆ *Be on the lookout for level 1, 2 and 3 conversations*

◆ *The inner 'Man Cave' has two levels: the first is an open door that welcomes acknowledgement, the second is the skull-and-crossbones, heavy-walled chamber, that only the man can navigate*

◆ *Allow men time to process, offer support and don't invade by being demanding.*

16. AN ACKNOWLEDGEMENT

I believe that very soon the world view of masculinity will change drastically and a man's character will be measured by his ability not only to love, but in his ability to allow himself to be loved, by his kindness, his humility, his gentleness, his receptivity, and his vulnerability. A man secure and centred in himself is a gift to the world.

— **Rundy Delphini**

I read Rundy Delphini's words in a book on sacred sexuality and they struck me as being of exquisite clarity, vision and hope. They aligned with my own views of being able to wield the sword and the harp, or being a man with both a Heart and a backbone.

Before masculinity can evolve to a place where these two complimentary states exist, we must first be willing as men to experience them, and as Delphini states, this requires a man to be secure in his vulnerability.

I hope by now that the landscape of contemporary masculinity has been sufficiently explored for you to understand that there is much to be done if we're to create healthier and safer environments, and in doing so, a better future for all our children. We have a long way to go before the majority of men feel secure in their vulnerability.

I doubt whether anyone would argue that the current situation requires continued scrutiny, as the social unrest and statistics speak for themselves. However, my experience is that there is a general malaise, a 'blind eye' attitude, where anyone who looks can see that the Emperor has no clothes. However, not all men wish to see. When we consider the pressures men are under in so many aspects of our lives, it should come as no surprise.

The irony is that we, as men, are fighting fires, fuelled by stereotypes and fanned by the media, when we could quite simply stand up and say, 'This is me!'

While it may be challenging to make changes by the time we reach later life, due to the often ingrained and entrenched patterns of behaviour, it's never too late to explore one's *inner landscape*. We can lay claim to our *Elderhood*. Men, secure in their vulnerability, do not shy away from the inner work needed to maintain their centre of gravity. They seek the company of like-Hearted men, hold women in the highest regard and respect themselves and the world around them.

There's a sea-change happening around the globe regarding men seeking connection with their Hearts and Australian men are leading the way, so the more we, as a society, discuss subjects such as health, depression, suicide, relationships and sexuality, the more chance we have of making the changes so urgently needed. The more we engage our kids, the more love they will feel and the more they will learn to feel. The more we as men decide that the stereotypes we've been branded with are out-dated, ill-fitting and from a bygone era, the more impetus we can muster to reclaim ourselves. And that means men doing what is necessary to get in touch with our Hearts as well as developing the backbone to do it.

In ensuring we support this movement that is gathering momentum, we will naturally demonstrate and express our care for *all* life, support boys and young men in their journey to functional masculinity and seek ways to contribute whatever we can to lead, mentor and educate. This will create an environment that turns boys into men, who understand they have access to both a sword and a harp, what is the difference, when to wield which and to what degree.

A leading men's organisation (www.menswellbeing.org/) expresses their mission as, "Developing the wellbeing of men to foster healthy relationships, families and communities." They clearly understand the relationship between physically, emotionally and mentally healthy men and the quality of the society in which we live.

To illustrate this, an international conference on men's health was held in Brisbane, Australia in October 2013 and covered a range of topics. One common theme to emerge from multiple countries was that female-centric teaching and female-focused curricula are failing boys at an alarming rate, with fewer boys completing high school. When coupled with the under-fathering epidemic in many Western countries, the concern is that we are collectively approaching what the conference termed 'a demographic winter'. By this, they were referring to possibly two generations of disconnected, disenfranchised and disengaged boys who will end up unemployable and unweddable. This is a real crisis facing the Western world today and in dire need of attention, focus and funding.

Men are also actively seeking opportunities to show respect and support for the evolution of the new feminine that is being expressed, one that does so *without a cost to men*. Being branded by ardent feminists as 'part of the patriarchy' (or as a female therapist derogatively said to me, "If you have a penis, you're a part of the patriarchy!'), it's as if both women and men have had enough of the gender war and can see that an opportunity exists for the first time in our human history, to acknowledge the past, let it go and move forward in a united vision.

Humans lived under the Goddess aspect of nature for millennia, where the Earth provided all life and continues to. The feminine principle was the guiding one, and there are still many indigenous-based cultures with matrilineal societies. However, history shows that over time, the feminine principle has been brutally oppressed and suppressed in both women *and* men. Perhaps we're entering a time where both the feminine and masculine principles are now maturing with an understanding that neither can dominate, since this creates conflict at the expense of life itself. A 'win-lose' scenario doesn't work for either.

So before we move on to look at some solutions, I would like to acknowledge all the men who are doing the challenging inner work, taking stock, looking inward, seeking purpose, and contributing immensely to the sea-change (or should that be see-change?), the men who organise gatherings, father-and-son weekends, rites of passage programs, men's sheds, men's groups, workshops and the like, for these man are the leaders of our time who will lay the foundations for future generations of men.

I'd also like to acknowledge the women who are supportive of this shift. It'd be easy for women to hide behind their pain from being on the receiving end of unaware and dysfunctional men, yet as you can see by the comments made by women I've been privileged to meet and included in this book, there are wise women who want men to live happy, fulfilling and meaningful lives themselves, and for their own Goddess to meet their God of choice.

This journey of restitution and resolution must be one that both women and men approach with openness and vulnerability, otherwise, it'll simply descend into another time of unconscious discord. We have substantial hindsight to understand the effect of this on our children, women, men and the planet itself.

We can shift our perspective to an ecological worldview but only if we embark on this individual and collective inward journey, together.

17. WOUNDEDNESS

How strange that we should ordinarily feel compelled to hide our wounds when we are all wounded! Community requires the ability to expose our wounds and weaknesses to our fellow creatures. It also requires the ability to be affected by the wounds of others... But even more important is the love that arises among us when we share, both ways, our woundedness.
– M. Scott Peck (author of The Road Less Travelled)

If you've never heard of male and female woundedness there is a plethora of information in books and on the Internet. My first exposure to such a concept, as mentioned in Chapter 7, was via Robert A Johnson's book, *HE: Understanding Masculine Psychology* where Johnson parallels the myth of The Fisher King with that of a modern man's evolution through life. Here, again, is a very brief summary of the myth, this time in relation to our woundedness:

> *The Fisher King was also known as the Wounded King where the health of the King is tied to the health of the land. The Knight's quest is to find the Grail Castle and ask the question, "Whom does the Grail serve?"*

> *It is foretold that only a wholly innocent 'fool' knows the way to the Grail Castle and that when he asks the key question, the King will be healed and so will the land.*
>
> *Young Parsifal is the innocent fool, an aspiring Knight, wearing a tunic made for him by his mother. When he first finds the Grail Castle as a youth, his mother's words of caution, "Never ask questions in someone else's house!" prevent him from asking the very question that will heal the King! Johnson eloquently explains this as the boy being "blinded by his mother's homespun" and a classic 'mother wound'.*
>
> *Years later, after maturing, Parsifal fortunately finds the Grail Castle again and this time, because he has healed his mother wound, he asks the question and both the King and the land are healed.*

(Johnson's book is filled with insights and beautifully written, transforming myth into modern relevance, so a highly recommended read.)

Franciscan friar Richard Rohr, an active commentator on our human condition, expressed this beautifully in his writing, *The Sacred Wound*:

> *When life is hard we are primed to learn something absolutely central. The huge surprise is that the place of the wound is the place of the greatest gift. No one wants to be wounded yet almost everyone is at one time or another. Some wounds are small, some are very large. Some wounds are physical and some are psychological, and some are both. All wounds require healing. Psychological wounds*

are usually more complex and take longer to heal. A core wound rarely stems from a single traumatic incident. More often it consists of a pattern of hurtful events or a disturbing dynamic in one or more important relationships.

It is not an accident, nor is it necessarily unfortunate that each person suffers from a core wound. Some say that the Soul orchestrates the wounding to catalyse a special type of personal development that requires a trauma for its genesis. By exploring your core wound you can render it sacred. You can facilitate the death of your old story and the birth of the larger story, a Soul story, one revealed by the wounding itself. The goal in sacred wound work is not to patch up your small story, nor is it to heal the adolescent ego. Rather, it is to realise your old story and become a vehicle through which your Soul story can be lived into the world.

Our core wounds often involve some form of betrayal. The betrayal always involves broken trust. The deeper the trust, the deeper the betrayal – and deeper the wound. The deeper the wound, the deeper the possible blessing. Our understanding is enclosed in the familial and cultural conditioning which must be broken through in order to discover the wisdom that lies within.

Emotional and physical pain are an indicator that something needs our attention and it may be a message that something needs to be released. Knowing this is true does not mean that it isn't perfectly normal to get perfectly lost in the story that surrounds our suffering. At times the deep trauma of our story may seem like the only thing that we have to hold onto. It's very important to be very patient with others – and even more patient with ourselves – when we return to the story again and again. Healing has its own timetable.

When I read this a few years ago, the depth of wisdom and understanding spoke deeply to me of my journey of identifying and tending my woundedness. I was already on my healing journey, so reading that "Healing has its own timetable" allowed me to be patient with myself and be more mindful of the journey I was on rather than any destination.

Every man carries his own psychological wound(s) whether he knows it or not, for it is born from the transition of childhood to manhood, when the boy-man is between worlds. We start our journey in the 'unconscious perfection' of childhood, which means we don't have the awareness to *know* that we're innocent and perfect. At some point in our growth, a boy will catch a glimpse of the imperfect nature of life itself, especially the adult world of responsibility, which often comes as quite a shock. It's almost as if an irrevocable awakening happens as the boy *realises* (in the true sense of the word) that he is headed for adulthood and the responsibilities that this will bring. Another way of viewing this is the awareness of the beginning of a shift in focus from 'me' to 'we', whereby the boy starts to see that he is, in fact, NOT the centre of the universe!

A boy starts to move from the unconscious perfection of childhood, into the conscious imperfection of adulthood. Sometimes a boy will find such an experience way too intense and initially recoil from it, as he is unsure what to do with such a numinous experience, like a glimpse of The Grail Castle. Other boys will not be consciously aware that such a glimpse has even happened, however, it will leave its indelible mark on the boy's emerging and maturing psyche.

As he starts to leave his boyish self behind, he must find the innocent aspect of himself and trust it, in order to successfully make the transitional journey. Failure to resolve this wound will result in a psychological boy in a physical man's body and evidence of this abounds everywhere. One only has to look at examples in both the corporate world and politics!

This table from Powerhouse Programs, who organise and facilitate Rite of Passage programs for teenage boys (more on this in chapter 18) and adapted from Richard Rohr's work, highlights the shift in focus that must happen, if boys are to psychologically grow into men:

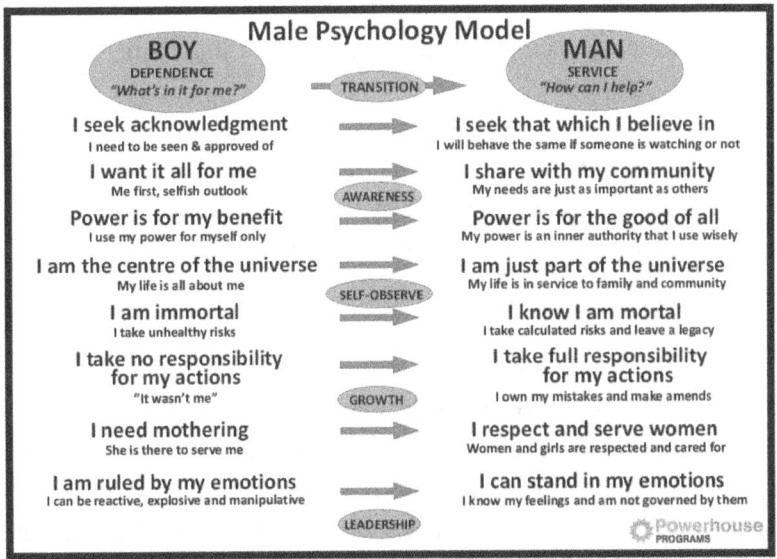

I'm sure on reading this you can identify boy-men you know or have met, so perhaps this enlightens you as to why this transition is vitally important, if we're to create healthy models of contemporary masculinity.

We've heard in earlier chapters about women saying 'they have children to look after, plus the man they marry'. Lack of understanding about this wound results in an incomplete maturing process in that the psyche of the boy never matures into the psyche of a man.

Consider the lack of male guidance from fathers, mentors and elders that we discussed earlier, which leads to boys not receiving the flow of masculinity they would have received only a few centuries ago. The result is generations of dispossessed and wounded men who never quite grow into their potential. Their compensatory mechanism is *power*: over things, places and people.

As a result, boys can carry both a mother-wound and a father-wound.

A mother-wound might emerge like this: a domineering mother continues to criticise her male partner/husband, that he can do nothing 'right' or after a messy separation, she talks to (or in front of) her son, about his dad being useless, incompetent, and good-for-nothing.

The boy, ensuring he continues to receive his mother's love, aligns with his her and denounces his own masculine capacities, effectively becoming psychologically castrated, thereby creating a deep mother-wound. This often manifests in later life, finding it difficult to have healthy relationships with women. Behaviours like people-pleasing, lack of purpose or direction, avoidance or being wary of male company, and inability to be emotionally regulated, all point to such a wound.

A father-wound typically emerges when a father, thinking that 'toughening up' his son requires criticism, put-downs and denouncing any competence or emerging emotional expression, becomes the modus operandi of the father-son relationship. Again, the boy, wanting love, support, encouragement and acknowledgement for who he is (and becoming), is replaced with a deep lack of self-worth, resulting in a wounded man who settles for much less than he's worthy, often choosing a partner who mirrors his father's critical attitudes.

And so the cycle continues when he then becomes a father.

Some of the stories I've heard from, and about, men around their father-wound have been tragic, often playing out for decades, until the man understood the impact of such a wound and decided to go on his healing journey.

In several workshops with men, when asked, "What could your dad have said to you during your teenage years, that would have made a difference?", the same things emerge: I love you, you're doing ok, I'm proud of you, I've got your back.

Many men have never heard any of these statements from their fathers.

I can share from personal experience that to confront and embrace one's inner wounds is not easy, especially in our fast-paced, dog-eat-dog world. It requires commitment, focus, honesty, courage and purpose, and really does provide each man with the opportunity for his own Grail Quest. Johnson notes that the inward journey is the one and only pioneering journey open to all, as a truly egalitarian pursuit, since neither money, social status, physical stature nor intelligence (IQ) provide any real advantage.

However, the issue for most men that prevents them from embarking on their inward journey is the degree of internal honesty required to admit that we need to initiate change. If a man is lacking in self-worth (and most are) then to admit we perhaps aren't as functional as we might be, requires an extraordinary degree of radical introspection, courage and faith, that firstly, we do need help, secondly that we can find it and thirdly, that we'll survive what we believe to be a perilous and fear-filled journey: *The Hero's Journey*.

So, the question we must address is this: is it better to live within our dysfunction and 'make do' reality or face the unknown, which is an uncertain future that might lead to liberation? Without embarking on the journey, we know 'doing nothing' will lead us to more of the same: pain and disconnection from ourselves and those around us.

If you remember, earlier I wrote about how boys are taught not to acknowledge their feelings. As a wounded man I am encouraged not to feel, since if I don't feel, I don't have to heal. Some men even avoid emotional pain at all costs and find all manner of mechanisms to do so, whether it manifests as serial relationships, marriages, high-powered careers or substance abuse. A man who lives in this way sees feelings as an irrational state and fears that if he heads there, he may lose his valued rationality.

We have, after all, referred to emotions like empathy and skills such as relational intelligence (RQ) as 'soft skills', usually afforded naturally to women, with the more masculine skills (doing, action, decisiveness) as 'hard skills', which does nothing to encourage men to consider just how important 'soft skills' really are. In short, they're essential for meaningful relationships, and there's nothing 'soft' about them.

If a man is a senior businessman responsible for others' welfare (and stock price!), he may be unable to afford to lose his rationality and navigate the world from an emotionally connected place, since that is not what is expected of him, and certainly not what shareholders value.

For a man or woman to be in a very senior leadership role, such as what's known as the 'C-suite', I'm sure it's a challenge to find the balance between what the role requires, then arriving home to their family and attempting to switch into a heart-centred parenting role.

"Hi Honey! It's been a difficult day. I've just decided to close several factories and fire 1,400 people since we're cost-cutting. I'll be with you and the kids in a minute."

Perhaps we can appreciate that the more recent move to working from home (aka WFH) for those whose employment situation allows this (while providing opportunity for being at home throughout the day), it also blurs the lines between work and home, which can challenge the home environment to not be both at the same time.

Our childhood wounds often surface when we're under stress and so we can become our childish, petulant, tantrum-indulging selves, allowing a less-than-mature version of us to 'escape', run rampant, and damage our outer world through words, moods and actions. How many times has this happened, and when we've finally let the dust settle, we're very aware we behaved inappropriately, and now have the added complication of needing to find a mature and meaningful apology.

For some men, disconnection from one's feelings can be pathological. At a workshop I conducted for mothers of late primary boys about to embark on their adolescent journey, one of the mothers asked if I'd heard of the term, *Alexithymia*? I hadn't so found a reference on Wikipedia that states, "The term alexithymia was coined by psychotherapist Peter Sifneos in 1973. The word comes from the Ancient Greek words *alexo* (repel) and *thumos* (soul, as the seat of emotion, feeling, and thought), literally meaning "pushing away emotions." Wikipedia goes on to say that some studies suggest that alexithymia may be more prevalent in males characterised by the inability to 'describe feelings' but not an inability to 'identify feelings', which means that men are capable of identifying that their partner may be angry, but have difficulty in feeling anger within their own body, and describing it.

Robert Bly comments that centuries ago, men had to be prepared for the brutality of war. They would be taken away from their families, spend time with other men practising their skills in training camps being prepared for combat, and then finally engage in battle. If they survived to return, they would not go directly back to their homes, but would be given time and ritual to let go of their posture for war, find themselves again, and reintegrate into their society. The old cultures knew that a man who had been to war and experienced atrocities, needed time to integrate his experiences before he could sit his or someone else's child or grandchild on his knee, and be present and tender with them.

Contrast this with the Vietnam War where conscripts, plucked out of their daily lives (teachers, accountants, tradesmen) witnessed unimaginable stresses and horrors, and at the completion of their 'tour' would be flown home to be dropped on the streets of New York, or wherever else they came from. The result is that more Vietnam veterans have died from suicide than soldiers killed in the Vietnam War itself.

The minefield of boardroom politics is little different, except that the scars are perhaps more psychological than physical. For Julius Caeser the *back-stab* was literal. For modern corporate people, it is an idiom. There is no transition time from making a hardened decision that can leave a thousand people out of work, to sitting at the dinner table and having a family conversation. To do this, one has to lose all connection with the decision, deny empathy and learn how to compartmentalise, so how can a real conversation at the dinner table, that might require empathy, take place? The term 'corporate psychopaths' is mentioned in a Dec '21 Forbes article titled "Senior Executives Are More Likely To Be Psychopaths" with research showing that while an estimated 1% of the general population might fit into the psychopath territory, among senior executives, it climbs to 3.5%. Are we seeing this emerge from men who are more deeply wounded?

It is easier to ignore one's wounds, operate from an unfeeling place and continue doing whatever it is we can do to just keep keeping on, since the alternative is so filled with fear, it is not even a consideration. Many men are unaware that just as rational processes resolve, so do emotional ones, yet as men, we have not been raised to understand this, so we rarely risk the journey.

Indigenous cultures understood this very well and specifically designed processes to ensure the transition from boyhood to warriorhood was done with precision and purpose, for to not do so would mean the warriors would not be men but boys. The very existence and survival of the tribe depended on each generation moving into manhood as a defined ownership of their wound through Rites Of Passage (which we cover in the next chapter) that ultimately moves a boy from a mode where he is the receiver of everything he needs – a 'me-centric' perspective – to a place as a warrior where he becomes the giver in a 'we-centric' community.

If this transition does not occur, the male wound can also express itself in the form of narcissism, whereby the childish view of being the centre of attention, or the centre of the universe, is never aligned into maturity.

Unaware men may also use their woundedness as a mechanism to manipulate a relationship by feigning stupidity or ignorance to their female partner, thereby eliciting sympathy that they really are so dependent that they can't operate a washing machine, vacuum cleaner, or cook a meal. In doing so these men can hang onto their woundedness and never face their underlying fear of letting go of their boyish self to move into manhood. It is only from a strong sense of self that a man can descend to a place of vulnerability and in doing so, experience true and conscious intimacy with oneself and therefore a partner.

If the man's partner is predisposed to being a *rescuer*, then the relationship becomes one of deep co-dependency, as each partner fulfils the needs of the other: the man needing a woman to mother him (victim) and the woman needing a man (boy) to mother (rescue). In a large majority of cases, eventually, the woman reaches her limit, becomes tragically unhappy, seeks external help through her social network and realises that she's trapped in a dead-end relationship. If she is a stay-at-home mother or has a part-time job, the prospect of losing her partner and the financial security that comes with him is a very difficult choice, yet many choose this path and become single-parent families. At the time or writing there are over 1M single-parent families in Australia.

If only women knew how to encourage men and not approach them from a position where the men feel nagged and that they need 'fixing' – and if only men could be brave enough to get along to a men's group, Gathering or Shed and open up just that little bit, to understand that they are very much not alone and missing out on a liberated life.

Once again EQ comes into play. I firmly believe that to be a good partner, husband, father, or leader one has to traverse the inner realm of our wounded inner boy(s), feel whatever it is that is hiding in that place and bring it forth to heal the Wounded King. Only then can a man step forward with confidence, knowing that he knows his own Heart with no need to manipulate, nor be manipulated, from this wounded place.

I've had the privilege of talking with women who have been honest enough to admit that in some relationships, they are aware of their partner's wounded aspect, even if he is not, and that this aspect metaphorically has a button on it labelled, 'Press here to manipulate me.' While the man bumbles along thinking he's making up his own mind about things or being clever in his approach, unfortunately, his cumbersome navigation is completely overt to women who specialise in covert operations! Listening to women openly and honestly discuss how they manipulate men was shocking and liberating at the same time.

An example that comes to mind is a woman who shared a story about her workplace. It was approaching the end of the pay month, so money was tight, yet a handful of women who worked together decided to go out to a cocktail bar. My friend commented that she did not have the ready cash to do so, but was assured that wouldn't be a problem. Perplexed and not wanting to miss out, she tagged along. The group of four women walked into the cocktail bar, seated themselves strategically near a table of four men, gave the appropriate signals to indicate they were 'available' (they weren't), had cocktails bought for them for a few hours while they flirted, then left when they'd had their fill, leaving the men out-of-pocket and most likely bewildered. Sounds familiar?

David Deida is another man on a man's mission and in one of his seminal works, *Way Of The Superior Man*, he notes that if a man discusses a decision with his female partner and she becomes aware that he has changed his mind to placate her, rather than making his own decision (which may or may not be aligned with her advice), the woman subconsciously loses trust in the man, since how can she bare her own vulnerable Soul in intimate moments, if the man cannot be trusted to walk his own path and therefore so easily manipulated?

It is from this inner wounded place that a man chooses to supplicate, since he has swallowed the stereotype that unless he does, he will never find happiness, a relationship or sex, hence why this place is open to be manipulated. He has bought the 'game' that women control the stakes and the only way to get sex is by convincing a woman that he has something to offer (or as O'Malley noted in Chapter 11, a *negotiation*), so it becomes an adversarial pursuit: she has it, he wants it. The saddest part of all of this, is that most women have bought the same game, when in reality, companionship, relationship, commitment, emotional connection, and the sacredness of sexuality and togetherness, is what both women and men truly desire, if only each could find the inner strength to own their wounded selves.

I'm also convinced that the armed forces purposely stimulate this wounded aspect of a boy's psyche with images of weaponry (usually large guns to insinuate a relationship with penis size) and mateship, coupled with the message of, 'Join the military, get a gun, be a man!'

A man who has connected with and integrated his wounded self would not generally be willing to go to another country as an occupying force and wound or kill others. Unfortunately, the path to manhood is not found at the end of a gun, nor in the distorted reality of war. It's not until a young man experiences the horror of war that he may realise that this was not the answer, but by then young men return physically and psychologically wounded, often with post-traumatic stress disorder (PTSD).

This is not to say that protection of one's home, family and country is not a noble act. This is the realm in which a man has an innate purpose to protect. It is more a question of why we as men do this and to raise our awareness to uncover whether we are fulfilling a noble purpose, or whether we're operating from a base level of our inner woundedness and trying to prove we're worthy, by being young men fighting old men's wars. Korea and Vietnam were classic post-second-world-war examples, followed more recently by the invasion of Iraq and Afghanistan.

If a man, centred in his Heart, who has connected with, touched, expressed and fully owned his woundedness actually contemplated going to war, he might decide that the ideals being purported are not his ideals at all, and choose not to go. If they are, he would engage from a very different place and maintain a level of awareness that would prevent him from *losing* himself. I'm convinced that the atrocities we hear about such as genocide, rape and murder, would be significantly reduced, if not altogether eradicated. Chapter 21 will explore this phenomenon further.

Ultimately, a man must find the courage to embark on his own inner hero's journey, with the sole purpose of connecting with his wounded Heart, to find what this is and means for him, and fully integrate it into himself to become whole. The very term 'heal' means 'to make whole' and a man can only fully heal by bringing this unconscious wound into consciousness.

As mentioned previously, there are various ways to do this. One of them is by finding ways to experience this for himself, through Rites Of Passage, which we will investigate in the next chapter.

Key Points:

◆ *A boy's psychological wounds come from a growing awareness of the imperfection of adulthood and moving from a 'me-centric' view to a 'we-centric' one, and can come from both mother and father*

◆ *Failure to address this results in a boy's psyche not maturing while inhabiting a man's body, and can lead to disastrous results*

◆ *Men are resistant to embarking on this inward journey and need all the support and encouragement they can get, especially from the women around them and other functional men*

◆ *Indigenous cultures know this and have developed processes to ensure this transition happens for the good of the boy and the community.*

18. RITES OF PASSAGE

Cultures have traditionally used passage rites as a means of transition between one stage of psychological (and social, physiological and spiritual) development and another. Ceremony and rites of passage are necessary for the social and personal psychological health of an individual. Passage rites prepare us for the next stage of our lives and give us reference points to mark the measure of our development; and ceremony gives us the method and tools for change.

All societies and cultures have passage rites: weddings, funerals and such. Even the humble birthday party is a passage rite: we are ceremoniously passed from one measured point in our lives to the next measurable bracket – from our xth year of existence to our xth + 1 year.

Society is becoming more intolerant of things that take time – in this modern rush along world we seem to seek immediate gratification. When we undervalue the moments of our lives, we undervalue our lives: the 'reward' will be a loss in self-esteem. You are worth every valuable moment of your life: you are here to live each moment.

> *Slow down and seek ceremony and rite to guide you –
> especially when you, from time to time, lose your way and
> need to be guided back onto the path you wish to travel.*
> **– Kakkib li'Dthia Warrawwe'a** (author of *There Once Was A Tree Called Deru*)

I've mentioned Rites of Passage in previous chapters and how indigenous cultures knew that something was required to mark a boy's evolution from boyhood to warriorhood, as the tribe's very survival depended on it. In 1909, French anthropologist Arnold van Gennep wrote about rites of passage and this has formed the body of work available today. Gennep noted that they marked the transition between stages of human development, and he named three states: pre-liminal, liminal and post-liminal. The word 'liminal' comes from the Latin word 'limen', which means 'threshold' and describes the in-between state found in Rites Of Passage. It accurately describes the teenage state of adolescents as they are no longer children and not yet adults. Expanding this concept, Gennep described the liminal rite of passage process as having three identifiable stages – *separation, transition and incorporation.*

What does this mean to us today and our current journey of understanding more about men?

Rites of passage specifically move a child from a 'me' to a 'we' centric perspective, from receiver to giver. Tribal cultures depended on their adult members' understanding that to survive and flourish, each person had to have a larger, more inclusive and holistic perspective. As the world becomes a global village this view becomes more of an imperative, yet our behaviour is becoming more and more me-centred with social media, look-at-me, be my 'friend' (Likes etc), narcissistic-centred, copy-catting behaviour becoming normalised, and therefore a major contributor.

If we look around at boys in the Western world, we see them searching for events to mark their transition, and if not provided by their community they will create their own 'initiations' such as losing their virginity, or getting drunk with their mates at 18, or their first pub-crawl.

For girls there are already several defined physical and psychological stages, such as the beginning of menstruation, marriage, childbirth and menopause. This is not to say that rites of passage are not important for women, which of course they are. It is however to note that there is a significant difference between how women and men are viewed, and how we approach these physiological and psychological transitions.

Joseph Campbell describes a hero's journey in *The Hero With A Thousand Faces*, which outlines 12 specific steps that a hero must take from beginning to completion, and can be seen reflected in many stories and movies today. George Lucas of 'Star Wars' fame noted that he had written his first draft of Star Wars when he came across Campbell's book and realised that Luke Skywalker's journey paralleled that articulated by Campbell. The universal appeal of Luke's story (and Star Wars' success) might very well be due to it aligning with the archetypal journey found in many historical narratives.

In line with the three liminal stages (separation, transition and incorporation), the hero's journey can also be summarised into three aspects as well: *Departure, Initiation,* and *Return.* These reflect how we in the West might view Indigenous rites of passage: a boy is removed from his childhood surroundings (departure), he experiences some form of secret men's business that he knows is coming but not what it is (initiation), then he is presented back to the community as a man (return). These stages align with Gennep's *separation, transition and incorporation*.

What's important to note here is that each culture that practices rites of passage processes distinctly knows these stages, plans for them, creates rituals to embody them (em-body is an important concept here) and marks the return of the man, even though the cultures themselves are in completely different parts of the globe. If we ever needed a sign that this process is a fundamental requirement to create an integrated and functional society that values each and every member, we need look no further. And if we need a comparison, simply look at our often disconnected and disengaged youth of today.

In the *separation* phase the boy is taken away from his comfort, his mother and all things familiar, and he begins to experience his wound of separation and grief, and that his world of childhood is coming to an end. He is being evicted from his Garden of Eden.

Many authors on rites of passage make a comment that this is often a boy's first experience of 'death' and provides an opportunity for him to understand the cycles of life, that endings are part of it and grief is a natural process.

In the *initiation* phase the boy experiences some form of physical challenge which is designed to test him, to allow him to discover his limits, how far he can go, and when to listen to his inner voice that warns him, he has reached his edge. Failure to heed the warning that he is approaching his limits may result in serious injury or death, so the emphasis is placed on really listening to that inner guidance and understanding this. The presence of wise male elders who have the awareness to know when a boy may be considering reckless or conservative behaviour is paramount, as is the requirement for a boy to respect his elder's wisdom. This prepares him for future adventures but also guides him to not be reckless or scared, since his life and his contribution are of significant value to the community.

In *integration*, the boy is presented back to the community as a man, usually in some type of ceremony. His body may be marked or painted, he may carry a scar, be given a totem or even a new name. Those around him then play their part in honouring the change, confirming to the new man that he has irrevocably crossed the threshold (post-liminal) into manhood, that he is now seen as a man and has transcended from one world into another. There's no doubt that his boyish world will surface from time to time, however, as the community around him chooses to allow this unfoldment, all the while continually engaging with him as a man, he becomes more and more confident in his role.

In one Native American tribe in North America, when boys turn 14, a ceremony is held whereby they are removed from contact with their mothers. For the next two years, they spend time only with men, and at an appropriate time are taken to a remote area where they climb a hill, alone, with only water to sustain them. The boy knows that this is his Vision Quest and that he's expected to receive a vision that will show him why he's on Earth and what his contribution to the tribe will be. While on the hill the boy hears the calls of mountain lions, which keep him awake, alert and focused. What he doesn't know is that these calls are being made by the men who have led him there and are guarding him to ensure he does not come under attack from real mountain lions, since the boy and his pending vision are of paramount importance to the community. Upon return, the boy shares his vision. It is not until he is 16 that another ceremony is held to reintroduce him to his mother, now as a young warrior.

Here we can see the same three stages of a rite of passage: separation (from his childhood mother), initiation (vision quest) and integration (returning to the tribe at 16 as a warrior).

When we compare these simple yet meaningful steps to the way we raise our boys today, we can see we fall far short of anything remotely resembling such a process. It's important to note at this point that I have often heard families comment that they will transplant a single aspect of an Indigenous rite of passage into their son's life, as if that single event will do the trick. If only it were that simple! Indigenous rites of passage have been refined for thousands of years and are specific to that culture's values, history and context, and in some cases span almost a decade of a boy's life. We cannot simply uplift another culture's process and expect it to have any meaningful impact. However, we can understand the framework and adopt it in context for our own sons.

Another aspect of rites of passage follows on from the previous chapter of *woundedness*. We might judge tribal rites of passage, especially the initiatory step, as being brutal, whether it is scarification of the skin, circumcision, loss of a tooth or some other physical trauma. Yet somehow these rituals transfer the *psychological* wound created by the dawning of awareness of adult responsibilities and separation from *mother*, into a physical wound, and in doing so, make it tangible. The physical marking is also a constant reminder to the boy that he's now a man, and it assists him in establishing the behaviour expected of him, as a man, and a contributor to the community at large. As mentioned earlier, a movement from 'me' thinking to 'we' thinking.

I've previously mentioned in Chapter 7 the importance of 7-year cycles. We planned an appropriate rite of passage for our first son, for his seventh birthday, to make it meaningful. It also served as a platform for his rite of passage program at 14, which helped prepare him for the adulthood to come.

Andy Roy and Stephen Halsall are facilitators of contemporary rites of passage programs for boys, with Andy being the author of *Raising Teenage Boys*. Having raised several teenage sons, he is certainly hands-on and experienced. Andy recommends that around the age of 12 to 14 is a good time to begin the process of initiation into a role of independence and responsibility.

Parents need to continually look for opportunities to discuss the expansion of their son's worldview, to be more 'we' centred, and when it's clear that any new responsibility is not being suitably managed, withdraw the freedom that comes with it by some degree, until a solid demonstration emerges, which indicates he may be ready to try again. I'm sure you can see how this might relate to a boy you may know, and I hope provides guidance, a framework and an interest to seek out other resources.

How does this relate to men of today?

The eminent psychologist Dr C G Jung wrote volumes on the process of becoming an individual, achieved by an inward-looking pursuit and engaging one's 'shadow side.' Jung named the process of becoming an individual, 'individuation', that is, a process of self-realisation. Remarkably, the process of becoming an individual is very similar to the hero's journey, and as mentioned in Chapter 17,

Johnson states that the inward journey is one that all people can experience. It is especially important for men since it awakens our ability to feel, to know we can play the harp as well as wield our sword.

Many a man who has undergone a defined adult rite of passage with the specific purpose of bringing the boy-man into himself as a complete man, has remarked how different their life might have been if they'd had such an experience during their teenage years. It is never too late, although the delay simply means that a life of disconnection from their masculine core at which lies their vulnerability, strength, relatedness, empathy and connection with their spirit, is unnecessarily postponed. The prolonged living in the place of 'in-between-ness' causes unnecessary pain.

In Tyson Yunkaporta's insightful and educational book, *Sand Talk*, he outlines the steps employed to domesticate an animal.

"To domesticate an animal you must:

1. *Separate the young from their parents in the daylight hours*

2. *Confine them in an enclosed space with limited stimulation or access to natural habitat*

3. *Use rewards and punishments to force them to comply with burdensome tasks*

Effectively, the Prussians created a system using the same techniques to manufacture adolescence and thus domesticate their people."

He then explains the history of our Prussian Army-based education system, that's still active today in our schools.

Yunkaporta adds, *"The [Prussian] government decided that if it could force people to remain children for a few extra years, then it could retard social, emotional and intellectual development and control them more easily. This was the point adolescence was invented – a method of slowing the transition from childhood to adulthood, so that it would take years rather than, for example, the months it takes in Indigenous rites of passage."*

And we might wonder why our education system is failing our boys?

It is not possible to over-emphasise the importance and criticality of ensuring that we as a community take note of the difficult world our sons face during their teenage years, and ensure we do whatever we can to provide a meaningful and relevant path for them, to avert their need to self-initiate, which we know can lead to disastrous consequences. As the African proverb goes, *"If we don't initiate the young, they will burn down the village to feel the heat."*

This is a timely reminder that without initiation into adulthood, the unbridled energy found in youthfulness when left undirected, can indeed "burn down the village." We only need to look at our Western cultures to see the role gangs of youths fulfil, most of which is destructive.

For a man, it is vitally important to hear the hero's call and take the steps necessary to become a complete and whole man, since it is only from the result of the inward journey that a man can claim his missing and disconnected aspects. Experiences buried in our psyche inform our behaviour daily, albeit mostly unconsciously. True leadership requires one to know oneself, which means *all* of who we are, shadow and all (more on this in Chapter 21).

Tom Heuerman is an author and speaker who put it well when he wrote, *"The millions of men and women who today do the hard inner work to redefine who they are and who model and nurture completeness for girls and boys, within and outside of organisations, are the real leaders in the world today."*

For women to support men who wish to embark on this path of self-discovery, words of encouragement and understanding as well as patience and allowance, are the tools that will assist them to embark on their hero's journey, and more importantly, stick with it when the going gets tough!

In the next chapter, we will explore the archetypes known as 'masculine' and 'feminine' and how they relate to men.

Key Points:

◆ *Rites of passage have been performed by indigenous cultures for thousands of years to turn boys into men*

◆ *Rites of passage have three defined states: separation, transition and incorporation, which align with the Hero's Journey of departure, initiation, and return*

◆ *We cannot borrow a single event from another culture's rite of passage process and hope it will make a difference in our culture. We can, however, design our own and ensure they have meaning and context*

◆ *Men can experience adult rites of passage, which although may happen late in life, can still be powerful and meaningful*

◆ *Our education system is not designed to help boys become men.*

19. MASCULINE & FEMININE

By healing our internal divisions and fully accepting ourselves as we are, we learn to accept and empower our sexual core, and we learn to honor our unique expression of Masculine and Feminine gifts. We fully incarnate in our bodies, at home and at ease in a man's body or a woman's body. And we learn to love with complete abandon, as free men and women, without rules or roles or guarded hearts.
— **David Deida**

In this chapter, we focus on masculine and feminine as *sets of characteristics* that fulfil particular aspects of one's life. Dr C G Jung defined them as *archetypes*, meaning 'from the original', explaining that we each contain both aspects, carried through millennia from our ancestry. Within each of us reside the primordial man (Adam) and the primordial woman (Eve), from which we're told all of creation stems. I refer to feminine and masculine as these archetypal aspects and unrelated to gender or sex.

Jung believed that every human has both masculine and feminine aspects or 'principles', even though most men would probably not want to know this! Unfortunately, these terms have been bandied around so much they have lost their meaningfulness and have even become tarnished and blasé. You might hear a woman talk about a man and remark, *"He's in touch with his feminine side."*

What does this even mean?

A few years ago, a female friend commented to me that a new male staff member had started at her workplace and was 'really nice to work with' because he was 'in touch with his feminine side'. This meant that he was easy to talk with, seen as pliable and most likely 'soft' in his approach. He might have been perceived as an 'emotionally-available man'.

I'd literally just come home from a weekend away with a group of men doing some deep 'men's work' at which one of the facilitators made the comment, "I want to get men in touch with their Hearts so they don't cut down trees!"

This comment really struck me, as I understood that an ecological worldview doesn't come from being in touch with either our masculine or feminine. It comes from being connected with nature and the world around us, recognising we're part of the whole and not separate from it. If we are in true contact with our Heart then we are in contact with other people, fauna, flora and all of nature, and this cannot be pigeonholed under a masculine or feminine archetypal label.

After my friend's comment, I quickly and short-temperedly retorted, *"Feminine? Feminine? What's wrong with his damn masculine side!? What is it with people who think that to be approachable, a man has to be in touch with his 'feminine side'? Do me a favour, head to Uluru, find a Tjilpi [Pitjantjatjara male elder] and tell him that to be an ecologist, he has to get in touch with his 'feminine side' and see what happens!"*

Needless to say, it was a pretty strong response after such an innocuous and casual remark, and I did get a wide-eyed reaction! Fortunately, my female friend knew me well enough and allowed me my moment of frustration and indiscretion, without firing back. But it did get me thinking about the number of times I've heard comments about men 'getting in touch with their feminine side.'

I'd like to offer an alternate point of view.

I prefer to use the term 'aspect' in place of 'side' since aspect doesn't create the image of two (and perhaps opposing) sides, but rather simply another part of who we are. The reason there's been a push for men to get in touch with our feminine aspect is that our incorrectly perceived masculine is dysfunctional, and what we see today, especially in Australia, bears witness to that. Unfortunately, we think this is masculine when it is *macho*.

As such, a phrase that's crept into the modern vernacular and really gets on my nerves is 'toxic masculinity' as a way of labelling bad behaviour in a sex-centric way. Does 'toxic femininity' exist and if so, isn't this too simply *bad behaviour*? I'd prefer not to excuse such behaviour from anyone, irrespective of how they 'identify', as this does a disservice to the whole archetypal model, which in its own right, bears millennia of wisdom and clarity.

There's no doubt that a man who is able to show his vulnerability by expressing emotions such as sadness or grief, must have some connection with his feelings for this to happen, however, this does not automatically assume that he is connected with his feminine. We only equate feelings with feminine because we've been taught to believe that feeling is a female (gender) thing, since 'boys don't cry' (we're often told it's a sign of weakness) and girls do. Hence if we see a man show any tenderness, emotion or feelings, he must be 'in touch with his feminine side', since if he was in touch with his masculine side, he wouldn't show any response at all!

And yet, our media is quite willing to use language that is counter-productive to such an emergence. When a man in public view, say a politician or sportsman, displays emotion such as shedding a tear, or being visibly upset, it's reported as *"Man Breaks Down At News Conference!"*

Really? So, a man who expresses emotion such as this, is 'broken'?

A boy, who on the sports field breaks a bone requiring an ambulance, hospitalisation and surgery, is "Such a brave boy!" if he *doesn't cry* to show how much he's in pain.

A woman might be capable of running a company as a high-powered executive, so we'd assume she has developed her masculine aspect, but if this aspect is expressed as a ball-breaking, lack of empathy, trouser-wearing and dominating persona, is this assumption true?

Johnson's books on feminine and masculine aspects of both men and women, do much to educate us about how these aspects cannot be combined into an androgynous mix, as this amalgam destroys the very essence of what each aspect contains. It's like taking something sweet and something sour and combining them in the hope they will unite, yet still retain their individual potency, when clearly amalgamating them destroys the very essence of each.

The challenge for a man is to acknowledge he has a feminine aspect, nurture it in whatever way works for him (I previously mentioned activities such as art) and learn to live 'between' his masculine and feminine aspects, in a central place of the paradox. Wisdom emerges when a man can call on both or either of these principles *at will*, and respond to life situations with awareness and balance.

Likewise for a woman.

Traversing the inner world of our masculine and feminine archetypes then becomes a *conscious process*, rather than not having any notion as to what's mulling around in our subconscious depths.

Jung named these aspects 'anima' (feminine aspect in a man) and animus (masculine aspect in a woman), and as they are opposite to chromosomal sex, he named them *contra-sexual* (opposite sex) *archetypes*. For a man, his anima 'animates' and brings with it an extraordinary opportunity for various stages of internal development, as he progresses through the four phases of his feminine integration, if he so chooses.

Initially, it starts with *Eve*, with a man's relationship to women as one of desire. If he matures beyond this image of woman as only a sexual and procreative partner, *Helen Of Troy* is seen as the second stage of development, where women are seen as worldly but perhaps not virtuous. The *Virgin Mary* is the third stage, whereby women are now seen to have virtue. Finally, a man moves into the fourth stage to his internal *Sophia* (the Greek word for 'wisdom') where he sees women as beings of wisdom that can be related to individually, having both positive and negative qualities. We can see in this process that there is a beautiful flow from seeing women as objects of desire, to being unvirtuous, to virtuousness, and finally as wise individuals relating beyond the earlier superficial levels.

According to Jung, women also have four stages of development of their animus, beginning initially with physical power or a 'primal muscle man' such as a Tarzan-like character. The second stage sees men as romantic and men of action. The third stage sees men as carriers of 'The Word' and dreams often contain images of professors or clergymen as deliverers of words. Finally, if the integration of the animus process continues, a woman begins to see men as having deep meaning with sage-like qualities. Jung noted that this stage of animus development is often experienced in women's dreams as a helping male guide. Again, a beautiful flow from a physical view, to action, to prose and finally as an integrated and wise inner guide.

While these stages of anima and animus development are a simplified summary and somewhat general, it's important for us as men and women to at least understand our own evolution, since the way we relate to our inner feminine (for men) or masculine (for women) aspects, greatly influence how we relate to the opposite sex.

In relation to this book and the understanding of men, it's necessary for us as men to be honest with ourselves, since only then are we able to determine where we are in the evolution of our relationship to our inner feminine. I'm sure in reading the above, either as a woman or a man, if you read the stages and are honest with yourself, you'll begin to see what is being mirrored in your outer life by the type of relationships you have with the opposite sex. These are an indication of where you are in relation to your inner archetypal aspect. We can of course actively traverse all four, once we reach the fourth stage, however, as each stage filters into our awareness, we now *know* we have the capacity to do so.

For men, it may come as somewhat of a surprise that seeing women purely from a sexual viewpoint reflects an immature inward relationship with one's own feminine. If, however, a man truly sees women as equals, travelling their own life's journey and holding their innate wisdom (albeit different from a man's), then he is engaging with the Sophia within himself.

As previously mentioned, and perhaps poignant in this example, *it's not what we're looking at, it's where we're looking from!*

If women are to support men on their inward journey, then it's equally important they understand the relationship with their own masculine (animus), since this will colour how they see and relate to men overall. If for example, a woman's animus is still in the early stages of maturity, then she will see men in the Tarzan stage and in doing so, miss all the other characteristics men may have and only be attracted to 'hunks' or 'bad boys'. They may find relationships with men, while initially 'hot' during the stage of limerence, soon lose their appeal as the relationship matures.

The dilemma for both men and women is; from where do we draw our functional feminine and masculine principles? By that, I mean as a man, from where do I learn what a developed feminine aspect in a man looks like, behaves like, feels like? I cannot draw this from a woman since her feminine aspect is completely different to that of a man. Again, likewise for women.

In reality, the only place for a man to have his inner feminine reflected back at him is from other men who've established a relationship with *their* inner Sophia. If you ever meet such a man he will exude an aura of completeness, solid in his sense of who he is, will treat women with respect, and care about his environment. He will also be emotionally mobile, have both Heart and backbone, and not be afraid to speak out when he sees injustice. He will demonstrate an acute awareness of his inner flow and appear as a well-rounded and balanced man.

Living in a patriarchal world makes it doubly difficult for women, since where does a woman find her guidance? This is why I believe we see some high-flying corporate women wearing suits and behaving like men, as they've learned from men that this is how to climb the ladder and play the corporate game. What women have learned is how a closed-Hearted, empathy-less, unfeeling and disconnected man navigates his way through the corporate jungle, and has therefore learned this is what a woman *must* do, to survive and climb the same ladder, which is sadly often the case.

If you've ever met a businesswoman who has been able to retain her feminine archetypal aspect, and has developed her masculine aspect in parallel, they are a breath of fresh air, as are men who run companies with what I term 'Heart-centred leadership.' We need many more women and men of this ilk, men and women who are in touch with their Sophia and Guide, to lead governments, educational institutions and businesses alike, and replace those with psychopathic tendencies, as explained in Chapter 17.

I also believe that adolescents would find early adulthood to be far less troublesome if they knew this about themselves, and could find elder men and women who were whole, who understood this process and were willing to mentor younger generations.

I opened this book at Chapter 1 with Marianne Williamson's comment about a generation of *"hard women and soft men"* and it's only in recent years that we've realised the experiment hasn't worked, much to the detriment of our children, education system and society at large.

While we struggle with equal status for women in employment and the gradual dismembering of a patriarchal system that has been prevalent for several millennia, we must support men and women who seek true partnership, who understand that no one is to blame, since that means there is a win-lose scenario operating, and so 'someone' has to lose.

We can do this by becoming aware of all the aspects that influence us daily, which lock us into a consensus view that male-female relationships, whether they be personal or interpersonal, are not ones that should be based on adversarial notions. They should, and can, be based on mutual respect, with each supporting the other as the counterbalancing principle that ultimately provides true balance to individuals and, therefore, society overall. This creates fertile ground for relationships based on a true sense of *interdependence*: not dependence, independence, anti-dependence or co-dependence.

Imagine a healthy intimate relationship, a functional partnership, where each person, irrespective of their identity or sexual orientation, has built an internal relationship with all four stages of their masculine and feminine archetypes. Each partner, seeing the other unfold in all their lifetime glory, bearing witness to that unfoldment, while holding themselves in their *differentiated* state. And their children, witnessing their parents doing this, unwittingly imbibe a highly functional relationship model so that they, too, can become whole and fulfilled during their lifetime.

What a lighthouse relationship that would be, and it would send out generational ripples.

Perhaps as David Deida's quote at the start of this chapter so eloquently states, if we build a relationship with our inner feminine and masculine archetypes, we become truly free and positioned to have much-improved relationships with others.

For this to happen, we must have a strong sense of *personal boundaries*, since these create an environment of safety (both personal and interpersonal), an opportunity for clear communication, radical honesty, and deep vulnerability. This can only come from inner work, since it is my view that the quality of our relationships, especially intimate ones, is a direct reflection of the quality of our relationship with our inner world, mirrored by our level of self-awareness, and coupled with a strong sense of who we are, so we *don't lose and abandon ourselves* in the relationship. In other words, a state of high self-esteem.

We will take a tour into the world of boundaries next, to understand what they are and why they're vitally important to any inner exploration.

Key Points:

- Men and women both have feminine and masculine aspects

- In a woman her opposite or contra-sexual aspect is her animus and in a man it is his anima

- If we're honest with ourselves, we can see how our relationship to the opposite sex mirrors the relationship we have with our inner opposite aspect

- Men and women can grow to see each other beyond the gender labels and engage each other with wisdom and respect.

20. BOUNDARIES

What you decide to tolerate more than once will inevitably become a pattern that will repeat itself. By not setting clear boundaries, you teach others – and yourself – that certain behaviors or situations are acceptable, even if they make you uncomfortable or hurt you.

– Johnny Depp

It may seem like an obvious and simple statement, but I'll state it anyway: *you can't give what you don't have.*

For example, if we met and I asked you to give me $1,000 in cash, on the spot, chances are you wouldn't have it in your wallet or purse.

Whether it is respect, love, self-worth, confidence or boundaries, if you don't have them *within* you, there's no way they can be instilled in another, especially children, as they mirror and model *what we do*, not necessarily what we ask of them. "Do as I say, not as I do!" just doesn't cut it anymore.

I wrote this chapter specifically on boundaries, as my personal journey regarding them has been one of both pain and freedom. So, let's explore what they are and why they are vitally important.

Boundaries inform us where the edge is, calibrate how far we can drift from our centre and provide some sense of how far we can move toward the edge without falling off. Imagine a football field with no boundary, no white lines or referees to tell us we'd stepped over them. Rules of the game, including the area in which it is played, are all contained within a necessary framework. Otherwise, any game without rules and boundaries would result in chaos and wouldn't be a game at all.

Why do boundaries matter?

I would go so far as to state that raising children without effective and consistent boundaries is setting them up for a miserable, indulgent and self-centred life, and is another form of abuse brought about simply by neglect. If children don't receive adequate parenting and a clear understanding of their and other's personal boundaries, society will ensure that in the world of adults, they will be enforced, often at great personal cost. The extreme boundary is of course incarceration or in some countries, death.

The head of a unique primary school focussed on the deep and sensitive personal development of primary-aged school children, commented to me that children are like the clay on a potter's wheel. When making a container such as a vase or pitcher, the inner hand is the hand of *love*, while the outer hand is the hand of *boundary*. It is only with a balance of both that a functional shape can be formed. Too much boundary from the hand on the outside and the creation is crushed. Too little and the inside hand spreads the clay all over the wheel, which collapses it without form or function. My own experience of boundaries is that, as with most people, in some areas I was seriously deficient. At times my behaviour would unwittingly transgress boundaries of another simply because I didn't know what I didn't know. So, I learned, often painfully, that my boundaries needed readjusting until I finally found a place within myself, a compass, a faint voice that would warn me I was approaching such an edge. And with persistence and patience, I learned to trust that voice which today serves me well … most of the time!

I like to think of that voice as an inner guardian and refer to him as my *Benevolent Bouncer*, the warrior at the door, whose role is to stand as a sentinel between my inner and outer worlds. He is like Heimdall from the Thor Marvel movies, the gold-eyed, broad-sword-bearing guardian of Asgard (played by Idris Elba). He alone decides who enters and leaves Asgard, so in effect, the 'bouncer'.

This might sound a little strange, so let me explain.

I'm sure you've experienced within you many voices of inner dialogue, influenced by what's happening in your outer life. If for example we're presented with a difficult situation, unless we've invested in some self-awareness therapy, we react without even thinking. Sometime later we might look back in ashamedness or embarrassment at our reaction or outburst and wonder "What was I thinking?" When we lose awareness we are not thinking much at all. In this case, a wounded (and by wounded I mean dysfunctional) child-like aspect of ourselves is let loose on the world, without us being aware of the 'escape', and it's not until the dust settles that we might realise it's happened, albeit after the damage is done. It's almost as if latent aspects of us are tucked away in a ready-made and well-stocked arsenal, waiting for any opportunity to defend the realm from attack. Unfortunately, there's little, if any, emotional intelligence on hand, otherwise, we might have chosen to respond with a different and more considered approach.

In these circumstances, we experience and initiate a *reaction* rather than a *response*.

Alternatively, we might come away from a situation feeling uneasy about something that's transpired. We're not sure what's happened but we feel tight, foggy, unsure, unclear and perhaps even screwed, dismissed or completely unheard. Without knowing it, we've allowed someone else's wounded child-like escapee to muddle our thinking and trash our sense of who we are, yet although we feel out-of-sorts, we don't really understand what happened. My experience has shown me that in each case the boundaries of behaviour and communication are blurred or non-existent, often filled with unspoken expectations and assumptions.

In the first case, we don't have an inner boundary or enough awareness to catch one of our wounded selves on its way out the metaphorical door while rallying the internal troops, lowering the drawbridge and heading off to battle with whatever it is we perceive as the threat. These events often result in an almost psychological carnage and, as I alluded to earlier, we often come away from such experiences almost as if we've been in a trance. We look at what we've done and either feel justified that we won the battle, or embarrassed that we over-reacted and created some collateral damage we have to now clean up. In the latter case, we don't have solid enough boundaries to stop another's army from gate-crashing our inner domain and trashing it.

Families and extended families are, unfortunately, exceptional at this, demonstrating *porous* boundaries. *"I was only trying to help!"* is the catch-cry of someone who's given unsolicited advice to a family member, in an attempt to control someone else's behaviour with sentences of 'shoulds'. Meanwhile, the receiver of the advice is thinking, *"How dare they speak to me this way!"* yet unable to speak aloud and set a boundary, for fear of ostracization, driven by our need to belong.

If we can *feel* what is happening inside us, we at least have a chance to listen deeply to what's occurring in our emotional self and interpret it. With practice, this can be developed into quite a rapid process and eventually becomes so automatic that we can learn to implicitly trust it. For men however, this is especially difficult, since our feeling function might not be as mobile as it needs to be, so getting help with learning to feel and identifying what it is we are feeling is not only a necessity, it is needed if we're to be confident and sense what's happening to us, both inside and out.

I referred earlier to the boundary between my inner and outer realm as my Benevolent Bouncer. This is because it has developed in me as a sort of witness process, whereby I am the observer to my own feelings and therefore not overwhelmed by them. Thus I can monitor what's going on inside and outside, and the benevolent bouncer at the door becomes a bit like a warrior.

When my inner world is in turmoil for whatever reason (usually due to living life!), as a guardian he ensures I maintain enough sense of who I am that I don't let my wounded five-year-old out into the world, have his tantrum, scurry back inside and leave the adult 'me' to deal with the aftermath and carnage.

Likewise, if another has let their wounded five-year-old out for a raiding party, my warrior at the door keeps a calm head, lets the others' five-year-old have his/her tantrum and ensures that he/she isn't allowed 'in' to trash my place.

If you've ever worked in an open-plan office or any office where petty politics is allowed to roam free, I'm sure you'll know exactly what I'm referring to. Everyone knows who the reactive ones are and what can and can't be discussed, so there are unwritten rules of engagement that mostly work to ensure no one gets hurt. All it takes, though, is someone like this to be having a bad day and look out!

So, in essence, the Benevolent Bouncer is the boundary, the warrior, the gate-keeper, the safe-space-keeper for me and the 'other', since its prime purpose is to keep a level head and in doing so, *keep the peace* as much as possible. He is the sword-wielder and the harp-player who knows exactly how much of either is required, and is ruthless in his application of each, without fear or favour.

If this all seems strange to you, I ask you to pause for a moment and ask yourself this: *what would it feel like to know that in these situations you would be able to maintain your emotional poise and not be knocked off-centre?* How would your life change if you *knew*, in the deepest recesses of your being, this impartial benevolent peacekeeper, your own internal United Nations Peacekeeping Force was keeping an eye on both sides of the door and would always act with authenticity and impeccability, and, as your creation, would want to do so in your and other's best interests?

For me, the sense is one of absolute freedom, since on the one hand I don't have to be cautious about engaging with people. On the other, I now know I can quite comfortably say 'no' when needed, not with any malice, vengefulness or edge, simply a gentle yet assertive unequivocal 'no'. I see in my two sons that this capacity alone has created a far more solid relationship between us since they understand that my 'no' is a 'no' and no amount of cajoling will change it. It is, in essence, a solid boundary that they rely on to keep them safe, and as a result, have learned to trust me. Too often, parents seek *approval* from their children and when that happens, it is the wounded child within the adult seeking approval from a peer, not a parent setting a boundary to keep their physical child safe.

The establishment of inner boundaries through self-awareness work is one way that I have experienced this state, and although it's not permanent – that is, I still lose it on occasion – my life has improved substantially.

The first step to establishing any sense of this is to be radically honest with oneself and try to gain some objectivity into our own behaviour. If you suspect, honestly, that 'something's up' then external help is the only way, whether it be through coaching, therapy, group work, mentoring or any modality that expands your view of who you are. I know from experience that who we think we are and who we actually are, are very different. Our waking consciousness would have us believe all sorts of things yet our shadow side is always there, awaiting its moment.

In Dr C G Jung's book, *"The Undiscovered Self"*, he writes, *"Since it is universally believed that man is merely what his consciousness knows of itself, he regards himself as harmless and so adds stupidity to iniquity. He does not deny that terrible things have happened and still go on happening, but it is always 'the others' who do them."*

In this work written at the end of his life, Jung explains that fanaticism, dictatorships and mob behaviour all come from simply an unwillingness to *own our own shadow*. A person weak in their own sense of personal boundaries will allow a group's mob attitude to influence their behaviour that would not otherwise happen outside of the mob situation. This is how genocides and atrocities happen through compliance, as individuals defer their own personal response-ability and value systems to the mob/gang/army/government. This has been repeated many times through history.

Only by owning our own capacity to be capable of 'evil things' do we allow the energy of our repressed shadow (more on this in the next chapter) to emerge into our broader consciousness, thereby exposing it and diffusing it of its potency. Those who choose to hold the high moral ground here, risk being overtaken by their own shadow, and we see plenty of this, for example, in various religious organisations where abuse abounds due to the repression of natural energies.

A man who has engaged with his shadow has seen more of who he is, has embraced more of himself, has tasted both his light and his dark, and can therefore travel through life with such an air of authenticity, that it is palpable. A man who has travelled this path is very clear in his sense of boundaries and therefore has no issue saying 'no' or 'yes'.

How does one even begin to unravel such deep aspects of oneself?

As with most journeys, the first step is the most difficult, yet the rewards are extraordinary. I am yet to meet anyone who has done this and hasn't said it was the most difficult thing they've ever done, and I also haven't heard anyone ever say they have regretted it. Without exception, they all would say it is so worth the effort, since the sense of completeness, confidence, strength, the feeling of wholeness and freedom is liberating.

To do this we must gain a different perspective, question our beliefs, assess our values and gain self-awareness. In time we become aware of a process separate from our normal day-to-day inner dialogue. As I gained awareness and became more mobile in my sense of feelings and intuition, I also became aware of what I termed a 'witness process'; another 'me' witnessing my behaviour and language to ensure I monitored what I was saying and how I was behaving, to express myself in the world, without hurting myself or anyone else.

At times, this 'witness' me, monitoring me and my engagement with the world, drove me to distraction as I couldn't shut it off, until, one day, I spoke with a dear friend who'd been a psychotherapist for many years. She completely validated my 'witness' view, advised that it is a normal step in the expansion of self-awareness and that in time, as I learned to trust myself in the world more and more, it would subside. It wasn't until some years later that one day I realised that the witness had merged with me, and I had indeed learned to trust myself and how I engaged and interacted with people. I had established my Benevolent Bouncer who had strong, clear boundaries, both inner and outer, that would serve as a protector of both worlds, without fear or judgement.

Now I had what I didn't have before, I could give from that place, since my cup of self-esteem was now full. This put me in an ideal situation to become a parent. I could now give solid, consistent and loving boundaries to my two sons so they would know where the edge was, and play as close to it as they wished, without falling off or hurting themselves or another. I've since learned that children are especially good at pursuing the edge, so if you're a parent I'm sure you can relate. And kids are absolute masters at finding holes in sloppy or inconsistent boundaries, so make sure yours are as solid as they can be!

Healthy boundaries are an essential part of life and a direct measure of self-esteem. If you're constantly putting yourself in situations where you feel downtrodden, or having to step in to rescue people, then it may be time to reassess your boundaries and perhaps seek support on how to do this, as it requires objectivity, honesty, trust, commitment and patience. Strong personal boundaries show others that you are a person of value and deserve to be treated with respect and dignity.

Author Cheryl Richardson wrote, *"If you want to live an authentic, meaningful life, you need to master the art of disappointing and upsetting others, hurting feelings, and living with the reality that some people just won't like you. It may not be easy, but it's essential if you want your life to reflect your deepest desires, values, and needs."*

Wise words in these times of social media popularity contests.

Ultimately, boundaries do not come at a cost to you or others. They are a cornerstone of all high-value relationships, providing a strong framework on which deep and rich interpersonal relationships can be built. Without them, it's a house of cards.

Women can support men with boundary issues by employing honest and clear communication. A woman clear in her boundaries, capable of asking for what she wants and saying 'no' to what she doesn't want, is a gift to any man. Men who have boundary issues are easily confused when 'no' means 'yes' and 'yes' means 'no', feeling like their head has been through a blender. The many men I have met understand a clear 'no' when it is delivered and they'll respect it. If you're a woman and have men close to you in your life, be brave and have a discussion about boundaries. If you're a man, dare to talk with a woman that you trust and gain her insight. You never know what wonderful wisdom might await you both.

As I've introduced some aspect of the psychological 'shadow' in this chapter, we'll explore that a little further in the next one, as it's a fascinating area and one that certainly requires some exploration.

Key Points:

◆ *Boundaries are necessary if we're to navigate life in a functional way*

◆ *You can't give what you don't have, so if you suspect you have boundary issues, seek help from a professional*

◆ *If we don't create effective boundaries for our children, society will, and they'll be much harsher*

◆ *The exploration of why we may not have solid boundaries can be a difficult yet highly rewarding experience.*

21. THE SHADOW

There is a crack in everything. That's how the light gets in.
— **Leonard Cohen**

No book of this nature about men would be complete without a mention of our psychological shadow. What is it and how does it relate to our everyday life? It wasn't until I read where the term 'shadow' originated that it finally made sense.

The Greek God Zeus was given the realm of the sky. One of his brothers, Poseidon, was given the realm of the oceans. Zeus's other brother, Hades, was given the realm of the underworld. The dead who dwelled in Hades' realm were known as 'shades', hence the term 'shadow' was used by psychologist Dr C G Jung to denote our personal 'underworld'.

In short, what's known in psychological writings as our shadow comprises *the unexpressed parts of ourselves*, both the 'light' and the 'dark', especially those 'unacceptable' aspects we learned not to express due to our carer's disapproval and that of our culture and other influencers. From the moment we're born, we're *tamed, domesticated and civilised*, and to be loved, we learn what's acceptable and what's not. In other words, we learn to become *acceptance-seeking* children.

In Gabor Maté's recent book *The Myth Of Normal*, he proposes that as a child, we have to choose between acceptance and our authenticity. When acceptance means food, shelter and nurture of any kind, and authenticity means being true to ourselves and risk becoming *unacceptable*, seeking acceptance will win every time as it's a smart survival strategy.

So, from a young age, we're programmed via this process to *abandon ourselves*.

Debbie Ford, author of many books on the human shadow noted that when we're born, 'we're a 1,000-room mansion of amazing possibility, yet by the time we reach adulthood, we're a 2-room bed-sit that needs a bit of work!'

I've had deep experience of my own shadow, and it can be both amazing and terrifying, sometimes at the same time. Jung described it well when he stated, *"The shadow is a moral problem that challenges the whole ego-personality, for no one can become conscious of the shadow without considerable moral effort. To become conscious of it involves recognising the dark aspects of the personality as present and real. This act is the essential condition for any kind of self-knowledge."*

I love that term, *self-knowledge*. Knowledge of self. Who wouldn't want to know more about who we are? In fact, this very concept of self-knowledge started me on my inner man's journey on a cold and wintery June long weekend, just north of Sydney in 1991 …

My relationship at the time was not going anywhere. We had been together since high school, lost our virginity together in naïve and romantic circumstances, had an engagement for a couple of years, then married in 1979 just 3 weeks before my wife's 21st birthday. I had turned 21 the previous year, so we were still very young and immature.

In early 1991 my wife had heard about a man who ran experiential workshops that changed people's lives. At the time, I believed I had no need to change anything (I was Mr Perfect!), so my partner attended a weekend workshop on her own in March of that year, followed by a '10-day Easter intensive'. I could see how quickly she was changing and learning about herself, and so I realised that if I didn't do something, I would lose the relationship. Somewhat begrudgingly, I attended the 3-day June workshop to see what this (and the facilitator!) was all about.

To this day I remember sitting there all of Saturday, as person after person dredged up their past attempting to seek some understanding, and hopefully resolution, for their life's dilemma(s). The facilitator left me alone until just before lunch on Sunday, by which time I was questioning myself in my smugness as to why I had wasted my long weekend and hard-earned money. I'd had a perfect childhood because I couldn't remember much of it, and certainly hadn't experienced any trauma like these people! I remember asking myself while sitting there, *"Why am I wasting my long weekend listening to these fucked-up people talking about their fucked-up lives?"*

The facilitator no doubt picked up on my arrogance and disconnection within myself, and I suspect, having worked with my wife, already knew some things about me.

He addressed me and asked me some innocuous questions, then out of the blue asked me a question about my mother. I don't remember the question, however, I do remember my response and it was one of releasing tears. I hadn't cried for as long as I could remember and it was this turning point, this unlocking of repressed emotion, that set me on a journey I could not have dreamed of. As we broke for lunch I went over to the facilitator and asked how he had done what he'd done, as from my perspective, he'd gotten under my skin and tapped into places I didn't know existed.

His answer, *"I know you better than you know yourself"* was the perfect thing to say to me because I remember thinking at the time that no one was ever going to know me better than me. This commitment became the impetus that was to drive me forward in my often-darkest hours, as I began to explore my own shadowy depths. The facilitator was to become one of my closest friends, and mentor me through perilous waters, as I continued the process of unravelling and owning my shadow, coming to know more and more of myself, until finally, I knew myself better than anyone else.

The concept of having a shadow is, for most people, a difficult one to grasp. We can't see it, touch it or taste it, so for men, its intangible nature defies our male analytical capacities. I know for myself that when I started my inward journey, the only reason I continued was because the facilitator had demonstrated that he could see aspects of my shadow leaking out in my behaviour. I didn't like to think that I might be 'broken', however, I also certainly didn't like the idea of not knowing what was lurking in my yet-unplumbed depths.

As life would have it, my relationship did end, after 17 years, in early 1993, as we both realised we had been drawn together for reasons that perhaps weren't in either of our best interests anymore, and my commitment to myself and my inner journey had become my priority. We were also childless, a decision my wife had made and to which I was ambivalent, so although a difficult time with deep co-dependency and entanglement, separation was much easier than if children had been involved.

Everyone casts a shadow, and everyone has a shadow whether we like it or not. To deny it is to deny such a fundamental aspect of who we are. We see this denial played out on the world stage, from fanatical juntas to fascist dictatorships and tyrannical police states and wars. It's off-balanced leaders tapping into this unresolved and hidden place in all of us, that causes fanaticism to flourish and people to behave in ways that they would never do alone. Many times, we see mobs on unsavoury missions or hear of atrocities perpetrated by one group over another. We may wonder how this can be, yet we see this time and time again where quiet, everyday people turn into an angry mob and commit all sorts of acts that they would not do otherwise.

Why is this important to men, women and relationships?

Unresolved personal aspects are unwittingly projected, like a movie, onto others without us even knowing we've done it. For example, you develop an irrational dislike for a co-worker as there's 'something about them' that rubs you up the wrong way. There's a good chance that whatever it is, it's actually something in *you* that is unresolved, and they have simply become a convenient screen on which you can 'project' what needs to be resolved in you. It's your movie, and whether you know it or like it, *you're the actor, producer and director.*

The challenge in these situations is that we are being asked to suspend judgement and own that it may in fact be us that is the issue, and not the other person, which of course means we have to take *responsibility* for our thoughts, judgements and behaviours. It seems to me that projection is an extraordinary opportunity to have some dysfunctional behaviour mirrored back to us, which is ultimately seeking to align and heal.

Once again, as mentioned in earlier chapters, *it's not what we're looking at, it's where we're looking from.*

For men, it means our dark and secret inner world can contain less than wholesome thoughts, or we may glimpse that our shadow is there, and we will do anything to keep a lid on it. Introduce alcohol or other substances that alter our view of reality, and we have a potent mix. Anyone who has been out late on a Saturday night in a large city, or to a sports event like the football and seen drunken violence, will relate to this.

The media often reports this as *alcohol-fuelled violence*, when in fact, the alcohol didn't create the violence; it was already there, buried in the unconscious of those who acted, and sometimes not that deeply. Alcohol removes the normal 'civilising' control mechanisms that keep it at bay. Depending on an individual's personality, this may cover a range of unexpressed emotions. Many a late-night phone call or cryptic text has come from a drunken friend or ex-partner espousing their love, or stating that you're their best mate/ friend/lover/partner/buddy they've ever had!

Sexuality is also another aspect that can emerge, and often in a sleazy or creepy way. Again, the substance doesn't make the sleaze: it's already there, normally under control, however, due to the lessening and loosening of boundaries, it's released on those around us – no warrior at the inner door here, not even a bouncer. Many people have engaged in sexual behaviour while under the influence and have profoundly regretted it the next day. Men are particularly at risk of not listening to someone's 'no', especially if they are in sexual pursuit, sometimes with disastrous consequences for all involved, as explained in Chapter 11.

Unexpressed shadow is one of the most damaging aspects of human behaviour resulting in a whole range of societal issues, such as gossip, manipulation, child abuse, relationship abuse, violence, rape, war, genocide and murder. Our willingness to live vicariously through the nightly news simply feeds our better-than-attitude and distracts us from having to look behind our façade and see what is really lurking there. It's easier to be 'holier than thou' than to find the courage to face our inner shadow, since we might discover some unsavoury aspects of ourselves, and then who would we be?

Our mask would slip, and others might see that we're not as perfect or *together* as we make out to be. Fear of being ostracised as a result, of being 'found out' or exposed, ensures we do whatever we can to hide our shadow, even to the detriment of ourselves and society at large. This prevents us from ever owning the possibility that we might have a shadow-self.

As mentioned in the previous chapter, Dr C G Jung's book *The Undiscovered Self*, is, for me, one of the most profound insights, almost like his life and learnings of 78 years (at that stage) were poured out via a single stream of awareness. I would sometimes read two or three paragraphs and have to put the book down, to ponder and process what I'd read, and often re-read (and re-read!) to digest. As a short book, it's the one that's taken me the longest to read, and having shared it with many people, without exception, they've remarked it is one of the best books they've ever read. If you're looking to explore the topic of shadow, I can highly recommend it.

My view is that if people in powerful positions made the time to read and understand Jung's insights, whether in politics, business or education, it would make a difference to our world. People in less powerful positions would understand how propaganda works, and why our collective shadow can be manipulated when we're unaware.

As Jung wrote in his book *Memories, Dreams and Reflections,* *"Resistance to the organized mass can be effected only by the man who is as well organized in his individuality as the mass itself."* In other words, we need to have built a relationship with our shadow, and have our inner house in some sort of order to understand its potency, so it/we cannot be manipulated through our unawareness. If not, we risk being pulled in by the masses, lose our sense of who we are and partake in mass hysteria.

Fortunately, enough men and women have found the courage to embark on their inner journey, into the realm of their shadow-self and have not only lived to tell the tale, but they have also brought back much of their journey's wisdom to this realm, to share with those willing to do the same. Authors such as Dr C G Jung, Maria Von Franz, Robert A Johnson, Debbie Ford, Deepak Chopra and many others have written volumes, not from theory, but from personal experience as journeymen, mentors, guides and therapists.

For a deeper understanding of the journey and the choices we will face, I particularly like Johnson's short book *Transformation*, where he takes the reader on a remarkable journey by viewing the evolution of the human shadow as three characters from fiction: Cervantes' *Don Quixote*, Shakespeare's *Hamlet* and Goethe's *Faust*, as two, three and four-dimensional characters, respectively, and surprisingly all of which have been turned into plays.

In Don Quixote, Johnson shows that we might start our journey as a dreamer, ungrounded in reality, never really seeing the world for what it is, and somewhat of a Peter Pan who doesn't want to grow up – the boy-man mentioned in several previous chapters. He is in denial of any aspect of his true self and especially his shadow, therefore, he is a 'two-dimensional' man.

If we do mature from a psychological boy to a man, we understand that we have to make decisions, and so we move into being Hamlet. If you've read or seen Hamlet, his ultimate indecision costs everyone around him the ultimate price: their lives! The 'to be or not to be' dilemma reflects a man's understanding that he now has the capacity to make decisions *but not the backbone to do so*. His indecision becomes his downfall. This is akin to knowing we have a shadow aspect, yet doing nothing about it, so it wrecks our outer life to the detriment of everyone, including ourselves. We become a 'three-dimensional' man, aware of this extra dimension of ourselves, yet unwilling to *act*.

If we take that next step and start to own our shadow, then we build a relationship with it, as Goethe's Faust did in naming his black poodle 'Mephistopheles' and, therefore, giving it an identity with which he could relate. Mephistopheles reveals himself as the Devil and a deal is written in blood, but eventually Faust ends up in heaven irrespective of his 'deal with the Devil'. In accepting his shadow-self he has added a further dimension to his psyche and has now become a 'four-dimensional' man seeking integration and resolution of his shadow-self, to become *whole*.

What Johnson is brilliantly explaining in this story is that a man's process of transformation can only be done through the movement from the two-dimensional dreamer, through the self-conscious and indecisive third-dimensional Hamlet, to a four-dimensional embracer of all that he is, warts and all. How else can we live a truly authentic life if we stay as two-dimensional or three-dimensional men, with so much of who we are remaining hidden? Only by embracing our shadow-self can we, therefore, know more of who we are and become accepting of it. To not be aware of our shadow is to be controlled by it, so we might think that we're free when, in fact, we are a prisoner at our shadow's beck and call. We think we're making free choices, but we're doing so *under the influence*.

Leonard Cohen's words about us all being cracked are very insightful, and I agree that's how the light gets into the shadowy and dark recesses of our being, to en-light-en who we truly are. Only by having the courage to face our shadow can we embrace all of who we are, for to ignore such a valuable and valid aspect is to deny such a fundamental component that influences us in so many ways, mostly without us even knowing it.

Our dreams often contain much shadow information, and there are many books on the subject of dream symbology, but be aware that dream interpretation, where a particular image is supposed to mean the same thing to all people, denies us the wisdom of why our unconscious chose such symbology in the first place. Beware of generalisations and trust your inner guide first.

Much of men's shadow is spread across the evening news, and some aspects of men's work these days begins with acknowledging our shadow-side, being honest about who we are, and in the company of other men, finding an important place of non-judgement from which inner healing can begin. This provides a stark and remarkable opportunity for men to own our shadow, so we change our image from one of being predatory, opportunistic, violent and unfeeling, to one of caring, safe, protective, vulnerable and *whole*.

The world needs more conscious and aware men, and we cannot become either while we walk around with a bag of shadowy and unresolved baggage on our backs. We're almost like Santa, carrying this large sack of 'stuff' around daily, often without even realising it. It's not until one day, for whatever reason, when life is not going well, and our backs are to the wall, that we decide to put the sack down, open it up and inspect its contents, and we realise that quite a lot of what's in there doesn't even belong to us!

At this point we're ready to commence the journey of becoming a whole man, a healed man, a functional man who is comfortable in his skin, commands presence and is not afraid of his own truth, the truth he needs to fulfil his purpose in this lifetime and bring his unique gifts to the world. And as Jung stated, it requires "considerable moral effort."

I hope that if you haven't yet embarked on your inner journey, you can find the impetus within you to do so, free yourself of unnecessary burdens and experience the feeling of liberation.

If you're already on your journey as a fellow traveller, may the wind be at your back!

Next, we're heading into the realm of what's become known as 'Secret Men's Business'.

Key Points:

◆ *Exploration of our shadow is the path to self-knowledge*

◆ *As men, we can transform our lives from Don Quixote, to Hamlet, to Faust and become more whole in the process*

◆ *To embrace all that we are is the only way to live a truly authentic life*

◆ *True freedom is impossible without internal liberation.*

22. SECRET MEN'S BUSINESS

Being a male is a matter of birth. Being a man is a matter of choice.
— **Ben Kinchelow**

I guess by now on our journey together into the inner world of men, that the quotation above from Ben Kinchelow comes as no surprise. We have seen that along the journey to becoming a man we must make choices that increase our awareness of who we are, in our entirety. One way we can do this is in the company of other men who have embarked on their inner journey, so let's explore more deeply what's known as *secret men's business*.

At a networking event I attended, we were asked to write our names on a sticky label and put something on there that our colleagues may not know about us, such as a hobby or a sport. I wrote 'Men's Business' and I was amazed at the number of women who came up to me, read my badge and commented 'Secret men's business?'

And that's how it's perceived by a lot of women ... and men ...

business so secret, that the large majority don't even know about it!

Simply because some of us, as men, are choosing to reclaim ourselves via men's groups, workshops, conferences, gatherings, rites-of-passage programs, men's sheds and other places where women are not involved, it is assumed that some 'secret' business is unfolding.

While it's true that men's groups and events I've attended require an agreement of absolute confidentiality, this is nothing out of the ordinary. Anyone who has attended any type of self-development workshop, group counselling or meetings such as Alcoholics Anonymous, is asked to agree that a participant *must not share another person's story.* This is done to ensure that everyone can be assured that whatever emerges, they can trust members of the group not to gossip. It's done to purposefully create a 'safe container', or as a close friend and co-facilitator of gatherings and workshops once commented, *"To create an environment so safe, that people feel safe enough to feel unsafe."*

To reveal one's deepest and sometimes darkest thoughts, especially in a group setting, requires agreement to create a sacrosanct space, otherwise, nothing deep emerges due to participants feeling *unsafe*. I believe it is because of this confidentiality that most women assume (incorrectly) that some secret business is unfolding, probably about them.

Let me challenge that perception.

Women generally deal with their thoughts and issues in a completely different way to men, primarily through open discussion within their (often) female-centric friends and social network.

Men, on the other hand, initially find talking in groups of men quite intimidating, and it takes time and courage not only to be present, but to decide to speak and contribute.

Also, if you ever walk into any 'spiritual' group or any workshop or event for personal development, usually the large majority are female, which leads women to think that overall, men are disinterested and aren't that motivated to improve who they are.

While it is generally true that more women than men embark on their inner developmental journey, they often seek out groups to do so, and are not concerned whether men are there or not. Oftentimes, I've been in groups where there are 80% women and 20% men. Men, on the other hand, who are brave enough to own their 'stuff', prefer to air their inner thoughts and challenges in the presence of other men, not only to avoid judgement and potential ridicule, but also to gain support from those who might have traversed similar and treacherous paths.

What goes on at a men's group, conference or workshop? It depends on several factors, however, some general themes often emerge.

The first has to do with fathers. As mentioned previously very few men have a functional relationship with their fathers. In *The Audacity Of Hope*, Barack Obama states, "*Someone once said that every man is trying to either live up to his father's expectations or make up for his father's mistakes, and I suppose that may explain my particular malady as well as anything else.*"

In an exercise I did many years ago at my first men's gathering mentioned earlier in this book, Andy Roy (who kindly wrote one of the testimonials for this book), co-founder of PowerHouse Programs for boys and author of *Raising Teenage Boys*, asked the group of some 20 men to break into groups of three (triads), and discuss, "What were the 3 things you wished you'd heard from your father during your teenage years, that would have made a world of difference?"

Each triad found a quiet place where we took turns to speak and reminisce about our teenage years, shared what words would have made a difference, summarised these within our small group and then returned to the whole group to share with them.

Remarkably, there were only four main themes: "You're doing OK", "I'm proud of you", "I love you" and "I have your back."

It was as simple as that!

Four short phrases acknowledging we were seen, understood, on the right track and that our dads were not only there for us, but also available and *present* with us on our teenage journey, after all, they'd already traversed theirs, albeit in a different time.

If you're a father reading this book, I urge you to remember this and create an opportunity that if your children are doing well, tell them, from your Heart. The impact of so few yet heartfelt words will resonate with them for their entire lifetime and influence how they are as fathers.

You can, of course, tell them more than once!

Another theme that emerges is how much dads love their children, and want to spend more time with them, yet often don't see how they can get off the work treadmill to do so. The funding of mortgage/rent, car payments, rising energy and food costs, childcare/preschool/school fees, credit card interest, saving for a holiday, and general living costs all take their toll. While I know mothers work hard and are sometimes the primary breadwinners, it's mostly fathers who carry the *financial* burden with some of them doing extraordinarily difficult jobs to make ends meet.

Relationships figure in discussions too but I've yet to be in any men's group or gathering where misogyny grabs a foothold. The reason is that men who have travelled some way on their journey have usually integrated any such tendencies as part of their personal growth, so when a 'newbie' braves the opportunity to share what he might be feeling about his partner or ex-partner, other men will allow his expression, without judgement, then gently suggest that there may be other ways of looking at the situation, by *sharing their experience*. This avoids 'advice-giving', which is often agreed to be avoided in group discussions, since any advice is always flavoured with the experience of the giver and their circumstances, and might not be appropriate, relevant or meaningful to the man who's sharing.

I specifically remember one men's weekend workshop that was co-facilitated by an older couple, both of which had run men's and women's workshops together for over two decades. I mentioned Diane McCann in Chapter 17 and her insights into men. At first, I was hesitant about having a woman jointly run the men's weekend workshop, since everything I'd explored up to that point had been men-only. However, I knew one of the men who would be co-facilitating, and he had invited me, so I trusted all would be ok. The presence of that one woman amongst 20 or so men, was enough to validate those who were having difficulties in their relationships, by acknowledging the men's intuition about what was going on.

One man was visibly angry on day one and quite bitter about his kids being taken away from him via the Family Court system. His language about his ex-wife was unsavoury, to say the least, yet he needed an outlet to air it and get it off his chest, to vent and be heard. The presence of the female facilitator did nothing to temper the anger that flowed from years of psychological abuse he'd endured. She listened with patience and empathy, and in the two days of the workshop, she had turned his strong anti-women views, amplified by the forced separation from his children, into a much more balanced view. He left that weekend a changed and much more centred man.

Strangely, a female friend of mine commented that a woman should not have been present at a 'men's business' event, and while I understood where she was coming from, one simply had to be there to see the very positive effect she had on the group overall. None of the men appeared to hold back because she was present ('present' being the operative word!) and I'd go so far as to say she provided considerable balance to ensure any dysfunctional perspectives didn't get a hold.

The level of camaraderie that emerges from men meeting regularly goes a long way to creating a sense of community for the men who participate. In one example, a man I know shared with me that he and a group of men decided years ago to head out to dinner once a month. The levels of trust and deep friendship that have built up over the years, resulted in a very deep bond and so the group has decided to keep it 'closed', meaning no new men can join. It also ensures that each man knows he is safe within that group and can discuss anything, without fear of judgment.

In support of this approach, a group called The Men's Table (www.themenstable.org/) originally met in 2011 intending to regularly catch up over a meal and provide a safe space for men to talk about their lives. The Men's
Table became an incorporated charity in 2019, and now offers the opportunity for men in a geographical area to become a 'men's table' with the support of the organisation. At last count, there were more than 2,000 men, attending over 200 tables across Australia.

Many organisations exist purely in the role of service to men, offering groups, events and gatherings, as well as private groups as well. Some are volunteer groups, others are not-for-profit, while there are also weekend paid events (such as gatherings) men can attend.

Often, groups that build a sense of strong (even small) community for men, can find themselves willingly supporting men in their group who may be experiencing difficulty. For example, the wife of an 'elder' in a men's group passed away. The couple had been married for a long time and so the man was grief-stricken and finding his sudden aloneness very difficult to navigate. His men's group rallied around him and ensured that each evening a man from the group would visit with a pre-cooked meal.

Another group, Circle Of Men (www.circleofmenqld.com/), founded in Tennessee in 1990 by an Australian man, found its way to Australia in 2005. It evolved due to the recognition of men in nursing homes
being in the minority, where the mix is 2/3 women to 1/3 men, with the staff also being mostly female. Circle Of Men attends

nursing homes and creates 'men's groups' to bring the men together (who might otherwise not socialise) for them to speak and share, like a traditional men's group.

There are many, many more examples of men supporting men in the most beautiful of ways, demonstrating the caring and functional support that men enjoy from a good, solid group.

Some events are men-only participation, and this is in keeping with much indigenous wisdom, especially in Australian Aboriginal culture where men's and women's business has very clear and defined boundaries. Boys and girls learn from an early age, which is which, and once matured, the boundaries are so ingrained that it's almost inconceivable for a man or woman to cross into the other's business and should they do so, the repercussions can be strong.

We in the West have much to learn from these cultures who knew the importance of such 'business' for the survival of their cultures, and as men and women, we can do much more to encourage each other to participate in events that support the notion that there are areas of 'no-go' for each gender, especially if the events are organised for personal growth. It also creates space for each party within a relationship to grow, and therefore the relationship itself to continue moving forward and mature, on the proviso that there is a deep and demonstrated level of trust.

For men in particular who are in relationships, have kids at home and don't usually have much capacity timewise to venture off to men's groups, events or workshops, it takes surprisingly little encouragement from our partners to get us there, and the return on investment to the man and his family can be tremendous. Due to COVID, there are also many online Zoom-style men's groups emerging, meaning online groups can now contain men from different regions, including overseas.

It's well known that women are far better at participating in a social setting whether it's school, sport or other venues where kids congregate. Women have much more opportunity to talk about the issues affecting them, as well as the conversation skills and emotional mobility to do so. Women learn this from an early age whereas, as we have previously covered, boys learn to shut down their feelings and therefore often struggle to have any communication around them.

For men, the pub is *not* the place, and I think when women discourage the men in their lives from congregating with mates, fearing it'll be a romp around the pub or club circuit that in reality achieves very little, no wonder it's frowned upon. Men's business on the other hand, in the form of a men's group, gathering or Shed, is a completely different story.

We really do need mentors and Elders to guide us through our stages of development. Whether you're aware of it or not, there is a quiet revolution happening where men, supported by other men and often their partners, are discovering how to heal from within, to embrace more of who they are, to become better husbands, partners, brothers, fathers and lovers, with the aim of ensuring their children have a better sense of who their father is, and therefore themselves.

The continued emergence of men's groups, men's sheds, men's conferences, and men's and women's gatherings are all testament to the fact that this revolution is happening. It's especially happening in Australia and provides much hope.

As the opening quote for this chapter notes, 'being a man is a matter of choice' and we must do everything we can to continue to support this groundswell of 'men's business' that doesn't have to be 'secret' men's business. In essence, this is the purpose of this book.

Anything that gets men together to talk about the real stuff, is invaluable and can even be life-saving. I know that if I'm feeling a little lost in my purpose or unsure as to how I'm being perceived in the world, which is often easy to do when we focus on our work, relationship and parenting, I will seek the company of men that I have learned to trust. I know they will not bullshit me, nor wrap their perspective in cotton wool, and whatever I am seeking will be delivered to me in a real and pragmatic way. For me, venturing into such realms becomes a way for me to *calibrate*: am I where I think I am in my personal and relationship development? When I am reflected back to me by other men with no agenda, the feedback is invaluable, and I'm grateful to those men, especially those older than me, my *elders*, who have kindly kicked my butt to lean in and consider a role of deeper service.

This book is testament to that exact process as without it, I would have most likely stayed in my comfort zone, and this book would never have been written!

If you're a man reading this and you think you're ready to try a men's group, check out the multiplicity of organisations and registered groups to be found on the Internet. If you're a woman reading this and you know a man in your life who would benefit, perhaps suggest it might be good for him to hang out with some functional and honest men. If he's a father, it'll make him a better dad, which in turn will help his children and therefore the next generation.

Happier men lead to happier families, which leads to happier and safer communities and societies overall.

Speaking of families, let's explore the vital role of fatherhood, next.

Key Points:

◆ *Men's gatherings often discuss fathers, children and relationship issues*

◆ *Men's groups assist men in dealing with difficult issues that may have already been faced by other men in the group*

◆ *Men find it easier to talk in front of other men that they do in front of women*

◆ *Happier men lead to happier families, leads to happier and safer societies.*

23. FATHERHOOD

When a child is born, a father is born.
— **Frederick Buechner**

No book exploring contemporary masculinity would be complete without a specific mention of *fatherhood*. Without the contribution of the smallest cell in a man's body, which found the largest cell in our mother's body, whether in-utero or in-vitro, none of us would be here!

While there's no doubt that the role of fathering has changed considerably since the Industrial Revolution, and in recent times is in an even greater state of flux, what does it mean to be a 'dad' today?

There's so much opportunity to improve our fathering role, especially with the emergence of various men's activities that support fathering as mentioned in previous chapters, but there's also increased pressure to put a roof over our family's head and maintain a lifestyle that is underpinned by consumerism. Families struggle to find the balance between standard of living and healthy parenting, and in many families, dads are mostly absent from their children's lives. When we add the high divorce rates (around 45% in Australia), our ideal of a complete and functional 'nuclear' family unit is even rarer. The doctor and author, Dr Gabor Maté, even argues that the nuclear family, a recent development in the timeline of humanity, goes against our very human nature and explains much about why we experience many social issues today.

If I had to describe my ideal situation as a father of two healthy, boundary-pushing sons, I wanted nothing more than to be able to be more available for them both, especially during their high school years, when testosterone kicks in, adolescence emerges and they're hurtling toward their own version of manhood. At the time of writing (2025), one is 16 and in year 11 (and learning to drive!), while the other, 22, has completed an electrical trade apprenticeship, thankfully with a smart, caring and competent small-business owner.

When a typical working week for most city-based dads includes hours of travelling, many hours at their jobs or shiftwork, with early departures and late arrivals home, weekends seem to be the only opportunity to connect with family. If the children do any weekend sports, then the life of most fathers becomes one of continued stress, with the only respite being an occasional annual holiday. With the pervasiveness of wireless hotspots (WiFi), touch pads and smartphones, we're never far from work, even while on holiday.

If we do take a long holiday complete with disconnection from the various forms of communication, on our return we know the good ol' email inbox is going to be filled with so much stuff that it'll take us days to filter and clear; all this while we're trying to catch up on what went on while we were away, and we're back into a more stressful situation than when we departed. I know men who keep in touch, read, clear and even answer their emails while on holiday, so they don't have to deal with the mess upon their return. Clearly, the accessibility that technology provides today has a downside and I see many fathers struggling with being this accessible while attempting to also be present with their families.

Insecurity of employment is another aspect we can add to a dad's burden. The Global Financial Crisis (aka GFC) of 2008-2009, changed the view of job security, and I regularly read news of business and factory closures, head-count reductions, downsizing and related job losses. Each time I hear this I can't help thinking that somewhere, a father, a primary breadwinner, has gone home to his family that evening to tell them that he no longer has a job, and I wonder at his sense of uncertainly, his loss of identity and whether, as a proud man, he feels any shame.

For the unaffected majority, he's just another number on a spreadsheet or a statistic in the news. I doubt if we'll ever truly understand the social cost of such 'economic imperatives'. The sad fact is that the results of decisions such as these will not manifest until the children of these families have reached adulthood and become parents themselves, and where boys are concerned who become fathers, we sadly have enough historical context to predict the outcome.

In the USA, a law student studying crime statistics noticed a direct correlation between the breakdown of societal values as measured via crime statistics, and absent fathers. The statistics speak for themselves; boys who don't have clear, strong male influences in their lives have greatly increased risks of incarceration, drug and alcohol use ... and early death. The effect of having a father (or father-figure) to guide boys through the turbulent adolescent years and their presence in minimising a boy's at-risk behaviour makes complete sense, as does the downside of a father's absence. There's no doubt that as a society we can do much more to ensure dads play a more active role in their children's lives and we can do this by understanding that most dads feel very alone and go through the daily routine, simply because that's what expected of them, while striving to provide the best they can for their family.

Thankfully, organisations are emerging that recognise this and to quote one example from www.fatherhood.com.au and their values, *"The Fatherhood Project is dedicated to building healthy communities by enriching the lives of fathers, their children and their families. We support mothers and fathers as earners and carers."*

Another is The Fathering Project (www.thefatheringproject.org/), whose mission is to *"positively impact fathering behaviour and fathers' engagement with children through evidence-rich programs and resources that engage, equip and support fathers, families, schools, employers and community organisations."*

Organisations such as these understand the correlation between healthy fathers and healthy communities and the knock-on effect that this produces. They are actively doing something about it. A couple of decades ago an organisation such as this would have been unheard of, and the advent of the Internet is providing wonderful opportunities for support groups such as these, to broadcast their message, support fathers and mothers in their emerging roles, and truly make a difference.

If we choose to look at the entire life-cycle of fathering, men are becoming more involved with family planning aspects with their partners, preparing for conception, pregnancy and birth itself. I know many men who have played a key role in supporting their partners during birth, respecting their partner's choice of birthplace and the type of birth their partners wish to experience. Many midwives are also supportive of fathers' roles prior to, during and after birth. It's no longer a rare site to see a baby strapped to its father's chest in a baby carrier or being carried or pushed in a stroller.

Australian author and father, Michael Ray (www./michaelray.com.au/), in his book *Who Knew*, has done a remarkable job of challenging fatherhood notions as a single dad raising a daughter and navigating all manner of bias  and inequality. For example, when his 4yo daughter, Charlie, who loves to dance, needed help to dress and prepare for her first stage performance, what does a father do when the organisers won't allow men back-stage? Had this been a role-reversal, a mother would have been welcomed to help their son, such is the complexity of situations like this, but sadly, this bias has become normalised. Thankfully, common sense and Michael's dedication to his daughter paid dividends, and his book is a refreshing perspective for fathers who parent daughters.

One aspect of fathering that I believe could make a difference in how we see our roles, came to me on the day my first son was born, at home, via a water-birth. We had friends in our house and one was whipping up a fabulous, nutritious meal in our kitchen, to ensure that after the effort of labour, there would be a celebratory and much-needed meal for the new mother. The willing cook happened to be a male chef who specialised in vegetarian food, so we knew we were in for a treat! About two hours after my son's birth, I brought him from our bedroom (where we had placed the birthing pool) and as I walked down the hallway, our generous food provider approached me, took one look at our newborn son and said, *"He is the paper, you are the pen. Write whatever story you wish."*

In that moment the awesomeness of fatherhood hit me: being a person responsible for a new life, of imagining my son as a blank slate, tabula rasa, and realising that every word and action he would be exposed to, would be absorbed by this newborn and innocent sponge, and would shape his view of himself, his world and his place in relationship to it.

Talk about being put on notice to be an aware and conscious parent!

While I've never forgotten those words of deep wisdom back in 2002, I have at times lost awareness of the responsibility they entail. I have, however, learned that children are especially resilient and respond well when, as adults, we explain to our children that our expression of emotion was sometimes not that well delivered.

I remember when my eldest was 10 years old and I was simmering on some unresolved personal issue. He asked a question that indicated to me that he held little gratitude for what had been an amazing and generous Christmas. At least that's what I convinced myself to justify my response. His question tipped me over the edge and before I knew it, I was off and running and laying down the law, berating him for his lack of gratitude. He knew what I was saying was true. However, he also knew my delivery was amplified beyond his minor indiscretion, so he simply allowed me my rant.

Before he went to sleep I'd calmed down, and as I tucked him into bed he asked for a hug, then told me he loved me. The following day, while playing Lego together, I took the opportunity to explain that my anger was out of proportion to the event, that I was angry about something else and I apologised for my over-the-top response. His matter-of-fact reply, *"I know, Daddy!"* surprised me, and he explained that he hadn't taken it personally, was okay with it all and had already moved on. Such is the mobility, resilience and understanding of children when we treat them with respect.

As somewhat of a straw poll, I've asked several fathers I know a key question: "If you could pass on one piece of advice to prospective fathers, what would it be?" Below is some of their collected wisdom:

- "Know that it's not all down to you, enjoy the small stuff." – David M
- "There are no 'silver bullets' to Fatherhood. When you spend time with your kids, be fully present with them, be authentic and extend them the same respect you expect from them." – Graeme G
- "Never wish for your child to be any age other than the one that they are right now." – Josh W
- "Love your wife and involve yourself completely no matter how tired you are." – Barry Z
- "Let them soften your Heart and show you the way to love everyone more." – Joe R
- "Men - bring your masculine to fathering. Be a 'man' dad." – Jonathan L
- "Be the kind of man you want your son to become. Treat women the way you want your daughter to be treated." – Brett C

- "Fathering is a gift, your tasks are to demonstrate character, authenticity, integrity, respect for people and the planet (our home) and self-sufficiency, then be willing to let them go test what they have learned." – Dale L
- "Make time to be fully present with your kids. 30 minutes of your full presence is worth so much more than 90 minutes when you are not fully there." – Nick C
- "Your son is not you. He is not here to carry your hopes and dreams, he is here to live his own. Your job as his father is to support him to know these parts of himself and feel confident to respond to them." – Kevin W
- "When your child is born take off your shirt and hold the wet young life to your chest for that needed close start." – Peter A

These comments about love, connection, care and focus may come as a surprise, and you may even think that they're not indicative of men at large. My experience is that if you assumed this, you'd be misguided, as most men I meet would hold similar views. It's just that as men we don't generally volunteer this stuff unless we're asked (as I did to obtain these insights). So, if you're a woman and you're perhaps now a tad curious, ask some fathers you know what advice they might give, or what they really value about being a father. You might be in for a surprise.

A recent article about house-husbands (dads who for whatever reason have opted to be the one staying at home and looking after children and the chores) stated that they no longer have 'sex appeal' to their wives, especially if the wives/partners are in powerful work positions. I found it strange that here we have men who have chosen a nurturing role for which men are often viewed as not being capable, now being viewed as losing something and making them less attractive.

This is quite a paradox when we consider all that we've covered previously in this book. On the one hand, I hear women complain about their husbands not being emotionally available, yet when a man steps into the role of nurturer, he is seen as possibly losing his 'sex appeal'.

I see this as further evidence that collectively, we're very much in a state of confusion about what it means today to be a man. This is why I believe that men seeking the company of other men is of such paramount importance as it provides us with a barometer, a mirror if you like, as to whether we are where we think we are on our journey.

When the mother of my children was six weeks pregnant with our firstborn, I remember being in the shower, pondering the unknown that was to come, and almost absent-mindedly asked myself a question in my head, not expecting an answer of course, *"I wonder what this child is here to teach me?"*

Quick as a flash, as if a voice from nowhere and everywhere infiltrated my awareness, the question was answered before I could think, "Selflessness!"

Fatherhood for me has been the most magnificent experience I could ever have imagined. It challenges me every day to be patient, present and loving beyond anything I ever thought I was capable of. Children truly are a gift, who ask of us nothing more than our full presence and respect, to be loved and in doing so, provide us with the opportunity to be fathers and experience *fatherhood*, for without them we wouldn't be.

Irrespective of whether you, as a man (or a woman reading this book), become a parent, we cannot escape the cycle of birth and death that we must all traverse, and in the next chapter we will explore the *seasons* of a man's life.

Key Points:

◆ *Technology prevents many fathers from switching off from work while at home or even on holiday*

◆ *Many working fathers invest a lot of their time and energy in their jobs, to ensure they keep their families as financially safe as they can, often to the detriment of their own wellbeing*

◆ *The relationship between a father's wellbeing and the quality of society as a whole is now being recognised, as happier fathers lead to happier families and therefore happier societies*

◆ *Organisations are emerging that support the role of fathering and its valuable place within the community*

◆ *Many men are starting to adjust their roles and become more active in their children's lives.*

24. SEASONS

In seed time learn, in harvest teach, in winter enjoy
— William Blake

In late 2018, I first met one of the men who I would come to hold in the highest regard and see as an Elder to Me. We met at a rite-of-passage retreat for men to explore the remarkable world of eldership, but more on that in the next chapter.

He introduced me to a seminal book about men, called Death Of A Hero, Birth Of The Soul, by psychologist Dr. John C Robinson. It had been a source of inspiration and although out-of-print since the late 1990s, it was *strongly* suggested that I find a copy, buy it and more importantly, *read* it!

And so I did, although the depth of the book was not something I could skip through. I found it deeply insightful, as if it had been written personally for me, and it took about a year to work my way through it, like a multicourse meal, one bite at a time, and often with a need to digest chunks of insight and re-read sections in between.

Robinson's assertion that we move through *seasons* of life really landed with me, and in sharing this with other men in various forms through coaching, mentoring, gatherings and event programs, I've seen it land with them too.

Robinson refers to the seasons naturally as Spring, Summer, Autumn and Winter, to reflect stages of our life's journey, which closely matches Alison Armstrong's Page, Knight, Prince and King stages mentioned in chapter 7 (from her insightful audiobook, *The Amazing Development of Men*).

Let's explore each of these in detail, so we can perhaps reflect how seasons have shown up in our respective lives ...

SPRING

Just like nature, Spring is the beginning of new life. In our Spring, we're new to the world, exploring in innocence the wonder of our immediate environment, looking to our carers for guidance and how to engage with the world at large. What are the rules? Are we safe? How do we 'fit in' and become acceptable to those around us? How do we make friends? What do we like and dislike? How do we socialise?

Other writers and observers of our human condition have stated that during this time, we learn to become acceptance-seeking machines, that is, we're tamed, domesticated, civilised, and told in no uncertain terms how to be acceptable. As we touched on in Chapter 21, Dr Gabor Maté contends in his book, *The Myth of Normal*, that as children, during our Spring we're often faced with a choice to assert our need for independence and possibly upset those who care for us with the risk of 'not being loved', or abandon the 'things' we feel the urges and passions to do, and in doing so abandon ourselves. They're known as The Terrible Twos for a reason, as children at this age, relishing their newfound mobility, test their boundaries (as well as their parents!) while exploring their surroundings. It's a time to test our *will* – what can I do, what is the outcome, what response or result will I experience?

A child facing the choice between acceptance and assertiveness will invariably choose acceptance, since being acceptable is how we stay safe. After all, the Big People feed, clothe, soothe and take care of us, so we don't want to upset them and risk not being loved and most of us learn this quickly.

Spring is also the time during which we are 'evicted from the Garden of Eden', as some psychologists call it, when we face some inevitable traumatic experience that creates such a shock, we can be deeply wounded, often unwittingly, by our immediate carers. The mother wound and father wound (discussed in Chapter 17) can take hold at this time and carry through into our adult life, often without knowing.

I had such an experience, aged about four, when I had done exactly what my father had always told me to do. *"Tell me the truth and there'll be little to no consequence. Lie to me and there will!"* had always been his mantra. I told the truth to a stranger about something my father had done, not quite illegal but certainly got him into some serious trouble, after which he berated me so heavily that I grew up with a subconscious belief that 'if I can't trust my own father who told me to always be honest and tell the truth, who can I trust?'

This played out in my life as trust issues with just about everyone, and it wasn't until my mid-40s, when it resurfaced, that I sought some help and embarked on a process of discovering just how deep this 'father-wound' was.

Father wounds run deep in many men and fundamentally change our relationship with our masculinity *at its core*. If we have a father who's incapable of acknowledging us as boys, we might grow into a man's body yet feel inadequate around other and often older men, subconsciously seeking approval – "You're a good boy!" – from them, without even realising it.

We are also mother-wounded during this time and this can manifest in many ways as well. If a boy's mother has had a difficult relationship with her own father, for example, then her unhealed, wounded and tarnished view of masculinity will be transferred onto her son, who might then decry his own masculinity.

And then there's what those who study psychological development call *The Great Wound*, which can be a traumatic or catastrophic event, like a boy losing his father or mother to suicide, an accident, health issue or other misfortune such as war. It can also arise from abandonment, rejection, neglect, relentless criticism, being shamed, violence, abuse (physical, emotional, mental or sexual) and many other behaviours perpetrated upon us. Fortunately, later in life, we can begin the healing of these wounds through various modalities, as they tend to surface during our late Summer.

It's in our Spring that we also form our primary character, test-and-measure our behaviour against societal norms that build our *social character*, travel through our teenage years, learn about love, loss and sometimes grief, find our tribe, lose it, find it again and lose it some more, until we settle into some steadier notion of who we are, what we value, and align with those we might eventually call 'friends'.

Spring is also the time of perhaps experiencing our first love, sexual encounters, becoming self-conscious, seeking initiation, starting work or higher education and leaving home. We are stepping into our warrior, looking for a mate, and this is when we start our search to be the *Hero*.

At some point though, we know we're changing. We no longer feel inclined to storm castles, rescue damsels and slay dragons, and there's a shift in self-perception as we approach our next season of life.

SUMMER

Throughout Summer, men typically reach the zenith of life, confident but perhaps not yet wise. We may marry or enter a long-term relationship, travel to broaden our worldview, establish a home, become a parent, complete a post-graduate degree such as an MBA, advance our career, build our sense of self, focus on finances and investments, and create a plan or vision for our future.

At this stage of his life, a young man seems to have relentless energy, primarily focused on building his adult life. For most men, Summer is the season where we're most productive, achievements are reached and new goals are set. It can also be a time of greatest growth and personal development, since the pressures of life, relationships, parenthood, logistics and career will test our grit and grow our resilience. It's sadly also the time when some 'fly too close to the sun' as Icarus did, and crash and burn, either to rise like a Phoenix from the ashes and start again, or in some cases, call it quits and exit life, either energetically or physically.

My experience with various life transitions and supporting younger men on their journey, has shown me that during early Summer, there's a 28-30yo transition point, which I can explain with this anecdote.

I was once at a conference in a coaching and mentoring support role, when a young man I knew approached me for a 'chat'. I'd developed a reputation within the business group for understanding the various phases and stages we men traverse, so in sitting with this 28yo man over a brief coffee, I could sense his discontentment.

I introduced the word 'ennui' (pronounced 'ahn-WEE') in Chapter 7, and during the discussion with this young man, it popped into my head. It means feeling weary, bored, dissatisfied, listless, a loss of mojo, and when I asked the man if this was how he was feeling, his look of surprise said it all. He was a little freaked out that I had been able, in a short space of time, to articulate exactly what he was feeling! Due to limited time, I arranged to meet him later in the event for a longer conversation.

Remarkably, during the same day, two other young men approached me individually, one 29yo and the other, a 30yo. I had similar, separate conversations with them, with the same surprised response, as if I was some sort of mind-reader, so I arranged to meet them privately at the same time and place I'd arranged for the first man.

I arrived a little early and watched each man as he approached. They were thinking it was to be a private 1:1 conversation with me, so they were somewhat surprised and perhaps a tad put-out to see the other men they knew from the conference, as they converged. I invited them to sit and asked their permission to share the gist of what we'd previously and privately discussed. They agreed, and so I shared. The wide-eyed look on each man's face when they realised they were each feeling the same feeling of ennui, was gold!

I explained this period of transition, while unique in context for every man, has some common elements, and a feeling of ennui was one of them.

At this age, it's almost like striving for some unknown goal, when the partying, relationship-chasing, castle-storming, dragon-slaying activities, and testing one's edges finally exhaust themselves, and we need to pause to reflect and refocus our often-disparate energies for the next phase of our life.

I also asked the men to start sharing their situation *with each other*, explained they weren't Robinson Crusoe, and so could support each other through connection, shared experience, purpose and friendship. Thankfully, they could see the sense in that and have remained in contact since.

While this is a small 'sample size', I have experienced this same transition in other men in their 28-30yo age range, and each has resonated with this same sense of transition. What I have learned from this is that when we think, *"It's just me!"*, chances are, it's not, and reaching out to either an older male mentor or trusted peers, can validate what we're feeling and help us realise we're not alone and that we walk on common ground.

Unfortunately, our previously unresolved childhood wounds remain ever-present and influence the way we approach life. For example, a boy who's experienced a deep mother- or father-wound will perhaps not realise that his perspective on friendships and potential relationships will be greatly influenced by them, as they continue to lurk in the depths of his psyche. It's not usually until mid-life (between Summer and Autumn) that such wounds surface for the healing and resolution they need.

MIDLIFE

Our midlife passage starts in our Summer/Autumn cusp and is typically around the age of 40-42. It's at the exit of this, which for some men can be in our late 40s or early 50s, when we begin the transition into the Autumn of our lives.

So, what happens in midlife?

I've mentioned earlier in chapter 13 on divorce that I once read about a man's midlife passage, summarised on one page, by Robert A Johnson, and it's synchronistic that John C Robinson's book's Foreword is written by Johnson, so they were very much aligned in their experience as psychologists.

To summarise Johnson's view here again, at midlife, we must build a different relationship with our ego to move forward more functionally, and a man's midlife passage, whether it's called a transformation, journey, tunnel, or crisis, *depends solely on the man's approach and awareness of his inner world* and how he navigates this tricky and unsettling time.

Johnson describes it as a 'shift in the centre of gravity of our ego, from master to slave', in other words, the externalising of ego-energy that fuelled our creative, building years (The Hero), must now be turned inward to relocate our ego to a more conscious place and one of service to our Soul. It's a time of great upheaval, a tectonic shift, a battle to 'lose the Hero and find our Soul', and certainly a time that requires external support. As mentioned previously, if not handled well, it can result in a man being in so much emotional turmoil, it can lead to suicidal ideation and sadly, loss of life.

Men who do not do this well often grow into brittle old men, incapable of adjusting, and by attempting to reinforce the edifice of their ego, rather than relocating it to an appropriate place of service, must use psychological energy to keep it all in place, often losing their very potency for life itself. It's as if the effort involved to maintain and carry the unnecessary load of a big black Santa sack of woulds, coulds, shoulds, what-ifs and regrets, rounds his shoulders and stoops his back, like Atlas carrying the weight of his unresolved inner world.

He can become dogmatic, acerbic, self-righteous, mean, verbally cruel, and drive away the very people he needs to help him through this, often creating disharmony around him such that adult children give him a wide berth. He can miss out on the richness grandparenthood can provide, which is the very relationship he needs to soften him as he grows toward his end, and tap into his elder wisdom.

AUTUMN

While there are no leaves to shed in our Autumn stage of life, it can generally be a time when, if we've had children in our 20s or 30s, they've grown, possibly moved out of home and living independent lives. We could be 'empty-nesters', or like me, could still be in an active parenting role yet aware of the diminishing feeling of youthfulness.

I remember realising in my 50s that during my 40s, something strange had happened. Instead of looking back at my life, my experiences and achievements, there'd been a gradual turning, from looking 'where I'd been', to 'where I was going'. I started to become aware of my mortality, that I had less time left than I'd already had, and was rapidly approaching the end of my life. I was well past halfway.

Where did all those intervening years go?

Many I've spoken with seem to have the same sense: that their children were born 'just yesterday', they clearly remember key aspects of their life, and life itself has become a blur of experiences too numerous to detail, yet filled with both the profound and profane, the happy and the sad, the pleasure and the pain, the light and the dark, as if we're all somehow a microcosm of the entire human experience, a holographic piece all mashed into an amalgam of our personal memories.

As Autumn comes to an end, we become further aware of our impending mortality, often losing parents, aunts and uncles, and those of similar age. This is the time to take care of our physical, mental and emotional selves, with exercise, diet, mental activities and anything that helps us keep an even keel in our inner world. Some find it in social groups, networks, business, entrepreneurship, charity work, supporting other younger men with mentoring … there are so many ways to keep active. It's important to do this so that in later life, when we may feel the yearning to tick off some bucket-list holidays, we have the cognitive and physical capacity to do so.

I've been into several nursing homes over the years and always find it challenging to see people who perhaps once had a partner, children, a family, career, a home, dreams and aspirations, sitting idle and staring at some meaningless TV chatter, with me wondering what wisdom lies behind their glazed stare. It's the one thing that motivates me to keep as fit and healthy as I can be, because I don't wish to end up in that situation, and I still have stuff on my bucket-list!

As we move toward the end of Autumn, funerals happen more frequently, an ache or pain can play on our minds (is it something to be worried about?), visits to the doctor or health practitioners become more frequent, and we start to contemplate what life might be like next year, a decade from now, or when we might be diagnosed with an end-of-life illness, as at some point, we know we will transition into our final season.

WINTER

Like all cycles of life, winter is the season where we notice more of our decline, either physically, mentally or sadly, both at the same time. Most of us start to depend more on the medical system, need a good doctor, get more than an annual check-up and blood test, discuss what's ailing us and do the best we can to deal with whatever our body and mind throw at us in their decline. We might still have some bucket-list holidays, and if we're healthy and fit enough, we might also still be financially able to do them, albeit perhaps more sedentary ones than before.

Either way, it's natural at this time of life to be reflective and perhaps wonder if we've made the *right* choices along the way, and maybe we have some deep *regrets*. I've learned the two most useless states of mind are guilt and regret. We can sometimes deal with guilt by redressing something from our past, especially if it involves someone else and we have access to that person. Regret, on the other hand, can paralyse us into a place from which it can be difficult to escape. We're all going to approach this aspect in our Winter, and in reality, we don't have a time-machine, so there's nothing we can practically do about it.

In Robert A Johnson's book, *Living Your Unlived Life*, he writes eloquently about acknowledging that we didn't achieve or try all the things we might have done, and so we must make peace with the parts of us that didn't get to experience them. He recommends a lucid-dreaming approach or 'active imagination', whereby we go inward to imagine we had made a different choice about an event or opportunity sometime in our past and make it an *internal adventure*. His book is remarkable for outlining a process to do this, so if you're reading this feeling a sense of grief or regret for what might have been, it could provide you with a method on how to let this go and move on.

Winter is also a time of preparation, getting our affairs in order, decluttering, giving away precious things to those we love, downsizing, planning our final years and letting those we love know our preferences for end-of-life care and yes, *our funeral*.

It might seem morbid to consider, yet by doing so, we unburden those we leave behind so they can be with their grief. I never had the opportunity to discuss this with either of my parents and there was no end-of-life discussion, so I only knew a couple of minor details, such as my dad was to be cremated, have his ashes spread somewhere he loved, and have Life Of Brian's, *Always Look On The Bright Side Of Life*, played at his funeral. I managed to provide all three in his case. With my mother, all I knew was that she loved a particular piece of music, Ave Maria, sung by Andrea Bocelli, and again, arranged that for her, but as for any other wishes, I had absolutely no idea.

In effect, by considering and eventually documenting this process, we're taking care of the details so those we leave behind don't have to guess what we might have wanted. As if there isn't enough to do when we lose someone we love.

Things to consider are:

Do you have a Will and an Executor in place?

Are you an organ donor and does your family know?

Do you have any Do Not Resuscitate (DNR) orders in place?

Does someone have a Power of Attorney and where is it?

Will your funeral be a cremation, burial or something else?

What about a chapel service, memorial at a private venue or public place, or someone's home?

A Wake or Celebration Of Life, maybe?

A playlist of music you love?

Is there any poetry, writings, compositions, art, videos, or anything that others might not know about you that you'd like to share?

Have you considered writing your own Eulogy?

As you can see, there's much to be considered!

This is also a time where our bodily autonomy may be lost (as well our functions), along perhaps with our dignity, as we hear others talk *about* us. This passage about frailty, kindly shared with permission and authored by Peter Efford, co-founder of the Menswork Project, is an extract from his Castle Without Walls series and for me, so eloquently sums up this time in our lives. Peter calls it *The Room Of Frailty*:

"Unless we die in an accident or because of a sudden illness, we will become frail. Somehow, even with the entire attitude we can muster, we will become physically or mentally diminished, or both, left needing the support of others. There is little quality to life.

There is much to learn in this unstable place. Our body is now unreliable; perhaps we are medicated, mentally alone, disabled, depressed, intolerant, agitated, angry or submissive. We will feel the force of indignity as others take responsibility for our well-being, our body functions, and financial affairs. We will be whispered about. Others will talk about us as if we were not there. We will overhear untruthful opinions about ourselves. Carers will care and not care all at once. Our routine will be merged to the convenience of others, and we will be left to sit and gaze at the television, fed soup and mashed up food. We will dribble, become incontinent. Our skin will become parched and patched. We will lose our sense of taste and our eyes will water. We may look in helpless agony as our partner struggles to keep us alive, as bewildered grandchildren gaze into our eyes and the family gathers for what might be the last Christmas together. This is the departure lounge. Friends are gone, a younger man that you have once witnessed, blessed even, visits, embarrassed and agonised at what you have become. Your reflection of how you can be for others, however courageous, is challenged.

It is time to go inwards.

For in this room is the wall of dark mirrors where at last we must be alone and see deep into ourselves to ponder why we have been given this lovely/lonely space to do so, just when we cannot change anything.

It is good to know of this place well in advance. To give it meaning while you can, for when it happens it might be too unbearable to contemplate. You might not even get the chance.

If you are lucky, you will be wrapped up in a blanket and put to sit out into the sun, where if you slowly lift your head, a light breeze touches you. Where did it all go, my beautiful life? My longing for back then is so great, almost as much as for my longing to die. Please give me a small time to put myself in order. I cannot regret myself, it is all so far away, and I am a living goodbye. Nourish me with my spirit; my dignity was keeping it away. I can be still, there is a great peace and at last I am in the moment."

(© Peter Efford, The Menswork Project 2009. The Elders Way. Edited October 2016. 2021. 2024 and shared with permission.)

And then, in the blink of an eye, our winter ends and we're no longer a physical presence.

My opinion is that in the West, we have done ourselves a disservice by compartmentalising birth (now mostly in hospitals) and death (we even use the sanitised Americanism 'passed' instead of 'died') because we somehow have come to view them as unseemly and not-to-be-discussed topics. Yet, both can be a celebration: one for the new life and the potential it holds, and the other to celebrate a life hopefully well-lived and the legacy left behind.

Seasons ... spring, summer, autumn, winter ... are a path we must all tread if we live a life untruncated by premature illness or accident. Either way, we all leave a legacy of some kind, and perhaps by considering this as we age, we can be more conscious of what we're going to leave behind.

Next, we will explore the rich world of Eldership and how, in our later years, we can rediscover our potency for life while sharing our collected wisdom with those who wish to hear it, and give back as an act of service.

Key Points:

- *We pass through 4 seasons - spring, summer, autumn and winter - each with its own defining characteristics*

- *It's important to recognise where we are in respect of progress through them*

- *Midlife can be a particularly troublesome time for men, especially if our identity is tied to the work we do or a primary relationship, and we have difficulty relocating our ego*

- *Winter is a time for what can be difficult conversations, as we consider our end-of-life plans*

- *Contemplating our legacy can be challenging, yet rewarding.*

25. ELDERSHIP

Men only talk about what really matters to them, to someone who is "safe", meaning non-judgemental, interested, and not competing for talk time.
— Alison Armstrong

Eldership.

I'd never given much thought to consider what it means to be an *Elder*, although I have mentioned in this book several times that I've had contact and friendship with men older than me, who I considered my elders, but never related this to myself. For example, when I get 'old', do I automatically become an elder? I know some of the characteristics I've experienced in these men, that almost automatically put them in that light for me, but once again, I hadn't given it much thought. The question that also rattled around in my head was, even if I knew, *would I want to be seen as an elder anyway?*

I can best explain my dance with the questions around eldership by sharing what unfolded for me, as I had started to 'do' (almost unconsciously) eldering behaviour anyway, so bear with me while

I explain.

In late 2018 after returning from a bucket-list holiday in Peru and walking the Inca Trail with my new partner (yes, I found love again!), I came across an email invitation to attend a Bali-based weeklong retreat for men, called *The Elder's Way*. I read the email with interest and despite my internal and logical protestations as to why I shouldn't go (just back from holiday, money, commitments, time etc), my Heart spoke otherwise. Within a day I was on the phone to the author of the email seeking some clarification, discovered he was one of the founders and authors of the program, and within a week I was on a plane to Bali!

For eight days I was embedded in a stunning location just south of Ubud, with a bunch of 7 other men I didn't know, trusting I'd made the right decision, eating local food and exploring what became the rich world of *eldership*. Being in unfamiliar territory with other men, doing a personal exploration of my relationship to Self and those around me, was not new, as mentioned throughout this book I'd previously attended men's gatherings and groups and often knew no one on the first day.

What was new, though, was a weeklong (not a weekend) deep dive into the rich world of eldership: what it is, why we need it, how to show up in my 'social circles', time for rest and reflection, amazing camaraderie, hearty home-cooked Balinese food and solid night's sleep under a fan to keep me cool and the mozzies away, all of which I found fascinatingly restful, rejuvenating and rewarding.

Like any verb, *eldering* is a doing word, related to the behaviour we exhibit around others, and is a rich world within itself. There are various definitions, some from religious organisations, but what they all have in common is that eldership is not something we can claim, but something that's *bestowed* on someone who exhibits certain characteristics, which we'll get to. It is also a recognition that the person, through life's experiences, has gained some universal *wisdom*, that when shared, might help others in their life's journey.

During that week, partaking in various processes using psychodrama and what's known as 'action methods', I was fascinated at the capability of the two original founders, one 77 (Peter, who wrote the foreword for this book) and the other 82 (Wes), both solid in their dual roles as facilitators and elders in their own right. They'd been running these retreats for over 20 years, and were evidently seasoned, wise, deeply focused and wonderfully caring.

I learned much that week: where I was hiding within myself, uncertain of how I was being perceived by my community back home, and most importantly, getting my butt kicked by Wes for 'hiding behind my book'! I didn't see that coming, but it landed, and I could sense that I was playing it safe for whatever reason.

At the end of the week, as we were preparing to return home after an extraordinary time for me of personal and focused growth, Wes pulled me aside and chided, *"We're getting too old for this caper and looking for some younger fellas to run with it. How about you come back next year and learn to co-facilitate with me, then we can retire, and you can run these retreats?"*

If you know the movie Sliding Doors, this was definitely one of those moments, and something about the ease with which I'd gotten to that moment, despite my initial resistance, heard me speak a definite and emphatic, *"Yes!"* and before I knew it, May 2019 had arrived and I was on my way to help Wes and dive even deeper into my own exploration of eldership.

We ran another in November 2019, then planned and sold out another for May 2020, but then COVID hit in March 2020, international travel was halted, and we had to cancel and refund all the deposits and payments. Ouch! Lesson learned.

I toyed with the idea of advertising again in early 2023, but instead, ran the retreat mentioned earlier on the vast expanse of The Nullarbor in August 2023. It wasn't until I attended the Tasmanian Men's Gathering (aka TMG) in March 2024, that a man who'd helped out at The Nullarbor came and hugged me and asked, *"Hey, JB, when are you going to run another one of those elder retreats in Bali?"* And so it started, with three other men, unrelated to the first, asking the very same question! I started to think someone had stuck a sign on my back, but no, serendipity had other plans ...

On my return from the gathering, I reached back out to Wes, who due to now being 87 declined my request to co-facilitate, but thankfully, Peter was willing and available. I started marketing to the various men's networks around Australia, re-jigged the weeklong program, found a new location in Bali for a larger, more up-market, 5-star experience, and in the first week of August, had 11 men and 2 facilitators (Peter and me) descend on a wonderful retreat space in the southeast of Bali for a week of eldership exploration.

For me, it was such an incredible experience to hold the reins, as it were, and invite Peter to simply fly in, co-facilitate, and fly home, with me managing all the logistics, coordination and the program itself. It was repeated in Nov 2024, with similar results, so this is what I, and the men who attended, learned from the new program.

One of the processes that always lands well is a *stocktake* of how we, as men, are showing up in our respective communities, and some of us have many: work, social, hobbies, sport, religious, service (think volunteer groups like Legacy, Probus, Apex, Lions etc), men's groups etc. If we're unaware of the nature of the type of behaviours that show, *"I am here as an elder"*, and therefore, we don't know what eldering behaviours are, then we're effectively invisible to the communities in which we serve.

Eldering is not something that naturally occurs in our Western world, nor emerges simply because we've reached a certain physical age. It is a demonstration of specific behaviours from a deep place of *service*, which advances those with who we come into contact, and not only those we know.

For example, you might eat at a restaurant and notice the young person serving you has a great attitude, is polite, respectful, customer-focused and evidently at ease in their role of service. Sure, you can leave a good tip, but you can also genuinely acknowledge them by speaking with them and positively commenting on what it was about them and their service, that made a difference to your experience. Imagine yourself in that same role all those years ago, and an older person noticing you, acknowledging you and complimenting you on your effort. I know at that age, I craved such recognition since it was absent from my father. I have done this on occasion with service staff and the results have been mixed. Some haven't known what to do with it (which tells me they live in a world bereft of adult recognition and don't know how to respond), while others have been deeply grateful for *being seen* and acknowledged. Either way, if delivered well, it's a *gift*, and what they do with that is up to them.

So, what are some of these characteristics we can demonstrate to those around us, and how do we create opportunities for them?

Attributes like presence, calmness, wisdom, well-travelled, courageous, empathic, curious, compassionate, aware, good listener, safe, respectful, accepting, gracious, generous, broadminded, positive mindset ... you get the idea. The important thing here is to become aware of what behaviours you might be doing well, what you might be partially doing, and what you might not be doing at all.

When I did an eldering stocktake of behaviours, I realised I was showing up well in about a third, another third I could see room for improvement, with the final third identifying that I wasn't showing up at all. This gave me some qualified insight into areas in which I could *choose* to do more because, ultimately, it has to be a choice and one we willingly make.

Running several elder events since that time in 2018 has also provided me with further insight into other men's self-exploration, and each time the participants have found such a self-assessment to be an invaluable experience.

One area in particular that we focus on as specific eldering behaviour is *blessings*. When I first came across this concept, to be honest, it felt a bit weird, as I associated it with a religious context but soon learned it had its own process. Looking back once I understood, and I could see that I'd been 'blessed' by many people, especially men in my various circles, and more so by elders. I had taken part in a group blessing process at the original Elder's Way with Wes and Peter back in 2018, so now understood the process and how important it was to both the *blesser* and *blessee*.

Blessing has now become something more active for me, as I've started to embrace opportunities to do so. As an example, a close friend recently had a milestone birthday, and a gathering of friends to celebrate it. Rather than looking for a gift, or the obligatory up-market bottle of champagne, wine or single malt whisky, I started to ponder what I would say to this man that reflected how I, as an older man, experience him showing up in his life: as a father, partner, businessman, mentor, and decent human being. I wasn't confident to do this in a public way, such as a speech. However, writing is my go-to way of communicating what I think and feel (hence this book!), so I chose to write a *blessing letter*. It would also then be something tangible for my friend to keep and refer to in the future.

The result was that he took a few days to respond after his birthday, and shared that he'd had to read it more than once to take in the depth of acknowledgement that he'd never experienced before, and knowing he sees me as an elder in his life, meant so much more to him than any purchased gift. This was the first time I'd taken this step, and I was nervous as to how it might be received, yet every word was considered and true from my perspective, and most importantly, *heartfelt*. It landed so well he asked for a PDF version so he could print it on separate pages to frame and put in his home office, to remind him in times of self-doubt.

What it has taught me is that as we age, we can *claim* our place of elderhood, while at the same time being generous of Heart and looking for opportunities to appease the yearning that many of us have: to be seen, respected and valued for all of who we are. This is especially true for younger people. Again, imagine you, as a young man or woman, receiving a blessing letter from someone you respected in which your attributes as a human being, and contribution to those around you, were noticed and reflected to you. I would have been so touched by such an experience and cherished an acknowledgement like this, and this is what reminds me to be on the lookout for opportunities to do that for others.

I've also learned from my elders that the more I do it, the easier and more eloquent my writing will become, so that encourages me to do it more.

If you remember Alison Armstrong and her model of *Page, Knight, Prince and King* (introduced in Chapter 7 from her *Amazing Development of Men*), she adds that for Kings, there can be a final stage. In the King stage, which emerges after our midlife passage if we traverse it well, we've burned away the non-important dross that no longer serves us, like a paring back of attitudes, values, beliefs and unwanted baggage. This frees us to be less burdened as we enter the Autumn of our lives, in preparation for our inevitable Winter.

Kings sometimes, therefore, want to change the world with their newfound wisdom and self-knowledge, thinking that they've found El Dorado and want everyone to know, so will often tell those around them how to BE and how they *should* be living their lives. Did they ask for advice? This is perhaps driven by some remaining and immature ego, yet to catch up and get with the elder program.

"Guilty as charged, your honour!"

It wasn't until I read Armstrong's book that I realised I'd been one of *those* Kings and so learned about the nature of the King Elder, a man who knows he knows what he knows, and is content *in his knowing*. He doesn't need to tell others, or broadcast what he knows, as he understands they, too, have their journey to travel and have gained their own wisdom along the way.

I'm reminded of the famous Chinese philosopher Lao Tzu, who noted, *"He who knows, does not speak. He who speaks, does not know."* The King Elder is more content to observe, listen, contribute where he feels he can add value, and know that those who see him, will gravitate toward him if they think or feel he has something to offer them, because he's made it clear he is *approachable*. This then becomes a beautiful and non-invasive way for a King Elder to support, acknowledge, and share his wisdom with those who might wish to know more.

The more I explore the deep world of eldership and continue to stretch my growing edges, look for opportunities to show-up, listen into my environment and the people I meet, catch myself when I'm over-talking and drop back into listening mode, the more enriched I feel.

I remember at the latest Elder's Way, when we were each checking-in as to how we were going on the third day, and I stated I felt like *a pig swimming in chocolate*. Perhaps a strange metaphor, but chocolate seemed so much richer than mud, and I like chocolate! I said this to the group because I wanted them to understand how rich my world felt, and that I was in the privileged position to witness so many heartfelt men exploring, finding and owning the eldership place within themselves. The change during that week was, as in previous events, palpable as each man grew into a larger version of themselves, with Peter and I knowing this would have effects for these men way beyond our week together.

If you're a younger man reading this then a rich world awaits you, and it has nothing to do with age, but perhaps does have something to do with how well you've lived your life and the wisdom you've acquired.

If you're a man in your midlife, simply know that the 'tunnel' has a purpose, and ultimately, despite your upcoming Autumn and Winter, the rich world of eldership awaits you.

If you're an older man who hasn't yet considered the possibility of exploring eldership, yet sharing your no doubt hard-earned life's wisdom with younger generations is something of interest, keep an eye out for opportunities to do so. Stepping into eldership can bring back or increase our potency for life itself.

And finally, if you're a woman reading this, perhaps you may see any older men in your life and social circles with a new perspective, and it might pique your curiosity about how they may see the world differently from you.

No matter who you are or where you are on your life path, eldership is a rich and rewarding exploration, and a way to give to younger people around you.

Key Points:

- *Eldership is not age-related, although an effective elder needs to have lived life and gained wisdom to share*

- *Eldering is a state of doing and being, consciously positioning ourselves with behaviour to serve and contribute back to society*

- *Looking for opportunities to 'bless' can be an amazing way to acknowledge younger people who often yearn for such recognition*

- *Kings can become King Elders, if we know this stage exists and we're prepared to move through wanting to tell people how to live their lives, and learn to listen more*

- *Eldership can increase a man's potency for life as it provides meaning and purpose.*

26. AUTHENTICITY

Only the truth of who you are, if realised, will set you free.
                                                           — Eckhart Tolle

When the first edition of this book found its way to the editor in late 2013, something niggled inside me for weeks, and it is a story I haven't shared before. The nagging question rattling around in my head was, *"Why did I write this, and why do I feel it's not yet complete?"*

I wrestled with this until my eventual 'Ah ha!' moment (fortunately before the editor had finished!), realising that the entire purpose of this book (along with the time, effort, and cost) wasn't to claim a spot on the New York Times bestselling list (although I wouldn't have said 'No!'). Instead, it was to encourage men at any age to embark on their journey of inner exploration and, in doing so, perhaps find some inner peace and liberation. Then, the word *authenticity* rattled into my consciousness, leading to the title of this final chapter.

So, as we near the end, I hope you've become familiar with my deeply held philosophy, and that is, to truly be *all* of who we are, there is an absolute requirement to delve into our deepest aspects: our emotions, feelings, self-talk, inner-critics, thoughts, trauma, patterns of behaviour, acculturation, beliefs and values.

Why?

As Eckhart Tolle states, *to discover the truth of who we are.*

Before I address that, let's look at what it means to be *authentic*. I know this word has been done to death in all manner of personal development and leadership courses, and it's all over social media selling. I'm sure you've had personal experience of people or businesses who've claimed to be authentic, only to discover it was mere lip-service. I know I have. However, if we look deeper at its *meaning*, perhaps we can resurrect and raise it to its original quality.

The origins of the word 'authentic' come from two Greek parts: 'autos' meaning 'self' and 'hentes' meaning 'doer or being', in other words, 'Being Self.' If we never delve into the shadowy recesses that contain all of who we are, not just who we think we are, how can we truly know ourselves?

The words "*Know thyself*" (from Greek Γνῶθι σαυτόν, or gnōthi sauton) is a philosophical maxim inscribed upon the Temple of Apollo in the ancient Greek precinct of Delphi, some 2,500 years ago, and since that eventful (and my first) weekend workshop in June 1991, has been my maxim ever since. If you remember, I mentioned how the facilitator challenged me by stating that he knew more about me than I did. This was a classic case of not knowing a single thing about why I was as I was, and this is very common among men. In the simplest of terms, *we don't know what we don't know.*

It's not possible for us to unravel our inner workings on our own, since we can never be sufficiently *objective*. It's even more difficult when we consider that what we believe we know of ourselves may only be 20%, with the other 80% being our *unconscious* Self. A pattern of behaviour that has become ingrained and has us running on automatic pilot, cannot be questioned, analysed or challenged by us since we may not even be aware of its existence. Even if we are, the simple fact that it has stood the test of time as a protective mechanism and delivered us safely to where we are today, albeit sometimes as a dysfunctional response, is an indication that it's probably more clever than we are.

As I read recently, we all have blind-spots, and the most common one is thinking that everybody else has them, but us! This is the reason why we must seek objectivity outside ourselves, either from someone referred by others we trust, or someone who can demonstrate that they have walked a deep path of self-discovery.

How do we know this?

Let me share some guidance that I think will serve you well as we come to the end of our journey together.

There's been much discussion about the role of mentors, especially for boys and young men. The evidence overwhelmingly shows that when we seek and select mentors or, if we're open to the idea they select us, irrespective of whether they relate to our business, professional or personal lives, they can have a *profound* effect.

This is how it used to be when we learned a trade from our fathers or were apprenticed to another to learn a particular skill. We were surrounded by older men who would see that we needed guidance in a particular area of our lives. Indigenous cultures also know this, and boys spend many hours with older men and women, learning from their collective wisdom. How else is a lifetime of experience passed on for future generations to capitalise on what we've learned about living, and be shared?

In a purely psychological sense, and as mentioned in Chapter 18 regarding rites of passage, the process of learning who we are, of becoming a true individual, is known as *individuation*. There's something strange that happens when we individuate: we begin to emanate a sense of completeness that others can sense, however, only if they're open to it. Other seekers somehow know that we've been on a journey that has taught us something, an aura of wisdom perhaps acquired during our journey, or with hindsight. We have been somewhere, experienced more of who we are and brought that back into awareness, which has made us *more whole*. Remember, to *heal* means to make whole, so our experience has healed some of our psychological wounds.

Gareth S. Hill, author of *Masculine And Feminine – The Natural Flow Of Opposites In The Psyche* put it well when he wrote, *"The individuated person is relatively free from personal complexes and has a quality of wisdom that implies a reflective relation to his life experience and a loving acceptance of his fate, those unbidden givens that have been formative or life-defining."*

In other words, when we meet an individuated person, we recognise the presence of something familiar, a settled awareness that our Soul might very well be yearning for.

Imagine for a moment that a particular aspect of our *Self* seems insurmountable. We're aware enough to know that there is a lurking shadowy aspect deep in our psyche. For whatever reason, we decide it's time to face the controller within and understand more of who we are. If we imagine that this may be as challenging as climbing

Mount Everest and we turn up at Base Camp in a t-shirt, shorts and bare feet, it's easy to see this isn't going to work. We may meet others on the way back down who have conquered their own mountain, and we can see that they're equipped for the journey, albeit a little weary and perhaps battered by the elements. However, *they do know the way*, the pitfalls and the nagging doubts, yet they have learned something about themselves that they didn't know before. They have made an irrevocable step in knowing something about themselves that they cannot now *un-know*. The feeling we get from those that *know*, is palpable, yet sometimes easily missed.

If, on the other hand, we remain blind to those coming down from their mountainous adventures and decide to head off from Base Camp unsuitably prepared, we might still make it. No doubt it would be far more difficult and painful than if we'd been prepared or had guidance. This simply may be the way some of us learn. For me, my independent/anti-dependent streak always wanted to go it alone, often not succeeding, yet perhaps my tenacity to *know myself* ensured I had another attempt when better prepared.

In my life, I would say I've climbed several metaphorical Mount Everests. Each one taught me something major about myself and each time I stood at Base Camp not knowing what lay ahead, yet I was better equipped than the previous time, since each experience had broadened my sense of Self. I did know, however, that after my first ascent, despite my psyche telling me I would die trying to protect patterns that were well passed their use-by-date, I knew I would survive, be enriched by the journey and be a better person for it. With each ascent (or descent into our abyss) we learn something very important about ourselves, remove the binding shackles that have kept us living small, and experience a sense of liberation like no other.

As noted by the author Eckhart Tolle in the opening quote, only the realisation of the truth of who we are can truly set us free. Otherwise, we're constantly at the behest of unseen forces, manipulating us often without us even *realising*.

It seems to me that to live an authentic life we absolutely must know who we are, otherwise, we'll always present a façade or multiple façades, as we continue to wear various masks to hide our true and unexplored Self.

In a recent conversation with a male coaching client, I was discussing authenticity and I asked him how well he thought he knew himself. The ensuing long seconds of silence while he pondered the question was followed by, *"I don't know how to answer that!"* This clearly showed that, in fact, the answer was unequivocal. Someone who truly knows themself, has been on their inward journey, has come to know more and more about who they are, and has individuated to any degree, would answer that question with an emphatic response that would leave no doubt. People respond to individuated people. People respond to authentic people. People want to be with people who don't play mind games, don't emotionally blackmail, don't gaslight, aren't dishonest, don't play politics, and don't manipulate others.

I firmly believe one of our main purposes in life is to understand who we are, why we are as we are, and to bring all the unexpressed and unrealised aspects of ourselves *into awareness*.

How can we lead others, in the true sense of leadership, if we don't know what makes us tick? Without self-awareness as the basis for authenticity, we're never free of our controllers and they will always influence our thinking and taint our interpersonal relationships. This is why there are so many political games in business boardrooms, government, offices and anywhere else where unrealised people gather. When we're all working from a pattern-survival mentality, where the need for power and control takes precedence over functional relationship intelligence, it creates a culture that is counterproductive to getting anything done well, and in this situation, people will do anything to ensure they survive, often at the expense of others.

Contrast this to working with people who are *doing their inner work*, and have at least delved deeply into their depths and become more whole. I've had this experience multiple times, so let me share an example. Firstly, as a somewhat individuated person, when you meet another, there's an instant relaxation that takes place. You can feel in your body that there's no posturing, no competition, limited ego, and that you don't need to watch your back. So, you're prepared to cocreate a platform of *trust*, a sort of innocent-until-proven-guilty arrangement. This doesn't mean that it's full steam ahead. However, it does mean that you can focus on what needs to be done and not be distracted by meaningless, mindless and unproductive psychological games.

Secondly, things move at a pace dictated by each other's ability to be *authentic*. When we understand that any relationship is not just the two people, it's the *space between* that we create, a sense of *ourness*, and is unique to every interpersonal relationship. Any time, therefore, that there's a disturbance in this between-space of a new relationship, it must be addressed respectfully, and a mutual resolution reached. This strengthens the bridge of trust and provides further foundational support on which a stronger relationship can continue to be built. As this cycle continues, the bridge becomes stronger and stronger, trust builds, and simply, stuff gets done. The focus is on the task at hand, not on who looks good, who gets credit, who sidles up to the boss, who gets recognised, etc.

True leaders cannot be leaders unless they *know* themselves. There will always be unconscious patterns seeking attention, which will disrupt the flow of creating authentic relationships.

I also firmly believe that individuated people create an individuated culture, which attracts individuated people, who further contribute to the culture. I've also seen how one unaware person can disturb a culture that is already strongly trust-based, although if the culture is truly based on these values, it tends to organically eject the 'bad apple' and self-heal, although sometimes, the apple will pull others down and be anathema to an already healthy culture. The disturbance, however, is often palpable and the elephant in the room must be addressed to get the culture back on track.

Leadership, and I mean true leadership, requires that we know ourselves better than anyone else, that we're aware of our foibles, strengths, qualities and blind-spots, that we have self-worth and therefore capacity to acknowledge it in others, and that we can give from a full cup rather than an inauthentic, half-hearted, protective and empty place. We need to build a solid core based on a sense of purpose and clarity that doesn't get distracted by others' realities, and that knows why we're here and what we're here to do.

For men, this is such a challenge for all the reasons explained within the covers of this book. We're not naturally adept at looking inward, expressing ourselves, explaining what we feel, acknowledging our pain or seeking support, yet I believe we do yearn to live as authentically as we are able.

Dr Elizabeth Celi is a PhD psychologist from Melbourne, specialising in men's mental health. Since 1996 Dr Celi has worked with many men, especially around our inability to connect with our authentic selves, which prompted her to write, *Regular Joe vs. Mr Invincible – The Battle For The True Man*. In her book, Dr Celi interviewed six men about their journey, what they've learned and what advice they would pass on to other men who might be interested in connecting with their True Man.

Dr Celi concludes, *"The True Man doesn't just fall into your lap. It takes drive and it takes focus. You have to put in the hard yards, make tough decisions, face the fears and be vulnerable when the situation calls for it. The more you connect with your True Man, the more you sense his true power in your daily life."*

Perhaps this is our Iron John?

Every time we choose to live an authentic moment, we give others around us permission to do the same. We challenge their fears by example and call on them to be truer to who they are, to liberate themselves from self-imposed shackles that in the end, serve no one. We invite them to experience a sense of freedom; the sense of which is impossible to describe and can only be *experienced*, and we invite them to be our friend in the times when our self-doubts consume us, and we forget who we are. These are the characteristics of someone who has journeyed deep into their abyss, and has come to know him or herself as a person aiming to live as authentically as possible.

Hopefully, this book has provided you with some concepts, guidance, ideas and deeper insights, so that you can ask yourself, *"How can I live and be more of my authentic Self, and what does that mean, for me?"*

In the final chapter, we will explore possible next steps you can take.

Key Points:

- *Authentic means 'Being Self'*

- *We need guidance outside of ourselves to unravel our beliefs, patterns and judgments*

- *We can learn to recognise individuated people as they emanate a solid sense of who they are and often exhibit hard-earned wisdom*

- *We cannot lead effectively if we do not know who we are*

- *By living an authentic life, we give permission to others to do the same.*

27. NEXT STEPS

Every day I remind myself that my inner and outer life are based on the labours of other men, living and dead, and that I must exert myself in order to give in the same measure as I have received and am still receiving.
— **Albert Einstein**

As we come to the end of our journey, firstly, I would like to thank you from the bottom of my Heart for reading this book, and I sincerely hope that its contents have been informative, thought-provoking and enlightening. Secondly, I hope it has affected the way you see men and broadened your view about how we men navigate our world, both inner and outer. I also hope that I have encouraged you to seek further information and read other authors' views on the challenges facing men today. I have provided a reading and resource list as an Appendix, so there's plenty of additional information out there.

If you're a woman who has read this book, then I particularly wish to thank you for being interested enough to discover more about the world of men. If you see men in a different light, if I have changed your perspective by challenging the stereotypes, if I have broadened your views and opened your eyes to some deeper workings of how men think, feel and relate, then that can only be a good thing. Men and women need each other now to meet in an *equal* place. This doesn't mean we forget about the past or sweep it under the carpet. It does mean that if we're to create a better world for our children, then we must work on our shadows, yet support each other in the process and be truthful with each other.

If you're a man who's already on your inward journey, thank you for reading and being part of the increasing number of men who are fellow travellers. Without you, there would be no *movement*, no improvement in relationships, no benefit to family dynamics and no change in society at large. I'm sure you know that the world needs you to share your learning and experience with other men who may be considering their journey. You can do much to lead and encourage others. Don't keep what you've learned, secret!

We need more women to understand the inner world of men, as we need more men to understand the inner world of women, for only in doing so can we begin to initiate the type of conversations that we need to have. You may or may not agree with what I have written and really, in the scheme of things it doesn't matter. What's important is that *together* we can move forward with *mutual respect* as our foundation, while supporting each other in the process, to be witnesses to our collective unfolding.

If you're in an intimate relationship and/or a parent, I cannot think of any other endeavour where we have the incredible privilege to *bear witness* to the unfoldment of another human being, as they travel through their life, its ups-and-downs, its learnings and lessons, its trials and tribulations and all its light and shade. And they do that for us, too.

We have much to learn from indigenous cultures that understand the importance of separate *men's and women's business*. If you are prepared to seek out such events, there are many to choose from. Embarking on the occasional women's and men's business events will empower each of us as individuals and enrich and strengthen all our relationships.

I am grateful to all the men that I have met in a multiplicity of circumstances, who have bared their souls and spoken from the deepest and truthful recesses of their Hearts. To all of you, I am truly humbled to have walked alongside you.

AHO!

To the men who are not already on the path of self-discovery, I hope this book inspires and encourages you to commence the most extraordinary journey you will ever undertake. If other men's journeys and mine are anything to go by, it will take you to places of the deepest pain and ecstasy, sadness and joy, rage and bliss, bewilderment and awakening. Within these experiences, you will certainly learn about *feeling* in all its dimensions, its nuances, discomfort and release. I guarantee that you will come to know yourself in ways you never dreamed possible, and in doing so understand what it means to be liberated, to be truly free and alive!

They say that the most difficult step of any journey is the first and if you're anything like I was back in 1991, I was an expert at avoiding what I knew I *must* do. Find yourself a men's group, visit a Men's Shed, look out for the various conferences and gatherings that focus on men, buy or borrow some books on men's business and take the plunge. It may be the scariest thing you've ever done, and I assure you, it WILL change your life!

If you've ever watched the first movie in *The Matrix* trilogy, remember the famous scene with Keanu Reeves (Neo) and Laurence Fishburne (Morpheus), where Neo chooses to take the *red* pill? Once Neo sees beyond the matrix, he asks why can't they wake everyone else up?

Morpheus explains to Neo, *"You have to understand, most of these people are not ready to be unplugged and many of them are so inured, so hopelessly dependent on the system, that they will fight to protect it."*

Will you fight to protect a system that is detrimental to both men and women, that maintains the status quo and continues the stereotypical portrayal of imaginary men, or will you work within yourself, connect with your Heart and other men, and choose to become a *Man … Unplugged*?

I hear a Hero's call!

Irrespective of where you are in your life's journey, my sincerest wish for you is that worthiness, self-acceptance, commitment, compassion, grace, courage, grit, potency, respect, inner peace, kindness, and *love* be your ever-present travelling companions.

EPILOGUE

I hope you've found your way through our journey together, and your precious time investment has yielded some insights to help you navigate your life ahead. I truly appreciate you making the time to read my words.

As a parting gesture, I wanted to share something with you ...

In December 2000, I was sitting on the couch in my lounge room one Saturday afternoon, contemplating the previous decade since I'd met my mentor, Stuart. He had died unexpectedly earlier that year, which pushed me into a deep grieving process, out of which I was now emerging and contemplating my road ahead.

As I sat, considering all the disparate elements randomly placed through time, and the synchronistic 'sliding door' moments that had greatly influenced my life up to that point, suddenly, I became aware of an almost out of body experience, that I can only describe as like watching a movie unfold on the screen of my mind.

It lasted for many minutes, and I later came to realise I'd truly had an epiphany, which an online dictionary describes as, *"a sudden, intuitive perception of or insight into the reality or essential meaning of something, usually initiated by some simple, homely, or commonplace occurrence or experience."* (www.dictionary.com/browse/epiphany)

During those minutes, I was shown, unequivocally, that all those disparate elements weren't disparate at all, and each choice was inextricably linked to each other, like a three-dimensional holographic tapestry, with each part interconnected. It truly was a profound and mystical experience that's deeply etched in my memory.

As the experience declined, I had this compulsion to write. I'd never been a writer, did poorly in English at school, yet here I was, driven by the need to document my experience. I had my laptop at home, so I sat in front of it, and out poured a 'piece' of writing, seemingly, from nowhere.

I finished it, printed it, and excitedly brought it out to share with my partner, who initially thought it was something I'd found on the Internet, but as she read it, she became aware it was me who'd written it. She then asked how long it had taken me to write something this eloquent, to which I looked at my watch and answered, "About 20 minutes!"

This experience opened an unexplainable door, and over the next few years, I would hear a comment, read a line in a book (I became an avid reader too), or a lyric, or a thought about life would pop into my head. It would sit, sometimes for weeks, until late at night just before bed, I'd feel the same compulsion and head for my laptop, write, never read or edit, and go to bed. I'd wake up the following morning, excited to open my laptop and read what had been written, since I had barely any memory of the content.

I came to learn later this was a form of *automatic writing*, or psychography, little knowing this was, in fact, my 'apprenticeship' to learn to write. The first edition of *Man ... Unplugged* is a direct result of this experience, because if someone had told me I'd one day author a book, I would have labelled them as crazy.

If you're a reader of books, you'll know that authors have a *voice*, and readers might like a particular author because of the way they write, or their voice, while others might be turned off by it.

During that time, I wrote many 'pieces', each of which has many muses, and don't really carry the voice of a specific author as such. Out of the many that found their way into words, as I was finishing this second edition, two writings in particular came to mind, and I share them here as a parting gift to you, the reader, in the hope they'll inspire you to ponder your journey ahead.

The first, entitled *Manhood*, describes the steps of self-realisation to becoming a whole man.

The second, *I Am Adam*, which for me was a fascinating piece as it poured out in minutes, continues to reverberate in my life. Perhaps an epitaph?

I hope they inspire you in some way, as they have me.

John

Manhood

Own your shadow, embrace one's woundedness.

Embrace one's woundedness, make a deal with Anima.

Make a deal with Anima, discover the Wild Man.

Discover the Wild Man, ignite the Zeus within.

Ignite the Zeus within, become a leader of men.

Become a leader of men, walk a path of Heart.

Walk a path of Heart, be humbled by the journey.

Be humbled by the journey, ignite your inner Divine!

Ignite your inner Divine, reveal your God within,

Reveal your God within, what else is there to say?

12 Aug 2005

I Am Adam

I am Adam
Primordial Son
Primordial Man
Aeons of ancestry lost in time ...

To love, to hate,
To release, to hold,
To destroy, to create,
To stay, to go,
To embrace, to deny ...

Infinite choices ingrained in my lineage
are all mine to make of what I Will.

Will it start with me or end with me?

I truly am the Alpha and the Omega
from which all endings and beginnings may emerge,
if only I can feel the Rock on which I stand.

The rock is my Heart,
the Heart That Knows No Violence,
connected to
All That Is,
for now and ever more.

The One Heart
The True Heart
The Connected Heart
The Joyfilled Heart
The Blissful Heart
The Heart that knows
All That Is.

I Am Adam!

Endless possibilities await all Men.

And those whose compass is their Heart
must now hark The Hero's Call,
to be one's own Adam.

The Beginning heralds the End,
A present nexus on which all future generations will stand.

I am Adam,
You are Adam,
We are Adam!

Feb 2012

Resources

The following list contains recommended websites, resources and books, some of which have been referenced in this book, and groups or organisations I have experience with.

Me first ☺...

For men who might want to attend either a younger man's (25-50) retreat program or the elder's rite of passage (for men over 50) mentioned in this book, all the details can be found at www.manunplugged.com.au where you can register your interest and join the waitlist.

Website	URL
Beyond The Ordinary	www.beyondtheordinary.net.au
Complete Men Foundation (Qld)	www.completemen.org.au
Good, Better, Best Men (SA)	www.www.goodbetterbestmen.com.au
Gotcha4Life (NSW)	www.www.gotcha4life.org
Man Alive Gathering (NSW)	www.manalivenetwork.weebly.com
Man Anchor (NSW)	www.www.mananchor.com.au
Menergy Gathering (Vic)	www.menergy.org.au
Men's Wellbeing (Qld)	www.menswellbeing.org
Mentoring Men	www.mentoringmen.org.au
Menswork Project (WA)	www.mensworkproject.org
Michael Ray	www.michaelray.com.au

Powerhouse Programs (Qld)   www.powerhouseprograms.org.au

Southern Men's Gathering (SA) www.www.southernmensgathering.com

Suit, Tie, Stroller   www.www.suittiestroller.com

TasMen (Tas)   www.www.tasmen.org

The Men's Table   www.themenstable.org

The Fathering Project   www.thefatheringproject.org

Tomorrow Man   www.www.tomorrowman.com.au

Author	Book
Armstrong, Alison	The Amazing Development of Men (audio)
Biddulph, Steve	The Secret Of Happy Children Raising Boys The New Manhood Stories Of Manhood The Secret Life Of Men
Bly, Robert	Iron John
Celi, Dr Elizabeth	Regular Joe Vs Mr Invincible Breaking The Silence
Coelho, Paulo	The Alchemist
Deida, David	The Way Of The Superior Man
Farrell, Dr Warren	The Myth Of Male Power
Goleman, Daniel	Emotional Intelligence

Gottman, John & Julie	The Man's Guide to Women
Hamilton, Maggie	What Men Don't Talk About What's Happening To Our Boys?
Hill, Gareth S	Masculine & Feminine: The Natural Flow Of Opposites In The Psyche
Johnson, Robert A	He: Understanding Masculine Psychology She: Understanding Feminine Psychology We: Understanding The Psychology Of Romantic Love Transformation Inner Work Owning Your Own Shadow The Fisher King & The Handless Maiden Ecstasy Living Your Unlived Life Beyond Heaven & Earth
Jung, CG	Memories, Dreams, Reflections Dreams Man & His Symbols The Undiscovered Self
Lashlie, Celia	He'll Be Ok
Millman, Dan	Way Of The Peaceful Warrior
Ray, Michael	Who Knew?
Robinson, John C	Death of the Hero, Birth of a Soul
Roy, Andy	Raising Teenage Boys
Ruiz, Don Miguel	The Four Agreements
Sommers, Christina Hoff	Who Stole Feminism?

Notes

Notes

Notes

Notes

Notes

Notes

www.ingramcontent.com/pod-product-compliance
Lightning Source LLC
Chambersburg PA
CBHW050337010526
44119CB00049B/583